The Teacher's Guide to to Big Blocks™

Amanda Loman,
Patricia M. Dorothy P. Hall

Carson-Dellosa Publishing Company, Inc.
Greensboro, North Carolina

Credits

Editor
Joey Bland

Layout Design
Tiara Reynolds

Inside Illustrations
Mike Duggins

Cover Design
Peggy Jackson

Dedication

We have had the extreme pleasure of working on this book with both Dottie Hall and Pat Cunningham. Five years ago, Four Blocks brought us together in professional work and lead to friendship. During the work we did together, we were fortunate enough to meet Dottie Hall, who in turn introduced us to Pat Cunningham.

The past five years have been an experience beyond words. We have been fortunate to see the model develop and change and observe two dedicated professionals work to seek out what is best for children. Dottie and Pat are wonderful professionals who find out about the latest research, the latest trends, and best practices and incorporate it into the Four-Blocks® Literacy Model.

In addition, they are fabulous people and we are pleased and proud to call them our friends. For all of their guidance and support, we dedicate this book to Dottie Hall and Pat Cunningham.

Amanda Arens and Karen Loman

In 1989, when Pat Cunningham, Dottie Hall, and Margaret Defee tried multilevel, multimethod instruction with one classroom of first graders in Clemmons, NC, they had no idea their efforts would lead to the framework now called the Four-Blocks® Literacy Model. The goal was to find a way to give all students more opportunities to learn to read and write successfully. During the next few years, more teachers and more grade levels began to try the framework. Four Blocks became a multimethod, multilevel framework to be used in first, second, and third grades.

As Four Blocks became more well-known and the successes were shared, kindergarten teachers became interested. Fortunately, the kindergarten teachers and their principals were advised that Four Blocks was not a framework for kindergarten. Because of developmental differences, kindergarten teachers would need to do things differently. These teachers were introduced to the Building-Blocks™ framework.

Similarly, as upper-grade teachers began to see the success Four-Blocks classrooms experienced and started getting students from those rooms who could read and write more proficiently than before, they wanted to try it, too. Once again, developmental differences and scheduling differences made it difficult to do Four Blocks beyond third grade. In recent years we have been working closely with school districts and upper-grade teachers to develop and define a framework for upper grades called Big Blocks™. Big Blocks incorporates the same instructional blocks as Four Blocks, however, due to curriculum requirements and students' learning needs, three of the four blocks require longer periods of time, or "bigger blocks."

Big Blocks is a framework for upper elementary classrooms—those grade levels beyond third still housed in the elementary setting. Each chapter of this book offers suggestions for what the framework might look like in middle school. In this chapter, we will share the definition of Big Blocks with you and provide sample schedules and classroom information to support that definition.

Multilevel Instruction

Big Blocks is a multilevel, multimethod language arts framework. Multilevel instruction focuses on the multiple learning levels and needs of all students in the class in a single lesson. A multilevel activity is an activity that is so rich, students at different levels have something to learn through the same activity (Cunningham, 2004). Unlike single-level activities, multilevel activities are not frustrating for the struggling reader and writer or boring for those who are more advanced. When teachers provide daily, multilevel learning opportunities, more students achieve the "mastery" desired over time (Cunningham, Hall, and Defee, 1998).

Big Blocks is multilevel because instruction in each block is differentiated to meet the needs of all learners. The Guided Reading Block differentiates instruction through the use of various grouping formats, instructional materials that are at or below the average reading level of the students, short texts and picture books, and small group instruction when possible and/or necessary. The Writing Block and Self-Selected Reading Block differentiate instruction through the use of mini-lessons at various levels, teacher modeling, and individual conferences that focus on the needs of each student. The Working with Words Block differentiates instruction through the use of easy and complex words, a focus on patterns and morphemes, and a focus on transferring the words and patterns to reading and writing. Big Blocks is multimethod because it provides instruction in all four approaches to reading through each of the Blocks.

Big Blocks

Big Blocks is not a program that dictates what is to be taught in a specified sequence or manner. Rather, it is a model that provides a framework for quality instruction that should be tailored to meet the needs of the students in your class. If your students need more time and focus on a comprehension strategy, then you should provide it. If your students are proficient writers and would enjoy learning more advanced writing strategies, then you should provide these strategies through mini-lessons and conferences. The Big-Blocks™ model honors your students as learners—with varying needs and learning styles—and it honors you as the teacher—a professional who knows students well and plans instruction for them accordingly.

The Big-Blocks™ framework differs from Four Blocks in its implementation based on the time devoted to each block and the frequency of each block. The differences from Four Blocks are the primary purpose for this book.

Why Not Four Blocks?

As students move into the upper grades, they have different literacy needs. Not only are most students reading and writing at more independent levels, more time is needed to teach the content area subjects. This content demand requires more time to be spent in social studies, science, and math and less time to be devoted to literacy.

Four-Blocks instruction requires that a primary teacher spend 30-40 minutes on each of the blocks each and every day. If students are to get a solid foundation of literacy in first, second, and third grades, that amount of time is essential. However, in the upper grades, each school—sometimes each grade level—has a different requirement for the amount of time spent on content area instruction. Therefore, the amount of minutes allotted for literacy instruction in the upper grades varies greatly.

Some similarities and differences between Four Blocks and Big Blocks are:

	Four Blocks	Big Blocks same as Four Blocks	Big Blocks new/different from Four Blocks
Self-Selected Reading	30-40 minutes daily instruction Read aloud, reading, conferencing, and sharing	Read aloud, reading, conferencing, and sharing	Instruction to equal 120-200 minutes per week Read aloud and some mini-lessons to model comprehension and decoding strategies Weekly written response to reading; daily reading log

	Four Blocks	Big Blocks same as Four Blocks	Big Blocks new/different from Four Blocks
Writing	30-40 minutes daily instruction Mini-lesson, writing, conferencing, and sharing Student choice and focused writing	Mini-lesson, writing, conferencing, and sharing Student choice and focused writing	Instruction to equal 150-200 minutes per week Increased time and attention to focused writing
Guided Reading	30-40 minutes daily instruction Comprehension Daily before-, during-, and after-reading activities Fiction and nonfiction texts A variety of after-reading activities	Comprehension Daily before-, during-, and after-reading activities Fiction and nonfiction texts A variety of after-reading activities	Instruction to equal 150-200 minutes per week We suggest one-third literature and two-thirds content-area texts with greater focus on content-area reading including nonfiction texts More frequent **written responses** to reading
Working with Words	30-40 minutes daily instruction Spelling patterns and high-frequency words Transfer to reading and writing	Spelling patterns and high-frequency words Transfer to reading and writing	Instruction for 20 minutes 2-3 days per week morphemes

Big Blocks

There are expectations and recommendations for each block in Big Blocks, too, but there is also more flexibility. On pages 17-20 there are several sample schedules from upper-grade classrooms. The variety of schedules demonstrates the many different ways teachers have incorporated this framework.

Big Blocks is a multilevel, multimethod framework that integrates language arts instruction with content learning. One way to increase the amount of time available for language arts is to look for opportunities to connect to or integrate with the things you are already teaching in content area studies. This integration accommodates the increased demands in content learning, increased use of textbooks to deliver instruction, and students' need for continued literacy support.

For example, Chapter 4 provides examples of Guided Reading lessons using social studies and science texts. Whether students are reading textbooks or trade books in these subjects, it is often the perfect time to guide their comprehension. Therefore, a Guided Reading lesson with a content focus is the answer. Another example would be to connect any focused writing (see page 62 for a definition and examples) to concepts in the content areas. For example, if your students will be writing persuasive letters, have them write persuasive letters dealing with the many issues of the Civil War. This integration not only helps with the time crunch, it also helps students gain a deeper understanding of the concepts they are learning.

Once students move past third grade, they spend much more time in textbooks. Frequently, these textbooks are written either at or above the reading level for that grade. If the textbook selections are content heavy with a lot of new vocabulary, the selections will work well for Guided Reading. However, if the reading level is above that of most of the students in the class, it is impossible to "guide" students through the reading. This text may be read to students as a part of your science or social studies time but would not be appropriate for Guided Reading.

As you begin to look at the Big-Blocks™ framework, it is important for you to know the reading levels of your students. Being familiar with their abilities will help you make solid instructional decisions. It will also assist you in deciding if your students are ready for Big Blocks. We highly recommend Big Blocks as a framework for use when the majority of your students are reading at a third-grade level or above. This allows for a majority of fourth-grade students to be a full year behind expectations. However, if more than half of your class is below a third-grade reading level, consider moving back into the Four-Blocks® framework. Although the Four-Blocks® framework requires that you spend even more time with literacy, in order for your students to be successful with complex texts, their literacy foundation must be solid.

One common problem we've seen in schools is the resistance to replace what is currently being done with something new. Instead, teachers and districts tend to "add" new things to the plate without taking anything else off. The plate remains the same size, and the school day remains the same length. Teachers can't continue to add new things without taking away something else. Think about your own instruction carefully as you read the chapters explaining the Big Blocks. Many of the ideas and strategies you read about will be things you already do. Where will the new ideas fit in with what you are already doing? What could these ideas replace? These are the questions that require answers when change is at hand.

Before you look at sample schedules, take a walk through a typical Big-Blocks classroom.

A Sample Day in Big Blocks

8:15–8:30 Arrival

Students trickle in from buses, breakfast, etc. During this time, some students take a few minutes to select books for Self-Selected Reading. The classroom library is open for business, and this is the perfect opportunity for each student to make sure he is ready to read. Other students turn in homework, put supplies away, mark the lunch chart with their choices, and sharpen pencils. Not everyone arrives at the same time, but early in the year the teacher spends a great deal of time teaching her expectations for the first few minutes of the day. In this classroom it is very important for students to be ready to roll at 8:30 since the older students are the first to go to their specials classes, and this group will be lined up and walking out the door at 8:35.

8:35–9:25 Specials Classes

9:30–9:40 Rest Room Break and Walk Back to Class

Again, students become acquainted with this routine as the year progresses. They learn that once they are back in the classroom, there will be no other breaks before lunch. Students are told to take advantage of the opportunity and to do it quickly! There is work to be done!

9:40–10:00 Working with Words

This is Monday, and the teacher has found it difficult to introduce new Word Wall words or Nifty Thrifty Fifty words in less than 20 minutes. Later in the year, students and the teacher are better at finishing the task in 15 minutes and still have 5 minutes for a quick review of the words already on the wall.

This is a Nifty Thrifty Fifty day. The teacher brings out her word cards for each of the four words she will introduce today. As she places the first word in the pocket chart, she explains that all four words this week include prefixes which signal an "opposite relationship." In other words, the prefix will cause the definition to change to its opposite.

The first word is **dishonest**. Honesty has been one of the character traits the school has focused on, and the teacher knows the students understand what it is to be honest. Her instruction connects to this example. Then, she explains that the word **dishonest** is the opposite of honest, or to be not honest. A few volunteers suggest sentences showing the meaning of **dishonest**. The teacher asks, "If the root word is honest, what is the prefix? Great. It is **dis-**. Let's chant this word. Listen to me do it first. I think I will clap, snap, clap. **D-i-s** (clap, clap, clap) **h-o-n** (snap, snap, snap) **e** (clap) **s** (clap) **t** (clap). Everybody stand up and let's chant it together. Ready?"

The students chant with her two times. Then, she asks them to say only the letters and forget the claps and snaps. She wants to listen to make sure they say the letters correctly.

"Now, sit down and write the word one time only. Please be sure to print and write the word only once. I am looking for accurate letter formation and accurate spelling.

"Our next word is **illegal**. Again the prefix, **il-**, changes the meaning of the word to the opposite. So, something that is **illegal** is not legal." Students volunteer sentences showing the meaning of **illegal**. "**Il-** is not the only prefix we've had that begins with i. We've had others: **ir-**, **im-**, and **in-**. Each of these has the same effect on a word—it signals an opposite. Listen to me chant this word. I think this word is short

Big Blocks

enough to chant the prefix together and then the root word together rather than doing syllables. So, it sounds like this: **i-l** (clap, clap) **l-e-g-a-l** (snap, snap, snap, snap, snap). Everybody stand up and let's chant it together."

The students chant with the teacher two times, and then she asks them to say only the letters and forget the claps and snaps. She wants to listen to make sure they say the letters correctly. The teacher continues this format with the words **misunderstood** and **irresponsible**. After students give sample sentences, chant, and write all four words, they check the spellings. The teacher spells each word again with the same rhythm, and each student places a small dot under each letter to show she has checked each word. Anyone finding an error erases the mistake and fixes it on the paper so that no mistakes are left on the paper.

Because it is Monday and the introduction of new words takes a bit longer, no other word activity is done today. See page 155 in Chapter 5 to see how the Working with Words Block changes across the days of the week.

10:00–10:50 Writing Block

Mini-Lesson (9 minutes)

Each day, the Writing Block begins with a mini-lesson. The teacher gathers the students in front of the overhead projector and proceeds to think aloud and write in front of them. Today's mini-lesson centers on figurative language. As the students settle in around the teacher, she begins to speak about her writing idea for today.

"You know, I was writing a piece about watching Merrill Kaye at her first dance competition. She has been dancing for 10 years now, and we just love to watch her on stage. While I was writing, I wanted to find just the right words to use so that you—and anyone else who reads my writing—could picture Merrill Kaye on stage. Do you all remember when we read *In the Time of Drums* by Kim Sieglson (Jump Sun, 1999)? It was a great story, and the author did such a super job of helping me see the story in my mind pictures. She used a technique called figurative language. You all have heard about this before. Remember? A simile is way to compare two things. Usually the words like or as are included in a simile. Here is a simile from *In the Time of Drums* to remind you: 'Twi's eyes glittered like moonsparkle on dark water.' You know, I am not even sure what 'moonsparkle' is. It may be a made-up word, but I can tell from that sentence that her eyes shone or sparkled. Can't you?

"Here is another example from the story to remind you: 'The old ways had slowly slipped away and been left behind like sweat drops in a newly plowed row.' I really like the way the author helps me picture her ideas.

"Anyway, the reason I brought up that book is because I want to try to do the same thing with my writing about Merrill Kaye. Here is what I have so far.

The J'ettes had never been in a competition. They were excited and nervous and so were the parents. As the girls entered the stage in their flowing nutmeg dresses, my eyes began to water. I have always been amazed at how the sight of Merrill Kaye on stage is such an emotional experience for me. It happens every time I watch.

The girls were dancing to a song called "Three Wooden Crosses," and I hadn't seen this dance yet. Much to our surprise, there was a short section when Merrill Kaye did a duet with one of the other girls. They came onto the stage with grace and poise.

"Now, this is where I want to tell about her part of the dance, but I want my readers to be able to 'see' her in their minds. I am going to try some similes to see if it helps. I just am not sure where to begin. Let's see . . . .

Merrill Kaye seemed as confident as a well-seasoned performer. Her smile radiated warmth—even at the back of the auditorium. Her movements and steps were as graceful as a swan gliding across the surface of a lake.

"Do you like that? I don't know if that is how I will leave it or not, but I think I am getting closer to the words I want to use. I think I will put it away for now. I know that leaving a piece of writing for a short time really helps me read it better and make solid revision decisions. Anyway, it is time for you all to write now. If you are working on a piece and want your reader to be able to 'see' the events of the story, you might find that figurative language could help. If any of you try it out today, let me know.

"Before you start your writing, get out your Big Blocks Notebooks and turn to the Writing section. Find the next blank page and write 'Figurative Language' at the top. You will use this page and leave two more pages after it open for more information on figurative language. That way it will all be in there together.

"Let's write this:

'Simile – a comparison of two things using the words like or as

   Example: Twi's eyes glittered like moonsparkle on dark water.'

"Alright, it is time to get back to your seats and get started on your own writing. Today, I will be conferencing with the orange group . . . ."

Big Blocks

Students Writing and Teacher Conferencing (31 minutes)

Every day, the students move from the "group" area for the mini-lesson to their seats for writing time. (Early in the year, the teacher established the expectation that this time is used for writing—or anything connected to writing—but only for writing.) Some students move directly to their seats, while others move to the shelf with their writing folders. Today, it is their turn to distribute the writing folders to their classmates.

Two students head over to the peer conferencing table to finish up going through one of the pair's rough draft. They understand the process is to be done quietly so as not to disturb other writers.

The teacher gathers her record keeping system for conferences and does a "Quick Check" of the class. For the Quick Check, each student responds immediately by saying the stage of the writing process they will be working on that day: brainstorming, drafting, revising, editing, peer conference, teacher conference, publishing, etc. (This is another procedure that was practiced extensively during the first couple of months of the school year.) The class can now complete the Quick Check in less than two minutes. The materials are distributed, the Quick Check is complete, and the room is ready to write.

Once all students are engaged in their writing, the teacher calls the first student from the Orange Group to conference. Lafe brings his folder over. He is ready to begin a draft on a new piece. The teacher asks to see his brainstorming work, and he eagerly shares his web. He is working on a new piece about elephants. He is the class's resident elephant expert and has been busy planning just how he might write about the animals he knows. The teacher listens as he explains his plan, and she knows the best plan for Lafe's conference today is to listen and send this anxious writer on his way. He is ready to proceed. She makes a quick note in her anecdotal records to check his progress on this elephant piece next week.

As Lafe leaves the conference, he is asked to quietly send Tracy to the conferencing table. Tracy brings a piece she would like to publish. After glancing through it, the teacher can tell that Tracy has been through the Writer's Checklist on her own and is ready for some revision suggestions. The teacher thinks a good revision suggestion would be for Tracy to read back through her piece and make sure the whole story is told in the same tense. Tracy has a tendency to tell part of the story in present tense and then flip to past tense. The teacher shows Tracy a couple of places where the tense is inconsistent. The teacher makes the suggestion and shows Tracy how this will improve all of her writing. Then, she sends Tracy off to make the changes. Tracy will have another conference to show the changes she has made. Then, the teacher will get the piece for the final edit before returning the piece to Tracy for publishing.

The teacher conferences with three more students, and the rest of the class remains busy with their own writing work. Students know it will soon be their turns for individual conferences with the teacher, and because expectations were so clearly explained and enforced from the beginning, they also know conferences are not to be interrupted.

Sharing (10 minutes)

After 31 minutes of writing time, the students hear the timer and know they have two minutes to wrap up the work they are doing today. The "warning bell" allows a student to find a stopping place and be ready to listen when the first student is ready to share. Sharing time must be limited to 5-10 minutes; therefore, each student knows he won't always get to share his whole piece.

Today, it is the Orange Group's day to share. Lafe says he wants to wait to share until he has more written on his elephant piece. Tracy decides just to share the revised lead of her story. Two others in the group read sections of pieces from their folders, and the last student in the group wants to wait until more of his piece is completed.

In 50 minutes, the students have had a very productive Writing Block. The time spent learning procedures is paying off, and the teacher is pleased with what she sees.

10:50–11:50 Math

11:50–12:30 Lunch and Recess

12:30–1:20 Self-Selected Reading

Teacher Read Aloud (8 minutes)
The teacher gathers students together once more for the read aloud. Though these are not primary students, they still enjoy the teacher read aloud in a "community" gathering. The teacher reads Patricia Polacco's *When Lightning Comes in a Jar* (Philomel, 2002). The students have enjoyed several Polacco stories over the past few days. It has worked as a type of author study, and the teacher makes a connection to this in the mini-lesson.

Mini-Lesson (5 minutes)
The teacher says, "I love that book by Patricia Polacco. Really, I love so many of her stories, but that one really gives me lots of connections. I think about family gatherings, church covered dish suppers, and traditions I would like to start with my own kids.

"However, we are not talking about connections today. I want to think about all of the Patricia Polacco books we've read so far. Let me list them on the chart paper.

> Just Plain Fancy
>
> When Lightning Comes in a Jar
>
> My Rotten Red-Headed Older Brother
>
> Thank You, Mr. Falker

Big Blocks

"There are many other Patricia Polacco books that I hope you might find and read on your own. After having read this many in class, can you think of some things that will help you read her work in the future? What did you learn about her as an author?"

After a brief discussion of ideas that the students think will help them with any other Polacco books, they are sent to do their own reading. This mini-lesson took only five minutes. The teacher sets the timer for two minutes, and students move back to gather their reading materials and find the perfect spots for reading. The Orange Group is asked to quickly find the books they want to conference on and join the teacher near the conference table.

Some teachers decide to establish conferencing groups and allow the same students to be the group for the day. In other words, reading and writing conferences will happen with the same group. The same students have an opportunity to get new books for Self-Selected Reading, the same students share during Writing and Self-Selected Reading, etc. Other teachers establish their groups and meet with different students during different blocks. For example, the Red Group gets writing conferences, the Yellow Group gets reading conferences, etc. This allows the teacher to see more than one set of students in the day. Choose the option that makes the most sense to you.

Students Reading and Teacher Conferencing (30 minutes)

With the exception of the Orange Group, all of the students are reading. They are not choosing materials at this time since their procedures are firmly established and they know that reading time is for reading only. Choosing books happens at a separate time of day.

Four students whose names are posted at the front of the room have special spots for reading if they would like to take advantage of the opportunity. One student sits in the teacher's chair, one student chooses the "chair in a bag" the teacher brought in, one student takes a beanbag on the carpet, and the other student chooses the large pillow on the carpeted area. The students know these special spots are offered to different students each day.

The students quickly settle in to reading, and the teacher gathers her record keeping materials to begin conferencing again. Today, she will conference with the Orange Group. These students are asked to sit near the conferencing area during Self-Selected Reading time. This will save time moving from one student to the next during the conferences.

Janet comes to the table for her conference and chooses to talk to the teacher about a book she has almost finished. *Maniac Magee* by Jerry Spinelli (Little, Brown and Co., 1990) is one of the teacher's favorite books, and she is looking forward to what Janet might share. "What would you like to share today during your conference, Janet?" the teacher asks.

"Well, I am really close to the end of the story, and I like it a lot. Maniac has a really strange life—I mean I don't really know anyone who doesn't have a home. Maniac has lived with so many different people in this book, and I think he is a good friend to lots of the different people he has met. I just wonder how it will all end."

"Do you have any predictions about that?"

"Yeah, I think he might decide to go back and find his aunt and uncle that he left at the beginning of the story. But I don't really know."

"Okay, well I'll wait to see what you find out. What do you think you will read next?"

"I would like to find another book by Jerry Spinelli."

"I have a couple of suggestions for you. You could try *Loser* (HarperTrophy, 2003) or *Star Girl* (Knopf Books for Young Readers, 2002). I enjoyed both of those. When you try one, be sure to let me know what you think."

Janet is sent to her spot for reading, and the teacher records a few notes on Janet's form. She indicates the title of the book Janet spoke about and her feeling that it was a good choice for Janet, too. The teacher also indicated the titles of the books she recommended in case Janet asks again.

Four more Orange Group students are called up to conference, and the teacher encourages conversations about their books by asking open-ended questions. The students have been taught that these conferences are a time to talk to the teacher "reader to reader." It isn't a time for the teacher to "quiz" them about the details they remember.

Sharing (7 minutes)
The timer rings after 30 minutes of reading time. Again, each member of the Orange Group is invited to share a quick recommendation of a favorite book or read a paragraph from the book she is reading. Each person knows she will have a minute or less to share.

1:20–2:00   Science

2:00–2:50   Guided Reading
On this particular day, the teacher has planned a Guided Reading lesson to connect to the current theme in science. The students have been studying simple machines, and they have a short passage to read on the types of simple machines, as well as a bit of history on how long simple machines have been around.

For this lesson, the teacher will use a Guess Yes or No format to help prepare the students for reading. (See page 112 for information on Guess Yes or No.) The teacher has written 10 statements about the text. Students will work through each statement and guess "yes" if they think a statement is accurate or "no" if they think a statement is incorrect. The teacher records the class guesses (determined by consensus) on the overhead with the written statements.

The 10 statements incorporate any vocabulary the teacher thinks students might need to see before reading and also includes some basic concepts she is sure students already

HINT

The requirements for the amount of time in content areas differ among grade levels and schools. Two common configurations for content time are (1) to give each subject area approximately 30 instructional minutes a day or (2) give social studies a one hour block for a two- to three-week unit of study and then switch to a one-hour science block for two to three weeks. Each approach uses approximately the same number of minutes across the course of the year. Some teachers like the flexibility to dig deeper, and the one-hour time frame allows for that. In addition, we recommend that more of your Guided Reading instruction be done with books connected to your social studies and science instruction. Therefore, when developing your schedule, you may want your Guided Reading Block to directly precede or follow your content instruction.

Big Blocks

know. After the class guesses "yes" or "no" for each of the statements, reading partners read the section of text with a copy of the 10 statements and 10 self-stick notes in hand. As partners read, they will mark the text with a self-stick note to indicate the place where proof for the statement is found. The teacher wants students to be able to provide "proof" for the statements during the class discussion at the end of the reading time.

The teacher circulates during the partner reading and listens to the discussions of where and whether or not the text provided proof for each statement. She encourages some students to do a better job of working together and praises others for doing so. At the end of the designated reading time, the class comes back together as a group to see how well they guessed. They change any "no" statements to reflect the information they read.

The teacher wrote the statements for the Guess Yes or No activity to highlight the concepts she knows students must attend to. This guides their comprehension well. At the end of the activity, the teacher asks students to think about what they read and write at least three sentences stating two things they learned from their reading about simple machines. The teacher will collect these "Quick Writes" (see pages 131–132 on Quick Writes) as a way to determine her method for proceeding with the topic at hand.

2:50–3:15 Wrap Up

This teacher has built in a good chunk of time at the end of the day. She considers it her "cushion" for when things spill over into other time periods. She has also established routines for this end-of-the-day time. She is trying to teach students organization and responsibility. Like many upper-grade teachers, she requires students to fill in a planner with homework assignments and upcoming due dates, etc. Today, she has time to buzz through the classroom and make sure these planners are completed. The room is tidied, and supplies are put away.

On occasion, there is time to read to the students again—perhaps a current events article or text that connects to the content area being studied. On some days, students read through the new words for the Word Wall or the new Nifty Thrifty Fifty words with partners. Or, students may place their take-home Word Walls in their backpacks. There are always a number of tasks to do at the end of the day, and this cushion of time allows for these to be completed.

Today, students finish the day with a read aloud using an article on the area community center from the local newspaper. Students are very interested in what is happening with the center's programs for students. The teacher will make sure the article is available tomorrow for Self-Selected Reading. After reading and discussing the article, students chant and write the new Nifty Thrifty Fifty words one more time.

The students' day is over, and they are headed out the door. The teacher takes the time to read through the Quick Writes from this afternoon's Guided Reading lesson.

Sample Schedules

We have tried to provide a wide variety of schedules. Some teachers have a consistent planning/ specials time every day. Others not only have different time slots, but may have two specials one day of the week and no specials at all on another day. These variations are part of the challenge in implementing Big Blocks.

In addition to a-week-at-a-glance sample schedules, which include all facets of school life, we've also developed some generic schedules with suggested time frames, or weekly minute requirements. Each schedule includes an explanation of why things were done the way they appear. It is not assumed that every Big-Blocks teacher should be able to find a schedule in this chapter to adopt. Rather, by looking at a variety of schedules, you may see a new approach to "finding" the minutes you need to make Big Blocks a reality in your classroom.

The following schedule only lists times allocated to Big Blocks. Notice that each Block does not occur each day, nor do the Blocks get the same time each day. This schedule features allocated time over the course of the week, which allows you to look for larger chunks of time. Although the Blocks don't have to occur in consecutive chunks, this schedule does just that.

	Monday	Tuesday	Wednesday	Thursday	Friday
10 minutes	WwW		WwW	WwW	
10 minutes		GR			GR
10 minutes	W		GR	W	
10 minutes					
10 minutes		W			W
10 minutes					
10 minutes					
10 minutes	GR				
10 minutes		SSR	SSR	SSR	
10 minutes					SSR
10 minutes					
10 minutes					

Time allocated each week: WwW—60 minutes; GR, SSR, and W—180 minutes each

The schedule on page 18 allocates 60 minutes per day for science **or** social studies instruction, with a focus on one of the two subjects for several days at a time. This provides for greater in-depth study.

Big Blocks

This schedule also has Guided Reading after content-area instruction so that students can connect the texts they are reading with the content-area activities they are doing.

	Monday	Tuesday	Wednesday	Thursday	Friday
10 minutes					
10 minutes					
10 minutes	Specials including art, music, PE, library, counselor, etc.				
10 minutes					
10 minutes					
10 minutes	WwW	WwW	WwW		
10 minutes				W	W
10 minutes	W	W	W		
10 minutes					
10 minutes					
10 minutes					
10 minutes				Math	Math
10 minutes	Math	Math	Math		
10 minutes					
10 minutes					
10 minutes					
10 minutes	Lunch and Recess				
10 minutes					
10 minutes					
10 minutes					
10 minutes	SSR	SSR	SSR	SSR	SSR
10 minutes					
10 minutes					
10 minutes					
10 minutes					
10 minutes	Science or Social Studies	Science or Social Studies	Science or Social Studies	Science or Social Studies	Science or Social Studies
10 minutes					
10 minutes					
10 minutes					
10 minutes					
10 minutes	GR	GR	GR	GR	GR
10 minutes					
10 minutes					
10 minutes					
10 minutes	Wrap up, end of the day jobs, computer lab				
10 minutes					
10 minutes	Planners				

Time allocated each week: WwW—60 minutes; GR, SSR, and W—200 minutes each

This schedule was designed for a school that has regulated daily instruction in both social studies and science. The schedule allocates a slightly longer time for Self-Selected Reading and Writing. This schedule works well if students are very engaged in their independent work. Time is also set aside to work with students who need additional support while other students work on homework.

	Monday	Tuesday	Wednesday	Thursday	Friday
10 minutes	Science	Science	Science	Science	Science
10 minutes					
10 minutes					
10 minutes	Specials including art, music, PE, library, counselor, etc.				
10 minutes					
10 minutes					
10 minutes					
10 minutes					
10 minutes	WwW		WwW	WwW	
10 minutes		SSR			SSR
10 minutes	SSR		SSR	W	
10 minutes					
10 minutes					
10 minutes					
10 minutes	Lunch and Recess				
10 minutes					
10 minutes					
10 minutes					
10 minutes	W	W	W	GR	GR
10 minutes					
10 minutes					
10 minutes					
10 minutes					
10 minutes					
10 minutes	Computer Lab	GR	Computer Lab	Remediation/ Homework	Remediation/ Homework
10 minutes					
10 minutes					
10 minutes					
10 minutes	Social Studies	Social Studies	Social Studies	Social Studies	Social Studies
10 minutes					
10 minutes					
10 minutes	Math	Math	Math	Math	Math
10 minutes					
10 minutes					
10 minutes					
10 minutes					
10 minutes					
10 minutes	Planners				

Time allocated each week: WwW—60 minutes; GR—180 minutes; SSR and W—200 minutes each

Big Blocks

Some schools don't have their specials at the same time each day. The following schedule allows for the Big Blocks and other subject areas even though specials are scattered among the days.

	Monday	Tuesday	Wednesday	Thursday	Friday
10 minutes	Science	Science	Science	Science	Science
10 minutes	Science	Science	Science	Science	Science
10 minutes	Science	Science	Science	Science	Science
10 minutes	WwW	W	GR	Art	GR
10 minutes	WwW	W	GR	Art	GR
10 minutes	Library	W	GR	Art	GR
10 minutes	Library	SSR	WwW	WwW	SSR
10 minutes	Library	SSR	WwW	WwW	SSR
10 minutes	Library	SSR	SSR	W	SSR
10 minutes	SSR	SSR	SSR	W	SSR
10 minutes	SSR	SSR	SSR	W	SSR
10 minutes	SSR	SSR	SSR	W	SSR
10 minutes	SSR	SSR	SSR	W	SSR
10 minutes	Lunch and Recess				
10 minutes	Lunch and Recess				
10 minutes	Lunch and Recess				
10 minutes	Lunch and Recess				
10 minutes	W	Music	W	Band	Science
10 minutes	W	Music	W	Band	Science
10 minutes	W	Music	W	Band	Science
10 minutes	W	Music	W	Band	Science
10 minutes	W	Music	W	Band	Extra minutes for WwW
10 minutes	W	Music	W	Band	Extra minutes for WwW
10 minutes	Computer Lab	GR	Computer Lab	GR	Remediation/Homework
10 minutes	Computer Lab	GR	Computer Lab	GR	Remediation/Homework
10 minutes	Computer Lab	GR	Computer Lab	GR	Remediation/Homework
10 minutes	Computer Lab	GR	Computer Lab	GR	Remediation/Homework
10 minutes	Social Studies	Social Studies	Social Studies	Social Studies	Social Studies
10 minutes	Social Studies	Social Studies	Social Studies	Social Studies	Social Studies
10 minutes	Social Studies	Social Studies	Social Studies	Social Studies	Social Studies
10 minutes	Math	Math	Math	Math	Math
10 minutes	Math	Math	Math	Math	Math
10 minutes	Math	Math	Math	Math	Math
10 minutes	Math	Math	Math	Math	Math
10 minutes	Math	Math	Math	Math	Math
10 minutes	Math	Math	Math	Math	Math
10 minutes	Math	Math	Math	Math	Math
10 minutes	Planners, end of the day jobs				

Time allocated each week: WwW—80 minutes; SSR and GR—200 minutes; W—210 minutes

Although we've suggested a minimum amount of 120 minutes per week in Self-Selected Reading and 150 minutes each for Writing and Guided Reading, you may find you have more time for one or more Blocks. We suggest that you strive to achieve an average of 180 minutes per Block per week (except for Working with Words, which should be 60 minutes) across the months and school year.

Classroom Materials and Layout

Big-Blocks teachers need a few essentials to be successful.

- **Materials for Students to Read**

  You will need a variety of genres at a variety of levels. If you have a basal or an anthology, start there. If not, that is fine, too. Include some class sets of materials. These can be trade books, textbooks, or articles. You will also need some materials for small groups of 6-8 students. These can be trade books, portions of an old basal or textbooks, or articles. And, you will need some individual copies of materials. These can be anything upper-grade students find interesting or engaging to read. Allington (2001) suggests a minimum of 500 different books in each classroom, with a note that in a study of exemplary teachers, they found collections of up to 1,500 book titles.

- **Materials for Students to Use When Writing**

  You will need paper and pencils, a place for students to store in-process pieces, and resources such as dictionaries and thesauri. You will also need charts and an overhead projector with individual sheets of transparency film for your writing and modeling.

- **Spaces for Reading, Writing, and Group Meetings**

  You will want to arrange your room to create quiet places for students to read and write. There should be places for small groups to meet and a place for the class to meet as a whole group. You will also need a space for the reading materials and writing materials to be stored and easily accessed by students.

- **Big-Blocks Notebooks**

  We suggest your students develop and keep notebooks as storage space for their learning. You may choose whether you want students to use three-ring binders with section dividers or spiral notebooks with dividers. The type of notebook you use is completely your choice, however, keep in mind that students will need at least three sections and will need to have these notebooks available on a regular basis. Three sections in the Big-Blocks Notebooks will be for Writing, Self-Selected Reading, and Working with Words. If you want students to keep their written responses to the Guided Reading selections, you may want four sections—one for each Block. During Writing mini-lessons, sometimes students will be asked to take notes. In the Self-Selected Reading section, students will keep a Reading Journal, a Reading Log, and notes from their Self-Selected Reading mini-lessons. The Working with Words Block will include activities that require students to collect words related to the studies they are involved in. All of these activities, notes, responses, and mini-lessons will be gathered in one location, and in each chapter, we will be referring to this location as the Big-Blocks Notebooks.

Big Blocks

The materials and room layout should be determined by your students' needs as readers and writers. The following chapters in this book will give you some ideas to consider. You might also observe students, talk with them about the available materials and space, and enlist their assistance in making your room a literacy-focused environment.

Big Blocks in Middle School

Middle schools generally have teams of teachers that provide instruction to designated groups of students. The teachers on these teams have established time for planning and preparing lessons that integrate learning from subject to subject. They also have established time to attend to individual student needs.

Some middle schools have identified reading as a priority, and all teachers are responsible for teaching students to read in their content areas. If this is the case, the content-area teachers teach most of the Guided Reading instruction using their content-area texts, ensuring that students develop comprehension strategies that will help them read nonfiction texts.

If there are both reading teachers and language arts teachers, the reading teacher teaches Self-Selected Reading and some Guided Reading. There will be a greater emphasis on Self-Selected Reading since content-area teachers are also teaching Guided Reading. The reading teacher will spend some time with Guided Reading, ensuring that students are continuing to learn comprehension strategies. The reading teacher's primary focus will be comprehension and applying what students know about decoding. The language arts teacher teaches Writing and Working with Words. There will be a greater emphasis on writing with only some work on words. The language arts teacher's primary focus is instructing students in various forms of writing along with the conventions of writing. The language arts teacher will ensure students have access to the Word Wall words and Nifty Thrifty Fifty words in the other Blocks by developing portable Word Walls that students carry from class to class in their notebooks.

If content-area teachers are not teaching Guided Reading, the reading teacher will want to place a greater emphasis on comprehension through Self-Selected Reading mini-lessons and more Guided Reading lessons; however, more time will still be devoted to Self-Selected Reading than Guided Reading.

If there is only one language arts teacher who teaches both reading and writing, then that teacher will need to strike a balance between Self-Selected Reading and Writing with some time devoted to Guided Reading and Working with Words. In either case, the team of teachers must work closely together to provide the most relevant and meaningful language arts instruction to students.

Departmentalization in Upper Grades

Although Big Blocks can be modified for middle school, it is most successful in self-contained classrooms where teachers can guide students to see the connections between literacy instruction and content-area reading and writing. It appears as though Big Blocks lends itself to departmentalization, with different teachers taking different Blocks. However, departmentalization does not allow the Big-Blocks™ framework to be as successful as it might be. Big Blocks is designed to allow for and to promote integration and connection among the Blocks. This integration allows for content instruction to occur through the Blocks and for students to transfer learning from one Block to another, with teacher guidance and assistance. Departmentalization does not allow for the guided transfer of learning, for teachers to really get to know the needs of individual students, or for as much differentiation as might be needed (Letgers, McDill, and McPartland, 1993). Although the Blocks may be used in a departmental setting, we don't recommend this structure for language arts instruction at the elementary level.

Professional Development Ideas

1. As you begin your implementation of Big Blocks, you may find it helpful to use this resource as a book study. Work through each chapter while trying ideas in the classroom. During book-study meetings, discuss what is working well and the areas you struggle with in your classroom. Learn to use your peers as powerful learning resources.

2. Choose to really focus on one Block at a time. Although you may be implementing all of the Blocks at once, you may choose to focus on one Block for a period of time. Use that time to try things new to you and to students. Use professional time with other staff members to share your successes and concerns. Look through the recommended professional resources at the end of each chapter to find books that will provide additional information.

3. Find schools in your area that have been doing Four Blocks and/or Big Blocks for a while. Take a day to visit their classrooms and ask questions.

Chapter 2 Self-Selected Reading in Big Blocks

Historically called individualized reading or personalized reading (Veatch, 1959), Self-Selected Reading is an instructional opportunity for students to select materials to read independently, choose how and what to respond to within the text, and share their reading with the teacher and/or other students. Teachers model effective reading strategies through read alouds, model comprehension strategies through mini-lessons, conference with individual students to support and guide their reading development, and provide a structured environment in which students can read and share.

In Big-Blocks™ classrooms, the Self-Selected Reading Block—approximately 180 minutes per week—includes the following:

- **Teacher read aloud and mini-lesson (5-15 minutes)**
  The Block begins with a read aloud and could include a mini-lesson that is designed to remind students how to decode or comprehend text when reading independently. Even if Self-Selected Reading isn't scheduled every day, each time the Block occurs, it begins with a read aloud and sometimes a mini-lesson.

- **Students reading from a variety of materials (20-30 minutes)**
  The classroom library contains books and magazines from a variety of levels, genres, and themes. Students select the material(s) they want to read.

- **Teacher conferences with students**
  While students read, the teacher conferences with several students each day, meeting with each child once during the week.

- **Weekly responses to reading**
  Students will choose how they will respond to the texts they are reading.

- **Opportunities for students to share (5-10 minutes)**
  Students share with the teacher and each other what they are reading and thinking.

The goals of the Self-Selected Reading Block in Big-Blocks classrooms are:

- to introduce students to all types of literature through the teacher read aloud

- to model strategies in mini-lessons that effective readers use

- to encourage students' reading interests

- to provide and encourage independent-level reading

- to provide instructional guidance and support as students apply decoding and comprehension strategies in their reading

- to engage students in conversations about their reading

- to build intrinsic motivation for reading

Self-Selected Reading Is Multilevel

Self-Selected Reading is the time when the skills and strategies learned in the Working with Words Block and Guided Reading Block are applied in students' personal reading. Because every child enters your class at a different place in their literacy development and will progress at different rates, instruction during the day must be differentiated to meet each child's needs. Self-Selected Reading allows the teacher to address each child's current level of reading development and encourage him to progress as fast and as far as possible.

Self-Selected Reading is multilevel because:

- students choose what they want to read

- the teacher makes materials available to all students in a wide variety of reading levels and genres

- the teacher uses mini-lessons to model strategies at a variety of levels

- the teacher tailors the focus of each student conference to the needs of the individual child

- students choose how to respond to the materials they have been reading

The Upper-Grade Reader

Most upper-grade readers have not mastered all of the skills and strategies associated with being proficient readers. They don't consistently demonstrate mastery of higher-level thinking skills (National Center for Education Statistics, 2003). They are still developing fluency (Ivey and Broaddus, 2000). They are also still learning about word patterns (particularly within big words), and they are still developing their vocabularies (Cunningham, 2004). However, with all of this learning to do, upper-grade readers have less school time devoted to reading than previous years and don't often choose to read for pleasure (Allington, 1975; Ivey and Broaddus, 2000).

Effects of Self-Selected Reading

There is evidence that the time devoted to independent reading affects many aspects of students' lives:

- The amount of time a person spends reading is the most powerful factor in the development of the reading processes (Allington, 1994).

- Students who read more become more proficient in reading fluency and comprehension, develop a larger vocabulary, and have greater cognitive development (Anderson, Wilson, and Fielding, 1988; Stanovich, 1986).

- Students who spend more time in silent reading at school increase their independent reading levels, score higher on comprehension tests, have significantly higher grade point averages, and develop more sophisticated writing styles than peers who do not engage in silent reading (Block and Mangieri, 2002; Block, 2001).

- Upper-grade students see silent reading as an opportunity to make more sense of the text at hand, since the time set aside frees them to concentrate, comprehend, and reflect without being disturbed or distracted by some other task (Ivey and Broaddus, 2001).

- Students who participate in ongoing independent reading in school are more likely to read outside of school and increase their reading levels (Greaney, 1980).

- When students don't read on their own, their general academic progress is in jeopardy (Worthy, 2002).

Self-Selected Reading in Big Blocks

Preparing for Self-Selected Reading

Self-Selected Reading is more than giving students time to read. This Block requires preparation and planning to create the environment and opportunities students need to become mature, engaged readers. Teachers must allocate adequate time, provide appropriate reading materials, and create an engaging literacy environment.

Time

Upper-grade students are expected to become independent readers, yet they often have few opportunities to read independently at school, explore their own interests in reading, read at their own pace, or make their own decisions about whether or not to read a particular book (Ivey and Broaddus, 2001). So, how are students supposed to learn to be independent readers if they never hav independent reading time? Many teachers assume that students will become independent readers by reading outside of school. While some students do this, often those who need to practice reading the most will not develop the disposition to read outside of school unless there is time to do so in school with teacher support and guidance.

In classrooms where students are motivated to read, teachers create opportunities for Self-Selected Reading (Morrow, 1991). We suggest 180 minutes per week be devoted to Self-Selected Reading in a Big-Blocks classroom; Allington (2001) suggests a minimum of 90 minutes per day. These large blocks of time allow students to "get lost in a book." Upper-grade students should be reading longer, more challenging books. However, with small blocks of time, students often can't get engaged in complex texts. If your schedule does not allow for large blocks of time on a daily basis, then find extended periods of time during the week that equal approximately 180 minutes (for example, M/W/F for 60 minutes or T/TH for 90 minutes). Whether large blocks of Self-Selected Reading time are provided daily or a few times a week, there should be a regular schedule. Don't provide Self-Selected Reading time only when there happens to be spare time or at the end of the day if time allows. Students need to be prepared for reading. Early in the year, you will want to start slowly to build success for you and students who haven't yet developed the habit of reading for long periods of time.

Materials

In addition to benefiting from time set aside to read, students benefit from choosing what they will read When students self-select what they will read, they expend more effort in learning and understanding material, have greater involvement with the text, use more sophisticated strategies than for assigned school reading, and enjoy reading at school (Gambrell, 1996; Worthy, 1996; Ivey and Broaddus, 2000). Practicing and applying cognitive strategies in self-selected texts will assist students in using these strategies later in assigned school texts.

Access to materials students are interested in reading has a significant effect on literacy development. Students (and adults!) report they are most interested in reading relatively easy materials. In fact, providing regular opportunities for students to read relatively easy materials is one excellent way to help students develop fluency (Ivey and Broaddus, 2000; Allington, 2001). Students should have access to a range of materials at a variety of reading levels and interests and not just the "best" books a teacher wants. Classroom libraries, as well as school libraries, should include a wide range of genre and topics at multiple reading levels if all students are to find appealing books to read day after day.

Self-Selected Reading in Big Blocks

Ivey and Broaddus (2001) report that the top three genre choices for upper-grade students are magazines, adventure books, and mysteries. Librarians report scary stories and books as most requested (Worthy, 1996). Other genres older students include in their most wanted lists are:

- Cartoon collections (Worthy, Turner, and Moorman, 1998)
- Comics (Worthy, Turner, and Moorman, 1998; Worthy, 2002)
- Jokes and humorous stories (Worthy, 2002)
- Magazines (Worthy, 2002)
- Series books (Palmer, Codling, and Gambrell, 1994; Allington, 2001; Worthy, 2002)
- Picture books (Worthy, Turner, and Moorman, 1998)
- Adult novels (Worthy, Turner, and Moorman, 1998)
- Materials about sports (Worthy, 2002)
- Books with relevant characters and themes (Worthy, 2002)
- Nonfiction (Ivey and Broaddus, 2001) Large amounts of nonfiction were reported as being read out of school compared with the near nonexistence of nonfiction mentioned for in-school reading!
- Books that had been read aloud to them or books that had been read by their friends (Palmer, Codling, and Gambrell, 1994) Reading familiar books fosters deeper processing and enhances learning.

High-quality, book-rich classroom libraries should be a priority in schools (Gambrell, 1996; Allington, 2001). Allington (2001) also suggests a minimum of 500 different books in each classroom, with a note that in a study of exemplary teachers, they found collections of up to 1,500 book titles.

Environment

Classroom and school library books should be attractively displayed. Books can be stored on shelves, in boxes, in bins, or in end-of-aisle displays such as you might see in a retail store—all with the covers facing out. Readers select books by their covers, not their spines. If wall space is available, house guttering can be used to create a wonderful open book display in any center. Mount two or more guttering clips so that the guttering is open to the room when placed inside the clips. Guttering can easily be cut to any size. The only construction needed is attaching the clips to the wall.

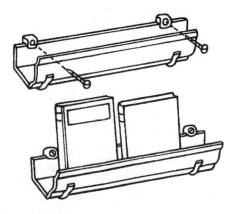

Self-Selected Reading in Big Blocks

Establish a checkout procedure in your classroom library that lets you keep track of your materials, allows students to have access to good books, and isn't too burdensome for either of you. A few suggestions include:

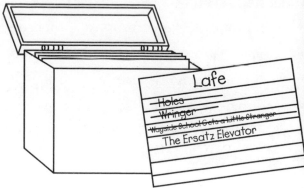

- Give each student an index card with his name on it. Students write the titles of the books they are reading on the cards. They cross the titles off when they return the books to the shelves. The cards can be kept in a small file box.

- Write each student's name on an index card. Place the index cards in a pocket chart. Students write the titles of the books they are checking out on different index cards that have been cut in half. (You may also choose to use different colored index cards for names and books so that they stand out.) Students place the cards with the book titles in front of the cards with their names. At a glance you can see which students have which books. Once the title of a book has been written on a card, it is placed in the book before the book is returned to the shelf, in order to be used by the next reader.

Kaitlin	Alex
The Lucky Stone	Blackberries in the Dark
Annabelle	Merrill Kaye
Letters from Rifka	Baby
Sidney	VeDrene
True Confessions of a Heartless Girl	Every Time a Rainbow Dies

- Have students write their names and the titles of the books they are currently reading on self-stick notes. The notes are dated and placed on a piece of poster paper.

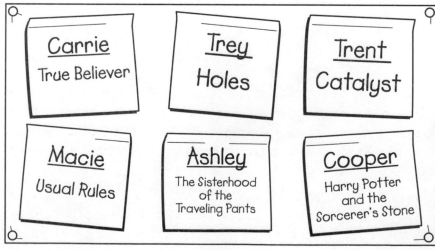

Book	Student	Returned
Holes	Lafe	10/4
Star Girl	Virginia	

- Keep a spiral notebook in the library area where students can log in and sign out books. A return date beside the entry means they have finished the book and returned it to the classroom library.

Develop book displays that highlight particular books, authors, genres, themes, etc. These may include posters, book jackets, and other "advertising" as part of the literature-oriented displays. Invite students to assist you in developing these displays. They are capable of developing quality displays featuring books they are interested in. It is important that the displays change at least once a month. Don't develop a display at the beginning of the year and expect students to remain interested all year.

The desire to read is promoted when comfortable seating is available in the reading area and throughout the room (Fractor, Woodruff, Martinez and Teale, 1993; Serafini, 2001; Pilgreen, 2000). Encourage students to find a special place to read. In addition to the reading area, look at other places in the room that are available to students during Self-Selected Reading. There should be a large gathering space for mini-lessons and sharing. The quality of conversation and learning will be greatly enhanced by having students gather together in a common area for the read aloud and mini-lesson at the beginning of Self-Selected Reading and sharing at the end. This space should serve double duty as students are reading in the space while you are conferencing during Self-Selected Reading.

Self-Selected Reading Read Alouds and Mini-Lessons

Read Alouds
Reading aloud to students has been found to be one of the most important things teachers can do to increase student achievement in all academic areas, increase vocabulary and fluency, and develop a love for reading in students (Block and Mangieri, 2002; Worthy, 2002; Ivey and Broaddus, 2000). Teacher read alouds allow students to access or develop background knowledge and learn about story elements and text structure.

Read alouds should include all types of literature and demonstrations of how books are used. You should read fiction, nonfiction, magazines and newspaper articles, poetry, plays, and any other type of literature that reflects students' interests and your curriculum. You may choose to read picture books,

Self-Selected Reading in Big Blocks

easy chapter books, or a segment of a book to get students interested. It is not necessary that you read an entire grade-appropriate chapter book. In fact, it may be preferable that you don't always read chapter books and that when you do, you don't read each book in its entirety. Long chapter books require weeks to complete and don't allow you to expose students to a wide variety of materials. Consider using the read aloud to motivate students to select books at their reading levels. For several days, choose books at the reading levels of those students in your room who persist in reading books that are too difficult. When you are done with a read aloud, make the book available to the targeted students. Students usually enjoy reading books you have read aloud. The goal is to show them how much fun it is to read books that are just right!

In addition to reading aloud materials that students might read, you should share your own reading experiences with students and emphasize how reading enhances and enriches your life (Gambrell, 1996). You may choose to read aloud a movie review from a magazine, a report from the newspaper, a book review or article from your professional materials, a passage from a novel, or you may choose to tell about something you have been reading. We believe an explicit reading model, a teacher who shares his or her own reading experiences, is more beneficial than a passive reading model, one who reads while students read.

Mini-Lessons

Read alouds provide valuable modeling for students. During read alouds, you can model comprehension and decoding strategies by thinking aloud—talking about your thinking—as students think along. Or, you may develop a mini-lesson that focuses students on the particular features of a genre or author. The mini-lesson should help students transfer key concepts taught in Working with Words or Guided Reading to their personal reading. We recommend a mini-lesson that focuses on decoding on the days when you don't have a phonics/spelling lesson in Working with Words and a mini-lesson that focuses on comprehension on the days when you do have a phonics/spelling lesson in Working with Words. It is appropriate to have a read aloud without a mini-lesson on one or two days a week.

In this section, six different types of mini-lessons will be discussed: procedural, comprehension strategies, decoding strategies, vocabulary strategies, literary elements/author's craft, and personal interpretation/response. Several mini-lesson topics will be listed under each type with a few topics described in greater detail. Before students can successfully engage in self-regulated, independent reading and apply the strategies you are modeling, behavioral expectations must be explicitly discussed and monitored. Plan to repeat mini-lessons several times throughout the year.

Procedural Mini-Lessons

Rules
Rules tell students how to behave. Some common rules are listed in the Self-Selected Reading Supplement on page 46.

Reading Materials
Share with students your expectations for using the reading materials in the classroom. Some mini-lessons might include:

- What each student should have for Self-Selected Reading
- What is available in the classroom library
- Borrowing classroom materials for Self-Selected Reading
- What is available in the school library; how to get materials from the library
- Reasons to abandon a book or reading material
- How to choose books and/or other reading materials (sample lesson on page 46 in the Self-Selected Reading Supplement)
- What to do when you are finished with your materials

> **HINT**
>
> Review rules frequently at the beginning of the year, after school breaks, when students become less focused, etc. Don't begin individual conferences until rules and routines are firmly in place and students are reading for a specified amount of time (e.g., 15 minutes). Before these routines are established, students need you to be circulating in the classroom. You should be listening to see if students are reading "just right" books and can respond to generic questions such as, "How's it going?" "Is this your first book by this author?" "What made you choose this book?"

Keeping Track of Reading
Students should be expected to maintain a written record of what they read. Show them what, where, and how you want them to record that information. Mini-lessons might include:

- How to fill out a Reading Log (daily record of what and how much was read; see sample form on page 37)
- How to complete a Reading Journal (weekly account of student reading and thinking; see mini-lesson on page 49 in the Self-Selected Reading Supplement)

How to Use the Classroom during Self-Selected Reading
Let students know what the classroom should look like and sound like during Self-Selected Reading. Mini-lessons might include:

- Finding a place to read
- Appropriate noise level/How to keep the noise level down
- How to take care of nonreading needs

Conferences
Student conferences are a critical component of the Self-Selected Reading Block. Additional information is provided on pages 34-35. Mini-lessons might include:

- Teacher responsibilities for conferences
- Student responsibilities for conferences

Self-Selected Reading in Big Blocks

Sharing

Sharing motivates and encourages students to continue reading. Additional information on sharing is provided on pages 41-42. One important part of sharing is giving and listening to book talks. A mini-lesson on the preparation and delivery of book talks will help students prepare for sharing.

Comprehension Strategies Mini-Lessons

Comprehension is the heart of reading. If you model how you think strategically while reading, it will reinforce students' thinking while reading. Comprehension think alouds during the mini-lesson will enhance students' transfer of critical strategies to their own reading. Mini-lessons might include:

- Using a variety of comprehension strategies (sample lessons on page 48 in the Self-Selected Reading Supplement)
- Marking interesting places or important parts in the text
- Interpreting graphic sources
- Looking for and finding relationships in and among texts
- Retelling a story orally or in writing

Decoding Strategies Mini-Lessons

Older students read materials with many new, unknown words. Modeling strategies that accomplished readers use when decoding new words will enhance students' transfer of these decoding strategies to their own reading. Mini-lessons might include:

- Put your finger on the word and say all of the letters aloud
- Chunking words
- Using Guess the Covered Word questions
- Reading "through" to figure out new words
- Using knowledge of prefixes, roots, and/or suffixes to read an unfamiliar word

Vocabulary Strategies Mini-Lessons

In addition to reading new words, students must understand the meanings of new words. Modeling how to determine the meanings of unknown words while reading aloud will enhance students' transfer of vocabulary strategies to their own reading. Mini-lessons might include:

- Determining word meanings using a variety of strategies (context, resources, background knowledge)
- Using morphemes to determine word meanings
- Noticing/marking interesting words
- Determining the meanings of multiple meaning words

Literary Elements/Author's Craft Mini-Lessons

Reading what the author has written requires more than simply decoding the words. Good readers think about the text and the author's intent. Literary elements will be the focus of many Guided Reading lessons in a Big-Blocks classroom. Self-Selected Reading mini-lessons offer opportunities to review the concepts taught in Guided Reading and to help students transfer the concepts to their independent reading. Mini-lessons might include:

- How the story setting fits the story
- How the setting affects the story
- How authors use the problem/event/solution pattern
- Characteristics of texts
- Read/understand analogies
- Read/understand foreshadowing
- Literary allusions from text to text
- Poetry
- Read/understand similes and metaphors
- Genre/genre studies
- Individual authors
- Characters' points of view
- Looking at leads
- Finding point of view

HINT

Many Literary Elements/Author's Craft Self-Selected Reading mini-lessons will connect to what students need to learn about writing.

Personal Interpretation/Response Mini-Lessons

Good readers have ideas about and responses to what they read. By recording these ideas and responses, students are able to reflect and share their thinking with others. Mini-lessons might include:

- Personal responses to text
- Recording ideas in the writing section of the Big-Blocks Notebook (connect reading to writing—How can I use my thoughts or the ideas I read to help me in my own writing?)
- How to use a Reading Journal and ways to respond to reading (sample lessons on pages 49-50 in the Self-Selected Reading Supplement)

HINT

Pay attention to conference conversations. When several students need help with the same strategy, develop a mini-lesson to share with the class.

Self-Selected Reading in Big Blocks

Reading

The majority of the Self-Selected Reading Block should be devoted to students reading books they have selected. There is one rule to be reinforced at this time: the only thing students can do is read! Reading time is not the time they select books for reading, sharpen pencils, complete unfinished work, or are up and roaming for any reason—this is time for reading. Students will be accountable for having enough materials ready and at their desks for the full reading time. They may need to select new books to have ready before Self-Selected Reading if they are almost finished with the ones they have. Book selection may be done before class begins, when students visit the library during the week, or as part of the weekly conference. Students should understand what reading time looks like and sounds like. If you have students who are unable to read for long periods of time, be sure they have a variety of short materials to read. Once a week, students should use some of the time to respond to what they are reading. However, the goal is to ensure that every child reads!

Conferencing

While students read, conduct conferences with individual students. The conference is an opportunity to engage students in conversations about what they have been reading, determine how they are progressing on a developmental continuum, and address the individual needs of each student. The mini lesson models the actions of good readers; however, the conference is where teaching and learning occur. It is the opportunity for each reader to learn and practice what is most relevant to her.

Conferences may occur at a common meeting area where the student comes to you, or you may choose to move to the individual student. In either case the conversation should be held in a quiet tone of voice to avoid interrupting other students who are reading in the classroom. During the meeting, you should take notes that reflect the conversation and learning in the conference. If plans are made or goals are set as a result of the conference, you should record it on your summary of the conference and on a self-stick note to be placed in the student's journal. For example, if a student has been encouraged to visualize while reading, you might write, "Visualize—What do you see in your head?" on a self-stick note for the student and a note on his summary sheet to ask about visualizing in the next conference.

Visualize—What do you see in your head?

HINT

Have students place their reminder notes where you can see them during Self-Selected Reading. Between conferences, make an effort to ask students how they are doing with their goals.

Self-Selected Reading in Big Blocks

Conferences should be 3-5 minutes long—longer for struggling readers and shorter for proficient readers. Schedule your struggling readers on different days of the week; schedule your advanced readers on different days of the week. That means your daily schedule will ideally include a struggling reader, a few average readers, and an advanced reader. Conferences should focus on meaningful conversations, encouraging students to apply strategies to become better readers, and assisting them in selecting new books when necessary or appropriate.

Questions to Stimulate Conversations with a Student Who Has Just Started a Book

- Why did you choose this book?
- What do you think it will be about? How do you know?
- How will you know if this is a good book for you?
- What do you think so far?
- Will you read a few paragraphs for me?
- What new information did you get from what you read?
- What do you think will happen next?
- When do you think you will finish this book?
- Is there anything else you want to talk about?

Questions to Stimulate Conversations with a Student Who Is in the Middle of a Book

- What is this book about?
- What has happened so far?
- Do you like it? Why or why not?
- Will you choose a few sentences/paragraphs to read for me? Why did you choose those?
- What new information did you get from what you read?
- Do you have any connections?
- What do you think (predict) will happen next?
- What questions do you have? What would you like to ask the character (or author)?
- What do you see as you read this part?
- When do you think you will finish this book?
- Is there anything else you want to talk about?

Be cautious about which questions you choose to ask. Don't ask them so that students "get" the same response you do. What is funny or interesting to you may not be to the student. If you find something interesting, funny, or if you have a connection and it adds to the conversation, then share it. If the student is leading the conversation in another direction, follow the student.

Self-Selected Reading in Big Blocks

Questions to Stimulate Conversations with a Student Who Has Finished a Book

- What was the book about?
- Did you like it? Why or why not?
- Do you have a favorite part? Character? Scene?
- Will you pick one (favorite part or scene) to read to me?
- Does this book remind you of anything?
- What questions do you still have?
- Would you recommend this to a friend? Which friend? Why?
- Would you read another book by this author? Why?
- What book have you selected to read next?
- Is there anything else you want to talk about?

Interruptions: Barriers to Self-Selected Reading Conferences

Student conferences are your primary opportunity to deliver a lesson that is meaningful to that student. Interruptions don't allow you or the student to focus on teaching and learning. The quality of the conference may be directly related to the frequency with which conferences are interrupted (Glasswell, Parr, McNaughton, and Carpenter, 2003). If a train of thought, conversation, reading, or instruction is interrupted, the opportunity for student learning is impeded. Include "no interruptions during conferences" on your list of rules and expectations. Let students know that when you conference, they are to "be kind to others" and not interrupt so that they won't be interrupted during their conferences.

Conferencing Variation: Group Conferences

Older students may participate in small group conferences. In this instance, the teacher may choose to conference with all of the students at one table or with a couple of students who are reading the same or similar stories. The benefit of this small-group conference is that students may be able to support and assist one another with reading plans or when they struggle. It may also lead to a richer conversation among students beyond the conference. The downfall of the group conference may be in the amount of time it requires. A single student spends 3-5 minutes in a conference; a group conference may be 1: 20 minutes in length, and not all of that time may be beneficial to each student. Older students enjoy working in groups and should have this opportunity when it is appropriate.

Keeping Records and Responding to Literature

Student Records—Self-Selected Reading Section of the Big-Blocks Notebook

Daily Reading Log

Students should record what they read each day in the Daily Reading Log sections of their Big-Blocks Notebooks. They should also indicate whether they have finished a book, plan to continue reading it, or plan to abandon it. A Daily Reading Log might look like this:

○	Daily Reading Log		
Date	Title of Book or Article(s)	Pages Read	F=finished C=continue A=abandon
2-23-04	Esperanza Rising	1-12	C
2-24-04	Esperanza Rising	13-30	C
2-25-04	Esperanza Rising	31-47	C

Having students record the pages they finished provides them feedback about where to begin the next reading and provides the information you will ask for in your Quick Check.

Reading Journal

Students should record their thinking and learning in the Reading Journal sections of their Big-Blocks Notebooks. The journals should be completed once a week. Responses may be Quick Writes or dialogues (Atwell, 1998; Educational Research Service, 1999).

A Quick Write is a 1-3 minute written response to a reading or to information learned on a given topic. Students use Quick Writes to:

- Preview—access prior knowledge or describe what they think a story will be about.

- Synthesize—reflect on how well a concept was learned.

- Summarize—succinctly retell the main points of a text. This can be done with what has been read to date and/or when the reading is completed.

- Character Response—respond to the characters in the story either by writing a letter to or from a character or a journal entry as the character

- Self-Assess—assess their understanding of, involvement with, and attitudes and emotions toward the text.

Self-Selected Reading in Big Blocks

Students may choose to develop a dialogue with the teacher through letters that describe their thinking that week. Educational Research Service (1999) offers the following guidelines for students who write in reading dialogue journals:

- Express their personal responses to reading—opinions, feelings, likes, and dislikes.

- Relate books to their own experiences; write about similar things that have happened to them.

- Expressing their thoughts is most important. Students should take care with spelling and handwriting but should not let these skills keep them from sharing their thinking.

- Talk about things they don't understand, or ask questions about what is happening or why something is happening.

- Make predictions about what will happen in the rest of the book. As they continue reading, students should keep track of which predictions came true but not worry about being wrong.

- Praise or criticize books, giving specific reasons why they feel this way, such as the writing style or subject matter.

Students may have great thoughts and insights while reading, but struggle to remember them when journaling. To assist with recall, students should note what they are thinking as they are reading. Self-stick notes or response forms may help students capture ideas quickly while they are reading so that they can reflect on them when journaling. Here is an example of a student response to *Sharks* by Sandra Markle (Scholastic, Inc., 1996):

○	Quote from text	Student Thinking/ Important Information
	"Look at the reef shark and the soldier fish. They are both fish."	Sharks are related to fish, not whales.
	"A shark's skeleton isn't made of hard bone. It's made of lightweight, rubbery material called cartilage."	Sharks' skeletons won't break as easily as other animals. Cartilage bends more than bones do.

Some things a student might think about and respond to are (adapted from Harvey and Goudvis, 2000):

- Connections
- Mental Images
- What I Think That Means
- What I Wonder
- What I Figured Out
- Predictions
- Important Information/Ideas
- What I See

You should be prepared to respond to students' journals. You may respond to journal entries in weekly conferences or in writing. However you choose to respond, it is important for students to know that what they have to say is important and that you are interested in their reading and thinking.

Teacher Records—Conference Forms

Conference conversations and plans should be captured in some way. This information will assist you in planning mini-lessons, following up on plans for individual students, and sharing information regarding student progress with parents and other adults.

One kind of information you might record is an ongoing compilation of the questions and conversations that occur in the context of the conferences. Later, this allows you to reflect and analyze student learning and needs. A sample Conference Summary form (see page 54) might look like this:

Student Name Kaitlin

Date	Conference Summary
2·26·04	Letters from Rifka
	Why this book? like stories in past; stories about girls
	Finished? no What happened so far? girl and family leaving
	Ukraine; she has to talk to guards so family can get on
	train without being seen How do you describe her? brave
	Why? risked her life Know someone like Rifka? not really;
	friends and family aren't in danger Any connections? stories
	about slave girl · can't remember book; Esperanza Rising

Self-Selected Reading in Big Blocks

There may be specific skills or strategies you are accountable for through your grade-level curriculum and/or grade card. Keeping a simple form with critical objectives will assist you in looking and listening for evidence of learning. A sample Reading Skills/Strategies Checklist (see page 52) might look like this:

Reading Skills/Strategies Checklist

Student **Kaitlin**	emergent	developing	fluent	Comments
Comprehension				
Thinking Strategies				
Making Connections			✓	9-25-03 OK 12-25-03 OK 2-26-04 OK
Predicting/Anticipating			✓	10-09-03 OK 11-20-03 OK 12-4-03 OK
Summarizing/Concluding				1-15-04 OK 2-16-04 OK
Questioning/Monitoring				2-12-04 OK
Imaging/Inferring		✓		2-19-04 sketchy
Evaluating/Applying				

Another form may be helpful in scheduling students and making plans for the coming week. A sample Conference Planning Schedule (see page 55) might look like this:

Conference Planning Schedule

	Student Name	**Conference Focus**
MONDAY	Kaitlin	Ck on Rifka; ck on imaging/inferring
	Alex	Ck on Wringer; ck on fluency
	Cooper	Ck on Harry Potter; ck on book difficulty
	Lafe	Ck on American Plague; ck on prefixes/suffixes
	Merrill Kaye	Ck on A Northern Light; ck on # pgs. read
	Virginia	Ck on Maniac, ck on fluency

Teacher Records—Status of the Class

Between conferences it is helpful to check in on each student's reading status. This can be done efficiently by using a Quick Check. Ask students to indicate when they have selected a new book (S), on what page they finished reading that day (not how many pages read), or if they finished a book (F). Then, say the name of each student. The student quickly responds with the appropriate letter and/or page number, and you record the information for later reference. The Quick Check should be completed in 5 minutes or less and can be done daily or a few times a week. A sample Quick Check (see page 53) might look like this:

HINT

It is preferable to ask students what page they read last rather than the number of pages they read to avoid a competition of who reads the most, which might translate into who thinks the least. It is also preferable that the Quick Check be completed without comment from you. If a teacher makes comments regarding the information, students may become hesitant to share accurate information or it may become another competition. Information gathered through the Quick Check should be addressed during individual conferences.

Quick Check															
Name	Date	2-9-04	2-10-04	2-11-04	2-12-04	2-13-04	2-17-04	2-18-04	2-19-04	2-20-04	2-23-04	2-24-04	2-25-04	2-26-04	2-27-04
1. Kaitlin		17	32	45	64	79	F	S	S	S	14	35	49	67	F
2. Alex		34	51	66	83	101	118	136	F	S	29	46	53	71	88
3. Cooper		53	78	99	124	156	175	199	223	247	270	292	F	S	36
4. Lafe		S	S	12	25	32	44	57	69	81	96	105	117	F	S
5. Merrill Kaye		117	F	S	24	55	81	104	132	165	224	269	294	F	S
6. Virginia															

Sharing

Students have ongoing opportunities to share what they are reading and thinking with the teacher during a weekly conference, in their weekly written responses, and with their peers during book talks or conversations. Social interactions and opportunities to approximate literacy activities motivate students to read frequently and to read a wide range of materials (Gambrell, 1996). When implemented thoughtfully and carefully, book talks and student discussions can have a powerful effect on student learning (Ivey and Broaddus, 2000).

Self-Selected Reading in Big Blocks

Sharing takes 5-10 minutes per day or a total of 25-50 minutes per week. Peer sharing may occur one student at a time through book talks to the whole class or with small groups of students sharing together. Book talks allow students to share what they have read and their responses to their reading, as well as to encourage others to read a particular book. A regular sharing schedule may be established so that students can prepare book talks on books they are reading or have read. Some teachers choose to have students share on the same day as their conferences so that the teacher can assist the students in preparing book talks if necessary. This is especially helpful to some students (and teachers!), and they should have this opportunity for additional support. Book talks should be short (less than one minute), interesting (students should be excited about their books), and creative.

Teachers may choose to have students share what they have been reading in small groups. Small group sharing allows for peer conversations (Palmer, Codling, and Gambrell, 1994; Gambrell, 1996). Teachers must decide if they want to structure the conversations to be academic or if they will leave the conversations to be student-driven. When young adolescents discuss their preferred books with their peers, the conversations do not resemble the book discussions most often seen in schools; the purpose is personal rather than academic (Ivey and Broaddus, 2000).

One group sharing opportunity is called Four Share (Cunningham, Hall, and Gambrell, 2002). Four Share is a group format with four students, each with a specific role. The first student shares by reading or telling about a few pages in his book in less than one minute. The second student says something she liked about what was shared. The third student asks a question. The last student tells something he would like to know more about. When the first round of sharing is over, the second student in the group shares, and all of the roles shift to the next students. Four Share takes about 20 minutes and would be more academically focused than student-driven. This is not a daily sharing activity but would be used occasionally.

Another way to organize small group sharing is through Partner Quickshares (Cunningham, Hall, and Gambrell, 2002). In Partner Quickshares, each partner has one minute to share something interesting, exciting, or important about what he has been reading during Self-Selected Reading. Partners should change each time so that students get to talk to many different people over a few weeks and learn about all different kinds of books. Quickshares can be used daily and may be more student-driven.

Incentives

When points, grades, or other incentives are offered for reading tasks, students are given the impression that reading is a chore not worth doing unless it is rewarded (Worthy, 2002). Be very cautious in your attempts to motivate students to read through means other than time, choice, and an interesting literacy environment. In a study of reading incentives, Gambrell (1996) found that rewards that were directly related to reading (for example, books, bookmarks, time to read, etc.) were effective; however, incentives were not an effective motivator in the long run. While many educational publishing companies refer to research regarding rewards and an increase in reading, they don't tell you about the long-term research on rewards. This research indicates that when the reward is no longer given due to summer vacation, new teacher, new school, new grade, etc., the behavior drops lower than it was prior to the reward, sometimes to the point of extinguishment (Kohn, 1992, 1999).

Struggling Readers

Access to engaging materials at appropriate reading levels is an issue for most upper-grade students. With limited range in materials in terms of both difficulty and interest, struggling readers may never have opportunities in school to practice reading books they can read successfully (Worthy, 1996; Ivey and Broaddus, 2000; Allington, 2001). In addition, upper-grade students, particularly struggling readers, still need explicit instruction in word skills and strategies. This instruction may occur in a mini-lesson or in the context of a conference.

Struggling readers are asked to read orally more often than proficient readers, and struggling readers tend to have their oral reading interrupted by other students and the teacher. One strategy that you can employ to curtail the usual interruptions of oral reading is Pause, Prompt, and Praise (Topping, 1987; Topping and Ehly, 1998). When the reader makes an error, you (and students!) wait until the end of the sentence to ask the reader to pause. This may be done verbally or with a nonverbal signal, such as a tap on the table. When the reader pauses, prompt the student by providing specific information on how to remediate the error. Then, ask the reader to try it again. If the reader self-corrects the error, provide specific praise or feedback as it relates to the application of the strategy. If the reader doesn't self-correct, don't offer the praise, however, do provide an accurate model.

Although strategy instruction is critical, be sure struggling readers aren't losing reading time to skill instruction. Reading will have the greatest effect on their overall academic achievement (Block and Mangieri, 2002; Worthy, 2002; Ivey and Broaddus, 2000). Regardless of the proficiency of the reader, the most important thing that occurs during Self-Selected Reading is reading. The most important thing that occurs during the conference is the conversation.

Challenges

There are many challenges to Self-Selected Reading:

- **Many students show a steady decline in reading attitudes and voluntary reading as they progress through school** (Worthy, Turner, and Moorman, 1998).

    Self-Selected Reading at school can have a positive effect on student attitudes toward reading.

- **A recent study found that the percentage of classrooms with libraries steadily decreases with each increasing grade level** (Fractor, Woodruff, Martinez, and Teale, 1993).

    Developing a quality classroom library, in addition to a quality school library, should be a priority.

- **The general purpose of school reading is to answer questions and to accomplish other academic tasks, not free read** (Ivey and Broaddus, 2001).

    Self-Selected Reading should have a personal reading focus; Guided Reading should have an academic focus.

- **It is difficult to set aside reading time due to pressure to prioritize explicit instruction over free reading time in order to prepare for tests and teach skills** (Worthy, Turner, and Moorman, 1998; Ivey and Broaddus, 2000).

    Protect Self-Selected Reading time just like any other content instructional time.

Self-Selected Reading in Big Blocks

- **Class studies of novels take up a lot of time, and that is time taken away from what students say they like most—time to just read** (Ivey and Broaddus, 2001).

  Short stories and picture books are not just for primary-grade students. Use them in Guided Reading lessons and Self-Selected Reading read alouds and make them available to all students.

- **School reading is based primarily on traditional texts. Teachers feel they must exert control over the materials that are available for school reading; therefore, class book lists typically consist of award-winning novels. Young adolescents don't list these books as top choices for independent reading** (Ivey and Broaddus, 2001; Worthy, 2002).

  Use student interests in developing your classroom library. Students will read more if there are books and materials available that they like to read.

Middle School

Middle-school schedules and content focuses don't lend themselves to setting aside time for Self-Selected Reading. Self-Selected Reading will be the primary focus of the reading teacher. If there is only one teacher responsible for all language arts instruction, then Self-Selected Reading and Writing will be the focus of most of the instruction with some time spent in Working with Words and Guided Reading.

In some schools where Self-Selected Reading has become a school-wide priority, it has been rotated among content courses with all teachers receiving staff development and information on mini-lessons, conferencing, journaling, and sharing. In these schools, read alouds have become a part of classroom instruction in all content areas.

Professional Development Ideas

1. Visit a local bookstore.

   - Look at how reading areas are created, how book displays are developed, and how customers access books and nooks.

   - Take time to look at the literature for students. Don't forget to look at a variety of genres and "easy" material that would be interesting for students of all ages.

2. Plan mini-lessons with your grade-level team.

3. Set a goal to read 10 new adolescent books this year. Join other teachers in reading books and doing book talks with and for one another.

4. Observe other teachers during Self-Selected Reading. Invite teachers to come observe and give you feedback.

Recommended Professional Resources

Allington, R. L. (2001). *What Matters Most to Struggling Readers: Designing Research-Based Programs.* New York, NY: Addison-Wesley.

Anderson, C. (2000). *How's It Going?: A Practical Guide to Conferring with Student Writers.* Portland, ME: Stenhouse Publishers.

Hagerty, P. J. (1992). *Readers' Workshop.* New York, NY: Scholastic.

Krashen, S. D. (2004). *The Power of Reading: Insights from the Research (2nd edition).* Portsmouth, NH: Heinemann.

Serafini, F. (2001). *The Reading Workshop: Creating Space for Readers.* Portsmouth, NH: Heinemann.

Sample Mini-Lesson: Rules for Self-Selected Reading

Some rules that can be discussed and posted for Self-Selected Reading are:

1. **Be sure you and your materials are ready for Self-Selected Reading.** Take care of biological issues and selecting materials before Self-Selected Reading.

2. **Read.** The only thing we do during the Self-Selected Reading Block is read. Occasionally, you will respond to what you have read.

3. **Work silently.** A quiet classroom will allow you and others to do your best reading and thinking.

4. **Conference quietly.** A soft voice will not interrupt other readers.

5. **Have more than one good thing ready to read.** Choose materials that look interesting. Be ready to abandon materials that you don't like after you have given them a good chance. If you abandon something during Self-Selected Reading, be sure you have something else to read.

6. **Keep track of what you read.** Be sure to record what you read and how much you read each day on the assigned form.

7. **Have a good time reading!**

Sample Mini-Lesson: How to Choose a Good Book or Other Reading Material

Note: The following mini-lesson includes a sample dialogue that a typical Big-Blocks teacher might use. It would not be appropriate for you to use this dialogue unless you have read and have access to the three titles referenced in the mini-lesson. You should choose titles that reflect your own experiences in choosing text.

"I am going to model how I select a book. I have three books here that I am thinking about reading. One is a nonfiction book on teaching reading, *Phonics They Use* by Patricia Cunningham (Allyn Bacon, 2004); one is a fictional book, *The No. 1 Ladies' Detective Agency* by Alexander McCall Smith (Anchor, 2003); and the other is a nonfiction book on making things, *A Thousand and One Formulas* by Sidney Gernsback (Lindsay Publications, 1920). I chose these books because they have interesting covers and are about topics I am interested in. First, I usually read the back of the book and a few of the sentences on the first page. I am going to pay attention to the words (Can I read most of them? Do I know what most of the words mean?) and try to find out what the book is going to be about (Do I know what is happening? Do I think I know what will happen?).

"This one, *Phonics They Use*, is about teaching children how to read. It focuses on how children read words and the ways teachers can help children. I am very interested in that. The back cover of the book shares information about the author but not about the book. This book has an introduction, which might tell me what it will be about. (The teacher reads aloud from the introduction.) 'They know the skills. They just don't use them!' These words express the frustration felt by many teachers who spend endless hours teaching children phonics only to find that the skills demonstrated on a worksheet or master test don't get used where they matter—in reading and writing.' Whew! That sounds just like something I would say. I think the author is going to tell me how to do a better job teaching so that students use the information I am teaching when they are reading and writing.

"*The No. 1 Ladies' Detective Agency* is by Alexander McCall Smith, a new author to me. A friend gave it to me to read. This book is set in Africa and is about a woman who decides to open a detective agency. (The teacher reads aloud from the back cover of the book.) 'With the legacy left to her by her father, Precious Ramotswe sets up Botswana's first and only detective agency run by women.' Sounds interesting. I don't know a lot about Botswana. I think it is hot there. I'm not sure what most people do there, but I think women must not do some things men do. 'My mission, she proclaims, is to help people with the problems in their lives. This she does with enthusiasm, entering into a world of missing husbands, imposter relatives, wayward daughters and abduction.' I love to read mysteries, and I think doing what Precious does sounds fun! I can read the words and I understand them so far. I think this might be a good match as long as it is interesting. I think it will be about Precious learning how to be a detective and convincing other people that women can be detectives. If I choose this book, I will have to pay attention since I haven't read anything by this author before and I don't know much about life in Botswana.

"I like to make things. *A Thousand and One Formulas* is about how to make glue, how to make perfume, how to cut bottles, and stuff like that. (The teacher reads aloud from the table of contents.) There isn't anything on the back cover of this book, but the table of contents says, 'Cements and glues, compositions of all kinds, glass and glass working, inks, etc.' I think I will check out 'Cements and Glues.' We never seem to keep enough of that around for Kaitlin. The first section is on leather belting cement. I am not sure I know what that is. (The teacher reads aloud the first few sentences of the chapter.) 'Take 1 part of Common Glue; 1 part of American Isinglass. Place them in a boiler and add water sufficient to just cover the whole. Let it soak 10 hours then bring to boiling and add pure Tannin until the whole becomes ropy or appears like the white of egg.' I know how to read all of those words, but I don't think I know what this is talking about. What is American Isinglass or Tannin? I know what rope looks like, but what does that have to do with glue?

"I think I will choose *Phonics They Use*; I need that information right now. I want to keep *The No. 1 Ladies' Detective Agency* until I take my next plane ride. It is usually quiet enough for me to really think and get lost in a good book. I don't think *A Thousand and One Formulas* is a good book for me. I don't know enough about what I read, and I don't think I am all that interested in this topic. The title and the cover didn't really help me, but when I read a little from a chapter, I found out it wasn't a good book for me.

"When it is time for you to choose a book, you will want to be sure you get one that not only looks interesting, but is interesting to read. Read the back of the book and the first few sentences in a chapter to see if you can read the words and understand what is going on. If you can make a good prediction and you think the book looks interesting, it is a good book for you. If you can't read the words or don't know what is going on, you should try to find another book. When we get together to talk about what you are reading, I may ask you how you picked your book. Be ready to tell me what interested you and how you sampled it to be sure it was a good match."

Self-Selected Reading Supplement

Sample Mini-Lesson: Comprehension Strategies

Note: The following sample mini-lessons will show how a variety of strategies can be modeled with any text. These lessons were developed for the book *Blackberries in the Dark* by Mavis Jukes (Yearling, 1994). *Blackberries in the Dark* is the story of nine-year-old Austin who visits his grandparents every summer. The story begins with his first visit after his grandfather's death.

Connecting (after reading Chapter One)

"I used to spend time in the summer with my grandparents. I didn't go fishing with my grandpa, but I used to help him with the animals on his farm. I remember how special I felt doing things with him."

Predicting/Anticipating (after reading Chapter Two)

"I don't think Austin is very interested in the doll, even though it is special to Grandma. I think he is going to ask Grandma for Grandpa's fishing knife."

Summarizing/Concluding (after reading Chapter One)

"Austin is visiting Grandma for the first time since Grandpa died, and nothing is the same. I don't think he is going to have a very good visit this summer. I don't think he will come back next summer."

Questioning/Monitoring (after reading Chapter Two)

"What is a 'big German brown?' I wonder why Grandma gave Austin a doll!?! I wonder if something like this happened to Mavis Jukes, and that is why she chose to tell this story."

Imaging/Inferring (after reading Chapter Three)

"I can just see Austin and his Grandpa when the game warden caught them with that great big, brown spotted fish. I am guessing they weren't supposed to catch it. They walked through the fence to find a bull, and they got caught! They must have been so surprised. I bet the game warden was surprised, too! Maybe they just all stood there looking at each other, not knowing what to say."

Evaluating/Applying (after reading Chapter 6)

"Austin did the right thing stringing the doll's beads for Grandma. He needs good memories with her like he has for Grandpa. I hope Kaitlin has great memories of things she does with her grandparents."

Self-Selected Reading Supplement

Sample Mini-Lessons: How to Use the Reading Journal

"There are many ways you can respond to what you are reading. You can describe what you were thinking as you were reading, what strategies you used, how you applied mini-lessons, or you can write a summary of the story. Over the next few days, I am going to share some examples of what you might choose to write in your Reading Journal."

Mini-Lesson #1: Recording My Mental Pictures

From *The Lucky Stone* by Lucille Clifton (Yearling Books, 1986)

	Quote from text	Image (mental picture)
○	"But we was all scared of them because they had real long fingernails on they fingers and long toenails on they toes."	I see two women that are dirty. Their fingernails and toenails are so long they curl under like corn chips (Fritos).
	"Girl, bring me a glass a cool water I give you a lucky stone."	I think she is just fooling with the girl so she doesn't have to get up to get a glass of water. I see her looking at her mama to say, "See how smart I am? I can get someone else to get my water."

Self-Selected Reading Supplement

Mini-Lesson #2: Using Self-Stick Notes to Record My Questions

You may choose to use self-stick notes to write your ideas and thoughts as you are reading through a book. When you are ready to respond, you can tape the notes in your journal and write your thinking beside them.

From *Baby* by Patricia MacLachlan (Delacorte Books for Young Readers, 1993)

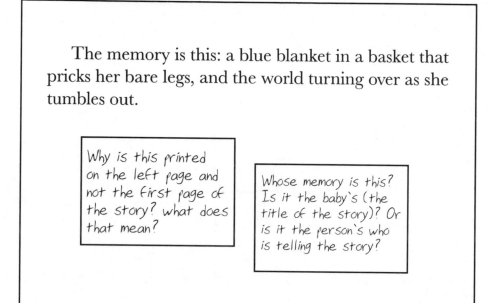

> The memory is this: a blue blanket in a basket that pricks her bare legs, and the world turning over as she tumbles out.
>
> *Why is this printed on the left page and not the first page of the story? what does that mean?*
>
> *Whose memory is this? Is it the baby's (the title of the story)? Or is it the person's who is telling the story?*

Journal Entry

○	STUDENT: Cooper	
date 1-16-04	*Why is this printed on the left page and not the first page of the story? what does that mean?*	I think this was printed on the left because it isn't part of the storyteller's story. It is the baby's memory not Larkin's, who is telling the story.
	Whose memory is this? Is it the baby's (the title of the story)? Or is it the person's who is telling the story?	I think it is the baby Sophie's memory of being left in the driveway of Larkin's house.

Self-Selected Reading Supplement

Sample Mini-Lesson: Writing a Summary

"I can best summarize the book *The Stranger* by Chris Van Allsburg (Houghton Mifflin Company, 1986) using a story map to organize what I remember."

Title and Author The Stranger by Chris Van Allsburg	
Setting Time-fall Place-Bailey's farm	
Characters (identify main character) Stranger-main character Farmer Bailey Mrs. Bailey Katy	
Problem Farmer Bailey hit a stranger with his car.	
Events Farmer Bailey took the stranger home. The doctor checked out the stranger. The stranger lost his memory. The Baileys took care of the stranger.	
Resolution The stranger remembered he had something to do with the leaves. The Baileys' leaves remained green until the stranger left. He returns every year.	

Summary:

One fall, Farmer Bailey hit a stranger with his car. Farmer Bailey took him home and had the doctor check him out. He was fine, but he had lost his memory. The Baileys took care of him until he remembered who he was. The Stranger remembered he had something to do with the leaves: they should turn bright colors and blow off the trees. As long as he was at the Baileys', the leaves remained green. When he remembered why he was there, the Stranger left. He returns every year, changes the trees, and leaves a frost-etched message, "See you next fall."

Reading Skills/Strategies Checklist

Student _____	emergent	developing	fluent	Comments
Comprehension				
Thinking Strategies				
Making Connections				
Predicting/Anticipating				
Summarizing/Concluding				
Questioning/Monitoring				
Imaging/Inferring				
Evaluating/Applying				
Word Analysis				
Letters and Sounds				
Patterns				
Analogy				
Roots, Prefixes, and Suffixes				
Meaning (Context)				
Sentence Structure				
Reading Habits				
Reads a Variety of Genres				
Spends Time Reading				
Selects Appropriate Materials				
Responds to Literature				
Other				

Quick Check

Name	Date														
1.															
2.															
3.															
4.															
5.															
6.															
7.															
8.															
9.															
10.															
11.															
12.															
13.															
14.															
15.															
16.															
17.															
18.															
19.															
20.															
21.															
22.															
23.															
24.															
25.															
26.															

A number indicates the page student finished; S = selected new book; F = finished reading

Student Name	
Date	**Conference Summary**

Conference Planning Schedule

	Student Name	Conference Focus
MONDAY		
TUESDAY		
WEDNESDAY		
THURSDAY		
FRIDAY		

Chapter 3 Writing in Big Blocks

With Big Blocks, the Writing Block format is still a "Writer's Workshop" approach (Graves, 1995; Routman, 1995; Calkins, 1994; Atwell, 1987). As students get older, they continue to need writing instruction and time to write. Two of the most significant changes in Big Blocks from Four Blocks are the time allotment and the amount of focused writing.

In Big-Blocks™ classrooms, the Writing Block—approximately 180 minutes per week—includes the following:

- **Mini-Lesson (5-15 minutes)**
  The teacher models the process of writing for students. She writes in front of the class and thinks out loud about what she is doing as a writer. She models making decisions, making mistakes, and how she puts words on the page. Students are gathered together to observe, and at the end of the lesson, they often take notes in the Writing sections of their Big-Blocks Notebooks.

- **Students Writing and Teacher Conferencing (20-30 minutes)**
  Students spend their time somewhere in the writing process: planning, drafting, revising, editing, or publishing. They spend most of their time on topics of their choice. They don't publish everything they write. Students work as writers work using the materials writers need.

  The teacher conducts individual conferences to differentiate the instruction and provide multilevel support for students. Conferences are held every time writing occurs. A conference provides a weekly opportunity to assess student progress and make appropriate instructional decisions.

- **Sharing (5-10 minutes)**
  "We write to be read." (Atwell, 2002). Many students will write just for the opportunity to share with their classmates. Sharing time is a critical component of the Writing Block. Students share part of their writing pieces in progress or read their latest published works.

The goals of the Writing Block in Big-Blocks classrooms are:

- to help students see writing as a way of telling about things

- to develop students' fluency in writing

- to provide opportunities for students to learn to use grammar and mechanics in the context of their own writing

- to help students learn about specific forms of writing during focused instruction to ensure that struggling writers are supported in order to maintain their motivation and self-confidence

Writing Is Multilevel

The Writing Block is the most multilevel of all of the Blocks. Any time students are given opportunities to write about things they have chosen because of their interests, the task is on their level. There are many other components built into the Writing Block that make it multilevel.

Mini-lessons are taught on a variety of topics and at a variety of levels. These lessons allow you to provide support to many different writers. In addition, the conferences are differentiated for each student. The one-on-one conversation is geared toward the concepts that the student needs.

Students can learn multiple things from mini-lessons and from conferences. You must get to know your students as writers to determine what kind of support they need. The framework of the Block allows for time to provide that support.

In this chapter, we will take you through each phase of the Writing Block. You will see ways to make students more accountable, mini-lesson ideas and conference techniques, as well as a list of valuable professional resources.

Shifting to a Writer's Workshop format is often a scary change for teachers to make. Most teachers were never taught to write in this manner. Their education didn't include someone who stood in front of the class and wrote his thoughts and feelings down, made changes, and struggled with the many decisions writers face each time they write. For teachers, it is a new—and often unnerving—experience. Realize that the power in teaching students to write comes from being willing to write in front of them!

Students will spend the majority of their time—or at least half of it—writing on topics of their choice. The Writing Block is not about story starters or prompts. Students will become better writers when they write about topics they are interested in, write about topics they know a lot about, and have opportunities to write on topics for multiple sessions.

Mini-Lessons

The Writing Block starts with a mini-lesson. The mini-lesson is one component of the instruction and happens each and every time the Block occurs. For 5-15 minutes, gather students together for a demonstration of writing. Without a mini-lesson, it is not Writing the Big-Blocks way. All young writers need instruction and a model of writing every time they are asked to write. However, it is also important that the mini-lesson doesn't last for 30 minutes. (That would be a maxi-lesson!) Students need instruction, as well as opportunities to try out the things they are learning about writing.

You will choose a method of writing in front of students using chart paper, an overhead projector, or document camera. For most upper-grade teachers, the choice is an overhead projector. You can face the students as you think out loud about the decisions you are making or the techniques you are trying. At the same time, students can see what you are writing on the screen. A document camera works much like an opaque projector. You can write in a notebook, and the camera will project your writing. Students can see you write with the same tools they use.

You may find there are certain mini-lessons you would rather do on chart paper. Chart paper makes a permanent record of the lesson. For example, you might be making a list of different types of writing for the students to choose from or be aware of during writing time (Hall, Cunningham, and Arens, 2003). You may decide to post the list you created so that students don't forget.

Writing in Big Blocks

Gather your students around you for the mini-lesson. It helps to build community when you have the students together—in close proximity to you and to others. Not all classrooms are conducive to gathering students together. However, if you decide it is important enough, you can make it work most anywhere. There are many rooms where gathering students together means moving two or three tables to make room. Give this job to specific students each time, and make it their job to see that the tables are pulled out of the way and then replaced at the end of the lesson. Most often, there are fewer management problems when students are gathered closer to you and away from the distractions in the desks.

What Is a Mini-Lesson?

A mini-lesson is a brief meeting where the teacher provides instruction to the whole class. A 5-15 minute Writing mini-lesson will almost always include you writing in front of students. It is absolutely essential for developing writers to see the process. This instructional phase must be focused on one particular concept, skill, or technique. The most common way a mini-lesson becomes a "maxi-lesson" is if you try to teach too many things in the same day. Students will have a much better chance of learning a concept if it is highlighted, modeled, and explained . . . but not in the midst of three other concepts.

You make decisions about what to teach during these mini-lessons in several ways. One way is to look at your curriculum or your state standards. These documents provide a view of what any fourth (fifth, sixth, etc.) grader in your school is expected to learn about writing. Use these document to keep you on track with your school's expectations.

Another way to make decisions about what to teach during mini-lessons—and just as important as the curriculum—is to look at students' writing. Your students will show you what they know and what they don't know. During every Writing Block, students will be drafting and producing text. Those examples give you excellent information about what type of instruction is needed. You will also be conferring with students during the Writing Block. Use the conference time to decide what concepts students are doing well and what concepts they may need help with. However, you should be cautious. It is easy to be overfocused on conventions and overlook important craft features.

Once you've made those decisions, use *Writing Mini-Lessons for the Upper Grades* (Hall, Cunningham, and Arens, 2003) and other professional resources to find ideas for teaching mini-lessons. You will find a list of recommended mini-lesson resources on page 90. These books can guide you in developing quality mini-lessons that fit the needs of your students.

One question that teachers often ask about mini-lesson instruction and the freedom of student choice is how to make sure students learn the concept being taught. For example, if you are doing a mini-lesson on using strong verbs, then send students off to write, what will ensure that they use those strong verbs? First of all, you must understand that very few mini-lessons will be taught only once or in only one way. Students need more instruction than that, especially on essential concepts. You will also address relevant mini-lessons in your individual conferences with students.

Types of Mini-Lessons

Big-Blocks mini-lessons typically fall into three categories: procedures, conventions, and craft. When teaching mini-lessons, there will be a combination of all three types presented throughout the year. An overemphasis on any one type of mini-lesson demonstrates an imbalance in what is important to a writer. Older students read and write more complex pieces. In the upper grades, there should be more mini-lessons on the craft of writing than on the conventions of writing. Conventions are important but don't require as much time for instruction as craft lessons.

Procedures

A procedures lesson is the type of lesson to use to set the structure and expectations of the Block. For each procedure you want students to follow, use a mini-lesson to model and teach the expectation. For example, you may have a certain way students will receive and hand in their notebooks/folders. Use a mini-lesson to teach that process. Let students learn the procedures well to make your Writing Block run smoothly.

Any time you feel a procedure needs fine-tuning, or a complete change, use a quick procedures mini-lesson to model that change. These procedures lessons will make up only a small portion of the lessons you teach all year; however, they will be among the most important. It is essential to have clear expectations and then demonstrate those expectations to your students.

Conventions

Mini-lessons that teach the conventions of writing are the lessons most teachers feel comfortable teaching. Conventions are more often known as mechanics. They are the agreements that govern our writing. For a reader to gain meaning from writing, it is most helpful to have words spelled in a consistent manner and punctuation to organize thoughts. Therefore, conventions are elements such as spelling, punctuation, capitalization, etc.

For most teachers, mechanics are easy to teach. They've been doing lessons on mechanics for a long time. Now, the key is to find a way to model using mechanics and editing mechanics in your writing, rather than simply "telling" students about mechanics. You also need to get away from having students practice mechanics in unrelated writing tasks. You need to model using mechanics in your own writing, look for examples in other writing, and demonstrate editing techniques in your own writing. You may use guided practice from time to time to allow students to put the concept into practice. (See page 60 for an explanation of Guided Practice.)

Craft

The craft of writing deals with the content. How do you write a strong lead? How do you write a powerful conclusion? How do you develop an interesting character? How do you narrow your focus? These are the things a writer uses to improve the ideas in her writing. The craft is just as important as the conventions. In fact, it is the craft that makes a piece worth reading.

For most teachers, these lessons are the most difficult to teach, especially when confidence in their own writing is lacking. Some teachers also wonder how to write a strong lead or use strong verbs to improve the mind pictures they try to create. How, then, do you teach it to someone else?

This is another area where professional resources are a great help. Look through the list on page 89 to become familiar with titles that can assist you in this area. Also, remember that your favorite children's literature is a great resource for finding quality examples. Spend time looking at the leads that draw you in. Explore the ways authors write titles. Good examples from published authors are an effective way to model in a mini-lesson.

Writing in Big Blocks

Guided Practice in Mini-Lessons

While guided practice is an effective way to allow students to try something out, it won't be necessary every day and won't work with every mini-lesson. Here is an example. You've just taught a great lesson on using strong verbs in your writing (Hall, Cunningham, and Arens, 2003). At the end of the lesson, you ask students to return to their seats, take out their writing folders/notebooks, and find one piece of writing they are working on or have worked on. You give them three or four minutes to look through their pieces for verbs. Do any of the verbs need to be changed? Do they need to be stronger? Would create a better "mind picture" for the reader if the verbs were stronger?

When the timer goes off at the end of three minutes, you may take a minute to read a couple of examples that students have written. Only share a few and share those you feel grasped the idea of strong verbs for the right reasons. Then, ask students to return to working on whatever they had planned for that day. Some students may find they want to continue working on beefing up their verb choices. If that is the case, allow them to continue. Most students would only choose to do that work on a piece that will be chosen for publication.

Other lessons that might be good for guided practice include lessons on editing, using the Editor's Checklist, reasons to paragraph, words to use other than "said," varying the way sentences begin, etc. This is certainly not an all-inclusive list. However, you can begin to see that some lessons have direct application to the process.

Some mini-lessons don't lend themselves to Guided Practice. For example, if you do a mini-lesson on writing poetry, the purpose may be to expose students to a particular form of poetry. This isn't a focused unit where you will be spending several weeks writing poems, therefore, when you finish the lesson, it wouldn't make sense to send everyone off to try this form of poetry for four minutes. Instead you leave it alone and return to it when you think you should. You might also suggest during conferences that some students try this form of poetry.

Later in the chapter (pages 68-76), we'll address conferencing. Understand that a conference is one more way to connect to the topics you teach in a mini-lesson. For example, in the strong verb lesson above, you might decide to use the following few days of conferencing looking for examples of strong verbs in students' writing or assisting students in making strong verb choices where these would improve their pieces.

On pages 90-96 are a few examples of mini-lessons. Remember to frequently write in front of your students and show them the difficulties they will face as writers. Adults and students alike face many challenges when writing. The mini-lesson is an opportunity to show students how to work through those difficulties.

Creating a Writing Handbook Section in the Big-Blocks Notebook

Accountability is important for older students. While it is still the teacher's job to provide solid instruction, students must take on some responsibility for learning and remembering what they have learned. Therefore, in Big-Blocks classrooms it will be important to introduce the concept of a Writing Handbook as one section of the Big-Blocks Notebook.

When students come together for the mini-lesson, they will bring their Big-Blocks Notebooks along. During the instructional part of the mini-lesson the notebooks are closed, and listening is the thing to do. However, at the end of the mini-lesson, direct students to open their notebooks to the Writing Handbook section and record snippets of the mini-lesson for later reference. Reif (1992) and Atwell (1998) both mention this tool in Writer's Workshop. There is also a mini-lesson in *Writing Mini-Lessons for the Upper Grades* (Hall, Cunningham, and Arens, 2003) that describes how to begin the Writing Handbook process with students. Writing in their notebooks shouldn't become the lengthiest part of the mini-lesson, but you should allow two to three minutes for students to make a record of what has been taught.

When beginning the Writing Handbook section, have students leave three to eight pages blank. Then, on the first page after the blank section, have students write the number one in the lower right-hand corner. The handbook section will be numbered like a book. After you have taught a few lessons and students have recorded them in the Writing Handbook section, it will be time for a mini-lesson on how to use the first three to eight blank pages to create a table of contents for the section.

Table of Contents	
Writing Lessons	**Page #**
Writing Ideas	1
Kinds of Writing (Genres)	2
Story Elements	3
Poetry	4
Poetry Example	5
Writing as a Gift	6
Paragraphs	7

Writing in Big Blocks

The hope is that once students begin to record what they are learning, the Writing Handbook section can be used during teacher/student conferences or even as a reference for students while they are writing. A table of contents makes finding the needed information even easier. It is impossible to know the exact order of mini-lessons you will teach throughout the year, so students will need to update the table of contents as items are added to the Writing Handbook section.

Deciding What to Include
In order for the Writing Handbook part of the mini-lesson to stay concise, it is very important to determine what will be written or recorded. In some cases, students will copy from a list you've created. Or, you may summarize the learning in two or three sentences and ask students to copy just those sentences. Other times, the writing involved may be lengthy enough that you decide to give students photocopies of the needed information later that day or the next. The photocopies can then be trimmed and taped into the notebooks. The information recorded is what is important. If recording the information will take 10 minutes, students lose writing time. You will know when the task is too long to have students do the note-taking themselves.

Organizing the Writing Handbook Section of the Big-Blocks Notebook
There are many options for organizing, and the only one that is right is the one that makes sense to you. For many teachers, the Writing Handbook section will be organized in the order in which mini-lessons are taught. Other teachers may want mini-lessons grouped together. For example, you may teach three mini-lessons on paragraphing one week and know that you will teach more paragraphing mini-lessons later in the year—maybe even next week. So, you ask students to number the next three pages in their notebooks but not to write anything on those pages. Then, when you come back to mini-lessons on paragraphing, students can turn back to the blank, numbered pages and add more information there.

HINT

You could label two sections in the Big-Blocks Notebook: Writing Handbook and Focused Writing.

It also can be helpful to reserve a part of the Writing Handbook section for focused writing lessons. Focused writing lessons are different than the normal lessons in a Writer's Workshop format, so a separate section in the Writing Handbook mirrors the shift.

Focused Writing
One of the differences between writing the Four-Blocks way and writing in Big-Blocks classrooms is the amount of focused writing that is taught (Hall, Cunningham, Arens, 2003). Upper-grade students should receive instruction in specific writing genres. Their need to know is embedded in the tests they will begin to take and in their desire to imitate the reading they engage in. Focused writing, therefore, assumes a more important role. This role is important because it consumes much of your instructional time. It is also important because students need to be taught how to write these genres. Unfortunately, teachers are often guilty of simply assigning students different genres of writing rather than teaching students how to write in these different genres.

Choosing the Genres to Teach

Teachers at every grade level and in every school or school district need to have conversations about which writing genres make the most sense to teach. Within grade levels, teachers can pool resources and their expertise to decide which genres to teach and when they should be taught. In addition, conversations between teachers at different grade levels help assure the teaching of necessary genres and the repeated teaching of those genres that pop up year after year. It is not enough to choose a genre because "it is fun" and "the students love it." Most states are now involved in high-stakes tests and curriculums that are aligned with state standards. Choosing writing genres well means studying the demands made on your students during those tests and looking at the curriculum to see where an interdisciplinary approach could be appropriate.

For example, many states teach state history in the fourth grade. Many fourth-grade teachers have students write reports about famous individuals from their states. One such district, Montgomery County R-II in Missouri, decided to teach students about the genre of biography. Each student wrote a biography of a famous Missourian rather than a "report," which is typically a school genre. Report writing is definitely not real-world writing!

If your state test requires students to write a persuasive piece as part of the assessment, it would only make sense that one of the focused units you teach during the year is persuasive writing. Having persuasive writing as one of your genres does not mean you have students responding over and over to persuasive prompts. Instead, it means spending a considerable amount of time and instruction teaching students how to write persuasively.

In elementary school, it might take five to six weeks of instruction to allow every student in a class to write a quality persuasive piece. On pages 94-96, you will find suggested mini-lessons for persuasive focused writing. Students need instruction on writing to prompts as practice for state tests and for connecting to the content areas. That would be another set of mini-lessons.

Make decisions about the genres that make sense for the ages of students you teach and are tied to your curriculum. Some focused writing is included in earlier grades, but focused writing instruction becomes more prominent in third grade as many state tests begin that year, too. Upper-grade teachers need to work with third-grade teachers to decide what kind of focused writing instruction each will undertake.

Preparing for Focused Writing

In order to teach a genre well, it is important to have many examples of that kind of writing in your classroom. If you teach biography as a focused genre, plan to use several biographies for your read alouds during Self-Selected Reading in preparation for writing instruction. The read alouds must come first so that you can connect to the knowledge that was gained. Have a collection of biography picture books that students can choose for Self-Selected Reading and have students read biographies during Guided Reading. Students need to hear multiple examples of the style of writing you are teaching. Another helpful resource is a file with examples of student writing. As you begin having students write focused pieces, remember to photocopy average and excellent examples and save for use with future classes. Remove the students' names for anonymity and consider the file of student examples as one more valuable resource in your toolbox.

Writing in Big Blocks

Instruction in Focused Writing

Most focused writing will take three to six weeks of instructional time. The idea is that during the mini-lessons, all instruction will focus on how to teach a specific genre. All students will spend their writing time in that genre until each student completes a final, published piece. Although you designate the genre, each student usually chooses the topic. It may make sense to have topics that relate to a content area study.

To develop focused writing mini-lessons, think through the process you would use when writing the same kind of text. What are the necessary steps? Each of those steps becomes a mini-lesson (or a series of mini-lessons) to allow you to model the entire process for students. As you model these steps, you construct your own piece of text for the students to connect to.

During a mini-lesson, it is necessary to do more than tell students how to do a step in a process. Model the step. For example, if you are doing anything requiring research, it is essential to model how to take notes. Most students don't have a good idea of what it means to take notes. Demonstrate by reading a section of text from one of your resources, then think out loud about how to turn that information into a short phrase that will remind you of what you've learned.

The focused writing we are referring to is different than writing to a prompt. In *Writing Mini-Lessons for the Upper Grades* (Hall, Cunningham, and Arens, 2003), one of the suggested focused writing genres is how to write to a prompt. It is important instruction that cannot be left alone. However, the most appropriate place for writing to prompts is in the content areas. See page 131 where the after-reading activity in Guided Reading is writing in response to reading. These examples are practical ways to include instruction in writing to a prompt for real reasons—not just test preparation.

Here is an example of how to decide what to write when taking notes (from *Writing Mini-Lessons for the Upper Grades*, Hall, Cunningham, and Arens, 2003, page 95):

"Since I am getting my information from other written resources, I need to make sure that I use my own words and not someone else's. For example, the text says, 'Martin was a good student. He finished high school two years early and was just 15 when he entered Morehouse College in Atlanta. At college, Martin decided to become a minister.'

"How could I take that information and use it tell about Martin Luther King, Jr.'s actions? What if I write, 'Martin found school easy and worked hard. He was smart and knew what he wanted to do.'"

Each mini-lesson demonstrates the individual steps taken to create one whole piece of writing. There may be some steps you want to model a few days before students actually write on their own. Other steps will work best if you model them and send everyone off to do the same thing.

When making decisions about focused writing mini-lessons, you may have an element you want to emphasize. Certain genres lend themselves to certain features of writing. For example, if your students will be writing essays, it would make sense to spend a good deal of time teaching them to write introductions and conclusions. If the focused writing is a narrative of some kind, it would make sense to emphasize strong leads. Perhaps your students will be writing traditional tales of some kind, and you would like to see them use figurative language. In that case, develop your mini-lessons to teach them about writing traditional tales but make sure you include several days on figurative language.

Independent Writing Time during Focused Writing

Students are all working on the designated focused writing. They know when their pieces need to be completed, and they are working toward that due date. Again, this reflects a difference from other times during the Writing Block. For most pieces, students use as much time as needed to write a quality piece. But when they are working on focused writing, you usually have an end date in mind and will share that date with students.

During focused writing, students will go through the stages of the writing process as usual, but you may give more directions as to when they should be ready for certain stages. In other words, you may set a due date for prewriting or brainstorming to be finished, then another date for the rough drafts to be completed. These interim due dates are helpful to students who need more structure. Students who meet a due date should be encouraged to move on to the next stage. Due dates like this can also be helpful to teachers who will be working hard to get all students published at about the same time.

While students are writing, you are conferencing. The conferences will center on the students' focused pieces. As the final due date looms closer, you may shorten your mini-lessons to increase the amount of time available for conferences and writing.

Sharing Time

Even during focused writing, there should be a sharing time. This time may be used to keep the focus on the genre being taught. You may have students share graphic organizers for their prewriting/brainstorming. They may read what they have written so far. They could share resources they used if research is a part of what they are doing.

It will be your decision on how to use this time in the Writing Block. If you are just beginning instruction on a new genre, you may decide to let students share whatever they are interested in sharing. As you get further into the unit of study, you could ask students to keep their sharing focused on the new genre.

Organization

The Writing Block only runs well if it is an organized environment. You and the students must know where the supplies are and where they are to be stored. A clear set of expectations is taught during procedural mini-lessons and followed to keep things going. To begin thinking about the organization you will use, consider time and materials.

Time

At the beginning of the chapter, we mentioned that approximately 180 minutes a week will be spent in the Writing Block. Sample schedules show the Writing Block lasting from 40-60 minutes. It is important to consider how to break down the allotted time. Once again, think about mini-lessons and consider what happens if a mini-lesson takes 30 minutes. The problem is that students don't have enough time to write. Independent writing is the time when students have the opportunity to practice what you have been teaching. Just as those students who read more read better, those students who write more write better.

That does not mean students can just write every day for 30 minutes and become wonderful writers. Instruction is critical, and you provide that instruction in mini-lessons and conferences. However, instruction can't take the place of writing.

Writing in Big Blocks

For these reasons, we see the breakdown of the Block this way:

   10–15 minutes—mini-lesson

   20–30 minutes—writing time

   5–10 minutes—sharing

Note: If your Writing Block meets for more than 55 minutes, increase the writing time; the mini-lesson and sharing time remain the same. For example, if the Writing Block occurs for 60 minutes, three times per week, then writing time would be 35-45 minutes.

Another consideration is the respect you give that time. In other words, when you send students off to write, how often do you interrupt the class to give another set of instructions? Do you stop everyone to manage the behavior of one or two? If you are trying to establish writing time as "sacred," you, as the teacher, need to respect the time as well. You show this respect by talking softly to individuals who are disrupting the class. You show this respect by making sure students get the allocated writing time every week. You show this respect by making writing a priority.

Materials

What do you need when you write? What are the materials you like to use? Students need materials that are readily available. Of course, the two most used resources are paper and writing utensils. For elementary students—and for most people—the best writing utensil is a pencil.

At times, it seems that students perform great disappearing acts with the pencils they bring to school. As frustrating as this can be, it is absolutely essential that there is a large supply of pencils ready during the Writing Block. There is no reason for a student to interrupt the important work of writing to tell you he has no pencil. Eliminate this as a concern and have a large container of sharpened pencils available at all times. Teach students to get the resources they need without interrupting the work of the teacher or other students.

The type of paper you use and how your students store it will be your personal choice. Here are some considerations as you make the choice.

Asking students to store writing folders or notebooks in their desks may be asking for trouble. The papers often become tattered and torn—or worse, they are lost. You may want to hand out and collect students' writing at the end of each Writing Block.

As students work on their drafts, they will need to revise and edit any pieces they choose for publication. Therefore, require students to write on every other line and one side of the paper only. **No exceptions!!!** If you have ever tried to edit a paper with writing on every line, you know how difficult it is. Begin on the first day with the expectation that all drafts will be written on every other line. You will also model this throughout the year in mini-lessons.

HINT

Have a stack of paper available with each page marked with a reminder to write on every other line. Use a high lighter or marker and make a small mark in the left margin on every other line. Make this paper available to use as drafting paper. When your stack runs out, have the students use high lighters to make their own.

Some teachers have students use spiral notebooks for their drafts. Other teachers have students use writing folders with pockets and loose-leaf notebook paper so that students can organize their work in the pockets of the folders. Another suggestion is a three-ring binder with dividers. This notebook or folder for drafting is separate from the Big-Blocks Notebook.

Other materials to consider are those you think students would find important to the process of writing. A partial list might include: self-stick notes, high lighters, index cards, colored paper, staplers, tape, correction fluid, erasers, pens, colored pencils, plain white paper, computers, and so on. You will make the decision about which materials make the most sense and seem to be used the most by the writers in your classroom. If the materials are to be used at will by the students, teach them where the materials will be stored and set the expectation that all materials be returned to their original locations.

The "teacher" materials you will need include chart paper, an overhead projector with plenty of transparencies, and/or document camera for writing in front of the class. You will want a number of transparencies because there will be times you'll want to save what was written on a transparency for another lesson. If a transparency is to be saved for a future lesson, write the mini-lesson in permanent marker rather than with write-on/wipe-away markers. Working markers that write clearly are essential for both the overhead and chart paper.

In the Writing Block, teachers keep everything. For that reason, you will need a place to store students' writing as it is published. You will also be keeping those things that are written but not published, and need to be cleaned out of the writing folders/notebooks to create room for more writing. One way to manage this onslaught of paper is to have a hanging file folder for each student. Any published piece is attached with a paper clip to the rough draft and any preplanning that was done. Once the materials are all clipped together, drop them in the student's hanging file folder. When you begin to notice that there is too much crammed into the writing folders/notebooks, you may need to have a "clean-out day." Ask students to look through their folders/notebooks and take out any pieces they feel they are finished with (pieces they don't think they will go back to or won't publish). Drop these pieces of writing

Writing in Big Blocks

into the hanging file folders, as well. Another way to store archival papers is in a pizza box. Clip papers in the same way and store with the latest writing on top.

Although you will be collecting a lot of paper, it will be a wonderful record of the progress your students make as writers. Unedited work is a true reflection of what students can do as writers. It is a powerful tool to let students look back at work from the beginning of the year and notice the changes i their own writing.

By keeping the published pieces of writing, you have a wonderful gift and portfolio to present to students and parents at the end of the year. On pages 83-84, you'll find ideas for hosting writing celebrations. The collections of published writing allow students to have a wealth of pieces to choose from when preparing to present at the celebration.

If you have students who want to share published writing with parents, or perhaps you want to show parents what students are accomplishing with their writing, make copies of the originals and allow students to take home the copies. Explain that you would like to keep the originals, but that you will give them back to the students at the end of the year. This way parents will know what their students ar writing, and you will have a wonderful collection of that writing, as well.

Conferences

The act of sitting down to conference with students about their writing is not only a great opportunity to get to know your students as writers, it is also an essential part of the instruction offered during the Writing Block. Without conferences, students go off to write with too little guidance.

You need to think of these conferences as conversations. Lucy Calkins says teachers need to think of what they can do during the conference to move the writer forward (Calkins, 1998). Don't focus your time on one particular piece of writing; rather, think about what needs to be taught to improve the student as a writer.

A conference on writing is a time to meet with a student in a one-on-one format to talk about the needs of that writer. The remaining students continue to work on the pieces in their folders and are not standing in line to meet with you. Students understand the expectation that you will be meeting with everyone and interrupting a conference is taboo as it causes you to pull your attention away from the writer in the conference. This expectation takes a bit of enforcement early on. If you allow students to come to the conferencing area or to approach you during a conference, your conferences will never happen. You will spend your days either troubleshooting students who demand your attention or telling everyone to sit down and write. You will also send a message to the conferee that her writing isn't very important (Glasswell, Parr, McNaughton, and Carpenter, 2003).

Ray (2000) writes about keeping conferences short. "We conference with students for a short amount of time. Not because it is the best way to teach, but because we have lots of individuals to teach." Conferences benefit every writer—not just the squeaky wheels.

Two of the most important steps in getting conferences started are:

1. Meet with students on a regular basis. Set up a schedule of conferences and keep track of who has had conferences.

2. Find a system for recording the essence of the conference. In order to remember what has been worked on, you will have to write it down!

Scheduling Your Conferences

If you have read any professional resources, you will find varying opinions on the best way to have conferences. Some teachers prefer to have students sign up for conferences when they are needed. Some teachers prefer to meet with students as they prepare to publish particular pieces. Other teachers say to meet with as many students as you can and keep track of where you left off. And some teachers elect to schedule students for conferences on particular days of the week. You will be the ultimate decision maker when it comes to how you choose to schedule your writing conferences. However, if you have never conferenced with students before, we would encourage you to set a schedule, post it, and stick to it. It is much too easy to get the Writing Block started and never find time to do the conferences. Without them, your students are not receiving enough help and instruction.

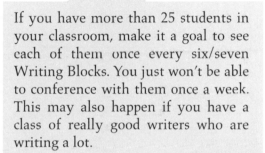

HINT

If you have more than 25 students in your classroom, make it a goal to see each of them once every six/seven Writing Blocks. You just won't be able to conference with them once a week. This may also happen if you have a class of really good writers who are writing a lot.

Much like the schedule used for conferences during Self-Selected Reading, it will be important to give some thought to the schedule. The goal is to meet with writers once a week. Therefore, divide your class into groups to determine a schedule. Think of your struggling writers and schedule one or two for each day of your Writing Block. Then, think of your best writers and schedule one in each group. Finally, divide the remainder of the class into the groups. This allows you to spend more time with the writers who need you. As Dottie Hall says, remember that what is fair is not always equal. On any given day, one writer may need a longer conference than his classmates. If that is what he needs, give it to him knowing it is a fair decision.

Once you have developed the habit of spending the independent writing time conferencing with students, you may find a better way to decide which students will get conferences and in what order. Throughout the process, always make sure every student is getting that one-on-one time and instruction.

Systems for Recording

On pages 97-100, you will find different reproducibles of recording forms. It is not necessary that you choose one of these forms to use. They are merely suggestions. You decide what format is the best for you.

HINT

If you want to allow students to sign up for conferences, allow sign-ups on Monday through Wednesday. Then, use Thursday and Friday to meet with those students who didn't sign up. Again, you will be meeting with everyone on a regular basis.

Each time a conference ends, you must take the time to make a note to yourself about the important aspects of the conference. It is fine to develop your own shorthand or system for recording. Include essential elements of the conference in your notes. Did you set a goal for the writer? Did you notice a strong improvement in the writer's ability? Was there a concern you want to note? Date the entry and include any relevant information. Two months later when you look back over those notes, you will be amazed at the clarity of your memory of that conference. Taking the time to do this may add a minute to the time you spend in each conference, but it may be the most valuable minute of all. Think of how difficult it would be to wait until the end of five conferences and then try to make notes on each one. Or worse yet, think

Writing in Big Blocks

about waiting until the end of the school day to try to recreate what was discussed. How you record your notes and what you record them on is not important. The fact that you take the time to record them makes a huge difference.

Another record keeping task is called a Quick Check. Because students are working on writing pieces and topics of their choice, it will be helpful to have a system in place to chart their progress in the process. The Quick Check, also called a Status of the Class, is a way for students to identify where they are in the process and for you to know who is working on what.

The following sample is from a Quick Check form. You should teach the class to respond quickly, as the whole check should take less than five minutes. Setting the procedure of your expectations for students will enforce the time frame. Students respond immediately when their names are called and tell you what they plan to work on that day. They need only respond with a word or short phrase: drafting, revising, publishing, etc.

Quick Check														
Name	Date	2/7/05	2/8/05	2/9/05	2/10/05	2/14/05	2/15/05	2/16/05	2/17/05	2/21/05	2/22/05			
1. Merrill Kaye		R/PC	E	C	P	B	B	C	D	D	D			
2. Alex			D	D	D	C	E	PC	B	C	B	D		
3. Lafe			C	P	P	B	C	D	E	PC	B	D		
4. V̶i̶r̶g̶i̶n̶i̶a̶			B	B	C	D	D	D	E	PC	B	C		

A Quick Check can be done each time students write or a few times a week. Students who can respond quickly to the Quick Check know what their writing plans are for the day. A hesitation will result in that student's name being skipped. It then becomes the student's responsibility to let you know what he will be working on that day.

Develop your own shorthand for the Quick Check, and in addition, develop with your students the language to respond to the Quick Check. They will have to know the stages they move through as writers. On the days students conference with you, you need only a simple response, such as "conference," since you'll receive much more information during the conference. You will find a reproducible form for the writing Quick Check on page 97.

Some teachers have other ways to track the students' progress at a glance. Teachers create bulletin boards with student names and systems for showing the stages in the writing process. For example, each student may move an indicator of some kind to an area on the bulletin board that shows the correct stage. Other teachers post the stages on a bulletin board and place note cards with the students' names on them to indicate where the students are in the process.

The illustrations below show two ways this can be handled.

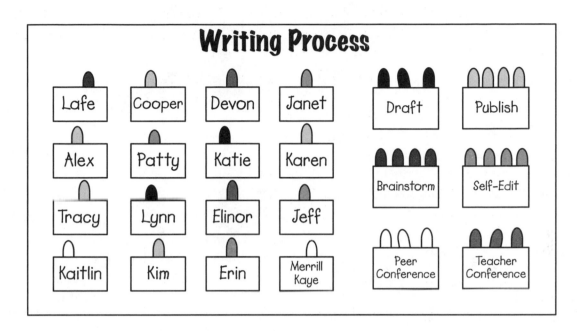

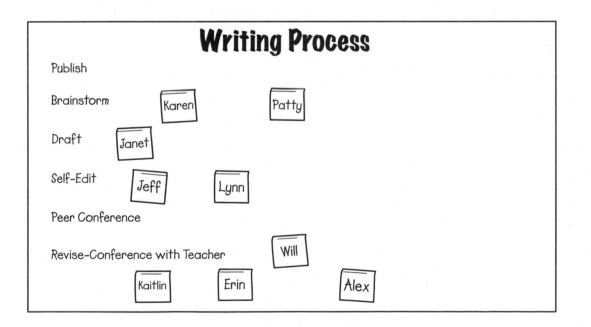

Writing in Big Blocks

Kinds of Conferences

One common misunderstanding is that all writing conferences are publishing conferences. Students will be writing every single day, and therefore, should be producing a good deal of text. An important idea to remember is that students will not publish everything they write. If all writers had to take everything they write to a "published" stage, they would not write as much. Publishing is hard work, and on page 78-81, we'll talk about how and why we publish. For now, just know that students will pick and choose those pieces to publish that they feel the strongest about.

Coaching Conferences

If you are familiar with the Building-Blocks™ Model the Four-Blocks kindergarten framework, you know that Building-Blocks teachers coach kindergarten students daily. But what does it mean to coach an older student?

At the time of the conference, you make the decision about what is best for that student. For example, as you walk over to get Alex for his conference, you notice he is really into his writing today. He seems to be on a roll and at ease with the process. You may make the decision that the best thing for Alex is just to let him continue with the writing he is doing. If so, you make a note to call on Alex last for his conference today or first thing on the next day.

However, the next student on your list is Lafe. As you sit down next to Lafe (or call him up to the conferencing table—again this is your decision), he seems to be struggling with where his story should go next. It would not be logical to help Lafe get this piece ready to be published if he hasn't finished it and may not even know if he'll want to publish it.

On the other hand, your conference could be the perfect opportunity to teach Lafe about prewriting or planning. Sure, you've done mini-lessons on using graphic organizers to get ready to write. Lafe has even used a few when you have required it of him. But this is different. This student is in the middle of the draft and doesn't know where to go. This is a great example of why a plan can help you write better.

So, you coach Lafe through filling out a graphic organizer using the ideas he has already included. Then, the two of you talk through what he will do next. This opportunity to teach the real need of thinking before writing will be a great benefit to Lafe as a writer in the future.

> Lafe, by next week's conference-use this graphic organizer to begin your piece. Bring it with you to the conference. I should be able to tell you used the info from the graphic!

HINT

If at the end of the coaching conference you set a goal for Lafe, not only should you write it in your conferencing records, but also jot the goal on a self-stick note. Give the self-stick note to the student. This is his reminder of your expectation.

Perhaps you sit down with Rhonda, and she says she has been trying to really draw the readers into her story. She wants people to want to continue reading. You are excited because she is talking about a strong lead, something you talked about a few mini-lessons ago. A coaching opportunity exists again. You may have Rhonda turn to the pages in her Writing Handbook where she has taken notes on strong leads. Then, as you work together, coach Rhonda in writing a few different leads for the same piece. Now, she has several leads to choose from and an even better experience of how to write a lead.

The instruction provided in these two examples may or may not lead to published pieces, but both are ways to assist students as writers.

Revision Conference

Once a student has chosen a piece for publishing, the next step is revision. Understand that prior to your working with a student on revision, he may have already done some self-revision and self-editing. Revision happens prior to the peer edit and the final edit, since it wouldn't make sense to edit something that may not even be included in the final draft. (See more about peer conferencing on page 78.)

When you sit down with a student to revise a piece of writing, you walk a very fine line. In your head, you are thinking, "This would be so much better if Merrill Kaye had written . . . ." Of course, you can think of things to improve the writing; you are no longer in fourth grade. With your students, you can make revision suggestions and require changes, but you can't come up with the words for the students. If you tell a student her lead would be much better if it said, "One warm, hazy evening . . ." the writing is yours and not the student's. However, if you remind the student that there are several ways to write a strong lead (start with a question, start with a quote, start with a conversation, etc.) and ask if she could make the lead better, you are guiding the revision without taking over. When helping with a revision, there may be times when you say, "Could you add more detail here so I can see it better in my mind?" The student author will reply, "No, I like it the way it is." You may need to bite your tongue and allow the author's decision to stand. Yes, you could get her to write a better piece by making your suggested changes, but this piece belongs to the author.

That is not to say there are never times when you, as the teacher, can't tell a student that a piece needs work. For example, if you have spent considerable time modeling strong leads, reading examples of strong leads, and guiding the practice of writing strong leads, you may decide to look for strong leads in student pieces during conferences. If Tracy brings her piece to you and the lead is: "Hi, my name is Tracy, and I am going to tell you about the day I went sledding and scalped myself," you, as the teacher, would definitely be right in saying the lead is not acceptable. You might even guide Tracy to the page in the Writing Handbook section of her Big-Blocks Notebook where you had students list leads that were no longer allowed.

This revision conference may become a coaching conference on writing leads and will move back to revision once the lead issue has been dealt with. Other topics of revision might include: staying on topic, organization or sequence, sentences that make sense, appropriate titles, format, etc.

Once students are finished with revision, they don't recopy the piece prior to editing. The more times students have to recopy pieces of writing, the more burned out they become on the whole process. Recopying a final draft should be the final phase of publishing and occurs after all of the conferences with peers and the teacher.

Writing in Big Blocks

A warning to those of you who have not worked with students on revision and editing: it is highly common for students to think that revision and editing means recopying their drafts in their neatest handwriting. Many students have a very difficult time making meaningful changes to their writing. Again, your modeling will be critical. Bring in pieces you are working on or have worked on in class. Do the hard work of revision in front of your students.

Editing Conference

While revision is done with the author making the final decisions, editing is completely up to the Editor-in-Chief, you the teacher. Prior to you doing the final edit on a piece of writing, each student has used an editor's checklist or Writer's Checklist (see pages 76-77) to check and correct his own writing. Students are accountable for finding and correcting all items on the checklist. This increases your expectations for student responsibility.

However, as the Editor-in-Chief, you have the final responsibility for correcting any errors a student couldn't recognize or that weren't on the checklist. Even though you are providing frequent writing instruction, there are concepts that are beyond upper-grade students.

Published work is ready for the public eye. Therefore, all errors in the draft are corrected, and the changes are incorporated into the final piece. Although Big-Blocks students are older and have hopefully been writing for years before they get to you, they still need and get an editor. All published writers have editors. It is also not feasible to expect parents to help with the editing at home. The work of revising and editing is to be done at school under your guidance.

One aspect of editing that changes as students get older is how and when it is done. You may decide to collect papers that have been revised and self-edited and are ready for your final edit. As Editor-in-Chief, you do the editing outside of the conference and return the edited paper to the author (hopefully not long after it has been given to you for editing). If there are many changes that need to be incorporated, it makes sense for you to sit down with the author and quickly point out the marks you made and the changes that need to happen. Mark changes clearly and use a consistent notation for the changes you will require. Be aware that students only learn from the items they find themselves. If you find the error, correct the error, and show the student where it was, that isn't teaching him how to correct it (Hillocks, 1986). If you want students to learn a skill, it must be on the checklist, and they must be accountable for finding it.

HINT

Colored pencil marks show up on the pencil writing your students do and seems a little less invasive than ink—particularly red ink. For the different phases of editing, ask for a different color for each phase. For example, when a student self-edits, he uses a blue colored pencil. During peer editing, he uses an orange colored pencil. Finally, when you do the last edit, use a green colored pencil. The different colors allow you to see what the student can do independently, with a peer's assistance, and with your help.

When you have a number of students who are ready to publish, provide mini-lesson instruction on how to recopy their final drafts into published pieces. In a mini-lesson, model recopying one of your own revised and edited pieces, showing how you transfer all of the changes. Many students will recopy and include all of the original errors. Teach students to be careful in the process of recopying. Teach them to look for the medium you choose to mark those errors. If you use colored pencils, have them look for the marks. If you use an ink pen, look for those marks.

Deciding What to Teach in a Conference

Just as you determine a focus for your writing mini-lessons, you determine a focus for the writing conference. What is the one thing you want to teach? As mentioned previously, teachers most often choose the one glaring error that would most benefit the writer. On occasion, you may also make the decision to use your conference to tie into the instruction you've provided during mini-lessons.

The types of conferences described on the preceding pages allow you to see the choices you have to make when a student brings a piece of writing to the conference. While it is a difficult task, the best way to get better at determining a conference focus is to do it over and over. As the teacher, there is a brief moment during the conference when you must make the decision about where the conference will go.

The ultimate goal in a writing conference is to teach students how to ask for the type of help they need during the conference. While you teach students this skill, you will be the one who makes the final decision. In other words, you may look at a piece of writing and make the decision that the best thing you can teach this student to move him forward as a writer is an editing concept. If editing is the first thing you conference on, revision may not be a big part of the process for that particular piece.

However, the assumption is that if you have chosen an editing issue, it must have been a glaring issue in the piece of writing. For example, let's say the student has brought you an on-topic piece of writing with excellent ideas and reasonable organization, but there is not one mark of punctuation anywhere in the entire piece of writing. It would be a logical decision to work on punctuation with that student. Including punctuation would definitely move that writer forward.

Another student may come to you with a piece that is connected with "and then's." This writer may have other errors to work on—some that deal with revision, others that address editing issues, but you make the decision to get this writer past the notion of connecting each idea with the words "and then." A focus on limiting the use of "and then" would definitely move the writer forward but would not allow time to go over editing mistakes, as well.

So, if you have spent several mini-lessons working on using strong verbs to make better mind pictures, you may tell students that during this week of conferences you will be looking for examples of strong verb usage, or you will help them think of stronger words to use. This connects the instruction to the whole class and the individual writers.

Making a decision about the one thing to teach during a conference is important. Students can't hold several ideas in their heads at once. If you try and teach a student about every kind of error he made in one piece of writing, your conference will take at least 20 minutes, and the student will learn nothing.

Conferences are not easy, and you may not feel equipped to move students forward as writers. Ray (2000) says that each teacher has a fistful of knowledge. For some teachers, that fistful may only include two things they can teach really well. If that is your case, teach those two things to the best of your ability. In the meantime, find resources that will help you

HINT

Katie Wood Ray (2000) suggests ending the conference with the student retelling what the conference was about. Rather than asking a student if he understands what you mean—and often getting a nod yes—have him tell you in his words what he has learned or what he will work on to improve the piece of writing.

Writing in Big Blocks

increase the fistful of knowledge you possess. Ray also reminds teachers that the time they spend with any writer in a conference setting is more time than any teacher spent with them as students in an effort to focus on their individual writing needs.

Writer's Checklist

The idea of accountability is not just for the upper grades. Even in first grade, teachers create checklists of skills/concepts that students are responsible for in their own writing. The Writer's Checklist continues from grade to grade.

Previously we mentioned that as the teacher, you are the Editor-in-Chief of your classroom. However, it is your job to edit for those things your students either haven't been taught or are not ready to be held accountable for. This makes your job easier and helps students see what they can and should do on their own.

A Writer's Checklist is a compilation of the writing skills/concepts you think the majority of students in your classroom can do independently. If a student didn't use the skill/concept correctly while drafting, he should catch his error in the process of self-assessment. The Writer's Checklist grows throughout the year. However, by the end of the year, upper-grade Writer's Checklists would probably have no more than 10-12 items. Remember, this list does not include everything you teach, but it does include the things you know students can and should be responsible for.

An example of a skill you will teach is comma usage. While you might expect students to use commas correctly in dates and in the greetings of letters, it would not be reasonable for a fourth grader to recognize all of the places he might need commas. There are ways to address any of these items on a checklist. Here is an example of a Writer's Checklist (Hall, Cunningham, Arens, 2003):

Writer's Checklist

1. I have included my name and date. (9/3/03)

2. I have used beginning capitals and correct ending punctuation. (9/15/03)

3. I have circled suspect words. (9/22/03)

4. I have used sentences that make sense and stay on topic. (10/5/03)

5. I have used capital letters for titles, specific people, events, and places. (10/21/03)

The checklist is written by the teacher and posted in the classroom. The dates at the end of each item indicate the day that particular item was added to the checklist.

As you can see, there are many skills/concepts included on this list. You never put something on the list until you have taught it. And more than likely, you will have taught it more than once. We recommend adding a skill/concept to the checklist when you begin to feel comfortable that most of your students can demonstrate it. Students may not have capital letters in all of the correct places, but you can see they have learned from the mini-lessons and are trying to get it right. Also, the items on the checklist are added gradually. They are added as the skills/concepts are taught. You might have the first four items on the list by the middle of October and then, you might not add any more until late November. If the Writer's Checklist below doesn't match what you need to be teaching or what your students can do, determine your own skills/concepts to add.

However, once you've implemented a Writer's Checklist, it is your job to hold the students accountable. When students come to conference with you, there should be evidence of the work they have done to check for all items on the list. You may give them half-sheet copies of the list, like the one below. As they look for each item in their papers, they mark it off the list. You might also have students write a number 1 at the top of their papers once they know there is a name and date. After they check for capitals and punctuation, they write a 2. The checking and numbering continues until they have completed the checklist.

Student Name:	Date:
Complete	**Writer's Checklist**
	1. I have included my name and date.
	2. I have used beginning capitals and correct ending punctuation.
	3. I have circled suspect words.
	4. I have used sentences that make sense and stay on topic.
	5. I have used capital letters for titles, specific people, events, and places.
	6. I have tried some transitions.
	7. I have used commas to separate words and phrases in a series.

If a student comes to a conference claiming to have checked for all of the items on the checklist and absolutely no changes have been made—and some changes need to be made—ask the student to go back to his seat and try again. If you make the decision to go ahead and conference with the student, you will be the one checking for all of the items on the checklist. The learning comes in the student finding his mistakes and making the corrections. Since there is so much to teach in writing, a Writer's Checklist allows you to have the students share the responsibility of editing so that you can concentrate on other issues.

It is certainly reasonable that a student may not find every error he is accountable for. It is also reasonable to require him to do part of the editing work. Setting an expectation for using a Writer's Checklist and maintaining that expectation will help students to learn and to be more independent.

Writing in Big Blocks

Peer Conferencing

Many teachers incorporate the act of working with a peer into the writing process. It is a great way for students to assist each other with the difficult process of writing. However, if you have a class that functions better without peer work, it is okay to leave this step out of the process.

The Writer's Checklist you develop should be the guideline students use for the peer conference. Ask students to work together to find any changes that may need to be made. You might ask the author to read while the peer looks on so that the author maintains control of the writing. Even though someone other than the author is making the suggestions, have the author make the appropriate marks on the paper. It is also a good idea to have self-stick notes handy during the peer conference. Students can write suggestions on a self-stick note and place it on the paper.

Just as you will be holding individual students accountable for the checklist, hold the peers accountable too. Develop a way to know which peers have conferenced. Perhaps they will both sign at the top of the paper, or the peers could sign the checklist they've used. It is important for students to understand that anything worth missing writing time for is significant. Therefore, you will be holding them accountable for those items on the checklist or to your specific expectations.

Publishing

Publishing means to make public. The purpose of writing in a Writer's Workshop format is to write for an audience. An audience should view published work. In other words, students will work toward making certain that some pieces are ready for public viewing. Remember, you will not be asking students to publish everything. You don't have the time, and they won't want to!

Publishing requires a great deal of work, and if students are expected to work that hard on everything they write, they won't write much. In addition, you will not be able to keep up with the conferencing necessary to get everyone to the publishing stage for every piece of writing. The idea that a student's piece is ready for public viewing means that the mistakes are removed. The revision and editing you have guided students through allow them to ready their work for the public. Understand that it is common for students to recopy a piece of writing and include the same mistakes in the final piece.

If you see a large number of students having difficulty seeing or incorporating the changes made to rough drafts, use a procedural mini-lesson to show them how to incorporate the changes. Students shouldn't be expected to recopy one piece of writing three or four times. Therefore, look at the final copy of the published piece and decide if it should just be left alone, or could the student erase the few mistakes and fix them on the final draft. It is also wise to keep some correction fluid on hand so that students can correct their mistakes.

Goals for Publishing

Beginning in third or fourth grade, teachers have to have expectations for how often students will publish. Every once in a while, students in first or second grade get into a habit of not ever finishing a piece. But most often with younger students, publishing is the "fun part." They enjoy finishing the writing and sharing it with friends.

As students get older, that may change. Sometimes students are writing longer pieces, and by the time they finish their rough drafts, they really want to move on to something else. Additionally, the thought of having to fix all of the spelling, punctuation, organization problems, etc., doesn't sound too exciting. As with any subject area, there are also some students who just aren't motivated to finish anything!

Therefore, Writing Block expectations usually include expectations for the minimum number of finished pieces a student will produce in a quarter or grading period.

As you decide on a reasonable number for your students, think about which focused genre you will be teaching. How long will it take? That should influence how many pieces of writing you think your students can do well. There may be some grading periods when one or two finished pieces is reasonable and other grading periods when four or five would be reasonable. The final decision is yours as you take into consideration what your students are required to write and how quickly they tend to move through the writing process. Be sure to allow plenty of time for first draft writing. Also, remember that you want students to experience the process of publishing. While you don't want to overwhelm them with published pieces, you do want them to publish as frequently as they can. Going through the process makes it easier to do the next time.

For the first couple of grading periods, you may need to have mid-period goals to keep students from procrastinating until the last week of the grading period for self-selected pieces. If more than half of your class is slow getting their drafts ready for conferencing, you will have more students needing conferences that last week of the grading period than you can physically or mentally get to.

If you want to adhere to the ideal of allowing students a lot of choice, but you want them to branch out on their published pieces, use your expectations to guide them. The following expectations are just some examples of how to encourage students to branch out.

First quarter expectation: A minimum of two published pieces; one is the student's choice, the other is the focused piece

Second quarter expectation: A minimum of three published pieces; one is the focused piece, the other two are the student's choice, but at least one of them must be a different genre than the pieces published in the first quarter

By setting expectations such as these, you are allowing students to have some choices but encouraging them to try something new. If these are to be your expectations, your mini-lessons will need to include instruction in genres other than the focused pieces. This may include a review of genres taught in previous grades. Students won't be required to write in these genres but will have the opportunity to see what they look like.

Don't be afraid to develop a yearly calendar with publishing deadlines and even drafting deadlines. Professional writers have publishing deadlines to adhere to. Your students can still take appropriate amounts of time to finish a piece and meet a deadline. You may feel more secure with grading period goals rather than yearly goals. Either way is a fine way to support the writers in your classroom.

There are many ways to make publishing more motivating. Think of interesting ways to allow your students to publish. By alternating several options, they won't feel as if they are in a rut.

Recopy—Sometimes, students will want to spend no more time than necessary to finish up a piece of writing. A simple clean copy is just as "published" as an elaborately bound and illustrated book.

Use a Computer—If you are lucky enough to have access to a computer lab, your students will love publishing on the computer. In fact, a lab is unnecessary. All you need is one computer in your classroom. Students can publish the text only or leave spaces open in the text for illustrations. The computer can be a real motivator. Students love playing with fonts and special effects.

Writing in Big Blocks

Illustrate—Young children are not the only ones who like to add drawings to their writing. You may find upper-grade students who love to add illustrations to the pieces they write. Your most artistic students may choose to spend too much time on the illustrations. Set an expectation and let students know how much class time is reasonable for illustrating. Just as with any other expectation, set a time limit if necessary. Students could also work on illustrations at home and bring them in to cut and paste into the final published pieces.

Make a Book—Many times, when a student chooses to add illustrations, she wants to put the whole piece together in a book form. However, some students may enjoy making books, even without the illustrations.

Use a binding machine to add a plastic comb binding for a little more permanence. Allow students to make dedication pages, "About the Author" pages, etc. Their books should mirror the books they love to read.

Check out the Web site *www.barebooks.com*. It is a site that sells books with blank pages at a reasonable price. The covers are made to allow for markers, colored pencils, etc. Students of all ages love having a real bound book to publish their writing in.

Use Acetate—The next time you laminate something, keep the excess film you trim off. Although it is time consuming, students love the chance to make books on small pieces of acetate or laminating film. Have the student decide how many pages will be needed and cut small pieces of film for her to use (4" x 6"; 10 cm x 15 cm). Allow the student to use fine-point permanent markers to write and/or illustrate the text. When it is time for sharing, the student places her book, page by page, on the overhead. If a student needs to erase, small rubbing alcohol pads work as a great eraser.

Patterned Paper—Fun, seasonal paper is always motivating for students. Be sure to have some on hand and available for students to use for final drafts. If the paper has a decorative border and no lines, create a line guide to place under the paper. It makes the final product appear more professional and often relieves your perfectionist students.

Sharing

Sharing a published piece—or a piece in its first draft—with a real audience is the reason for the Writing Block. Every day, Big-Blocks teachers offer students the opportunity to share the things they have written with an audience. For some students, this sharing time will be the reason they continue to write. For others, as they get a little older and a little more aware of their peers, it will be an intimidating process.

> **HINT**
>
> Create a line guide with a piece of notebook paper. Use a ruler and trace over the lines with a black, fine-point permanent marker. Students will be able to see the dark lines through the patterned paper, but the lines won't be on the final draft.

Nonetheless, have a sharing time every day you have the Writing Block. There are many ways to modify and vary the sharing time so that students don't feel like they are always doing the "same old thing."

A student should never be required or forced to share a piece that is too private. On the other hand, set the expectation that everyone shares a few things. In most places, oral language and speech are parts of the language arts curriculum. Students need opportunities to practice the skills of speaking and reading in front of a group. This sharing time is the perfect opportunity. Decide on a reasonable number of times for students to participate in sharing their pieces of writing with the whole class and make this a part of your expectations.

Writing does not have to be published in order to be shared. Remember, published means ready for the public eye. When sharing, a student may hold his paper, and no one else needs to even see the writing. Therefore, a piece may be shared at any stage in the writing process.

Sharing time is the last part of the Writing Block and seems to get left out by some classes. You know the way it is: you look at your clock and quickly say, "Oh no, we've got to go to lunch. We don't have time for sharing!" Even if you have to share when you come back from lunch, make sure you share every Writing Block. Remember, it only takes 5-8 minutes

Author's Chair

Probably the most well-known and most often used form of sharing is the Author's Chair. The idea is that one student is allowed to sit in the Author's Chair (a special chair or any chair in front of the class). While seated in the Author's Chair, a student shares his selected piece of writing with the rest of the class.

Many teachers prepare students for peer conferencing by allowing individuals to offer feedback after the reading in the Author's Chair. Some students respond well to the "Two Stars and a Wish" format.

Writing in Big Blocks

The "Two Stars" are positive comments and must be specific. The "Wish" expresses a need for clarification. Perhaps there is a question the reader/listener didn't get answered by the text. Maybe, there is confusion with characters or overuse of the pronoun they. The wish, too, has to be specific. The author can then use the information to make changes to the writing.

In order for this feedback to be helpful for the writer, and to continue to build your classroom community, teach your students what effective feedback sounds like. (Aha! Another mini-lesson topic!!) Since the "Stars" and "Wish" have to be specific, a comment such as, "Oh, I like that! It was so good!" serves absolutely no purpose. What was good about it? Tell the author why you liked it. Did you make a connection? Could you really see in your mind what he was talking about? Again, for your students to be able to offer effective feedback like this, well, you will need to model as the one offering the stars and the wish.

Partner Sharing

A quick way to let everyone in your room have a chance to share is through Partner Sharing. Ask each student to get together with a partner and take a piece of writing she would like to share. Give each partner two minutes to share something from his writing folder. In about five minutes, everyone in the room will have had a sharing opportunity. For students who prefer not to be in front of the whole class, this is much safer option, and it still provides an opportunity for students to work with oral language.

If you have a little longer than five minutes, incorporate "Two Stars and a Wish" (or "One Star and a Wish") for partners. This could be a precursor to peer conferencing.

Focused Shares

Another way to maximize your mini-lesson instruction is to connect it to sharing time. For example, perhaps you spent the past three days modeling lessons on choosing strong verbs. Word choice is important in creating mind pictures for students. So, after your strong verb mini-lessons, you realize that students need even more experience with the concept. You might announce that for the next two or three days during sharing time, students will share with the whole class sentences or paragraphs that use examples of strong verbs.

Allow as many students as you have time for to share their strong verb examples. This allows students to hear many examples of verbs and how they might incorporate the lessons you've taught into their writing.

Think of other mini-lessons that might be enhanced by allowing sharing time to focus on just that concept: figurative language, strong leads, specific nouns, transitions, etc. You wouldn't want to do this every day since students need opportunities to share the pieces they are most excited about. However, focused shares are an appropriate variation.

Out of the Classroom

Students also enjoy the opportunity to have a variety of audiences. Most often they will remain in their classroom and share with their classmates. However, it is perfectly acceptable and even encouraged to get students out of the classroom to share.

Ask another teacher in your building—a teacher of **any** grade level—if there is a five-minute window when you might send in one or two students from your class to share with his students. Again, each student can take a published piece of writing or one she is working on. Students in the other classroom, might only hear the first part of a story by a student from your class. They will be very anxious to hear how things turned out, which might create an additional opportunity for sharing the next week.

Sharing with other classes at the same grade level is fine, but don't be afraid to send your students to classes at different grade levels. Students enjoy hearing any other student's work. This is the reason you have sharing time.

Getting Published

In addition to sharing within the school community, look for opportunities to get your students published in the larger community. This is not something that happens frequently, but is one idea for enhancing the ways you celebrate success with your students.

An easy way to make your students' writing public beyond the school is to photocopy a published piece, or portion of one, on the back of your parent letter each week. Make sure students know and ask their permissions for displaying their work in this manner.

On page 96, you will find a list of Web site resources where students can safely publish their writing on-line. This allows students to share their published work with people at home and even those living far away. It is one publishing medium that you can offer to your young writers.

Local newspapers may be willing to publish student work, even if it is only once or twice a year. Students love seeing their work in the newspaper.

Celebrations

Allowing students to share their work is a great way to celebrate the work they do as writers. Often, Big-Blocks teachers go even further and plan celebrations specifically for showing off the work their students do as writers.

Publishing Party

For a Publishing Party, designate a date of celebration. This date helps students share published works with an audience outside of the classroom. On the day of the Publishing Party, students display their pieces on their desks, on bulletin boards, or in the hall. Other classes are invited to see and sometimes even hear the published work of others.

In addition to students from other classes, adults—including parents and school personnel—are also invited. This is one more opportunity to move the audience beyond the walls of the school. If it is a safe environment, offer those coming to view the writing a chance to provide feedback. Students may stand by their displayed writing waiting to answer questions as attendees read. Or, you may have note cards available for written validation.

A Publishing Party might be held a couple of times a year or even once a grading period. It probably isn't something you want to do monthly just because of the time you would take away from writing and any other subjects or Blocks you might miss because of the party.

Writing in Big Blocks

Young Author's Day

Another version of the writing celebration is Young Author's Day. This type of celebration usually involves the whole school and is therefore only held once or twice a year. Each school tends to develop and design its own version of the day. At the heart of any Young Author's Day is the sharing of students' published work.

Many schools invite adults from the community into classrooms or assemblies to share how writing is important in their jobs or lives. Other schools bring in published authors to talk about their writing and the publishing process.

Students are then grouped in cross grade level sharing groups to read aloud the pieces they have selected. Again, different schools have individualized the process for selection. At some schools, students are allowed to choose from any of their published works for the Young Author's Day. At other schools, students may write particular pieces for sharing.

We feel this day is better when a competition is not involved. Writing celebrations are not about winning awards. They are held to celebrate the risk any author takes when he is willing to share his published pieces.

Struggling Writers

When students are given time, materials, and choice, they will write on their level. The benefit is a developmentally appropriate choice in instruction.

The Four-Blocks® and Big-Blocks™ models both hold that one goal of the Writing Block is to maintain the motivation and the self-confidence of struggling writers. Conferences allow teachers to address students' individual needs and encourage students in the areas of their own successes. Struggling writers can also be made to feel successful when they have opportunities to share stories with other classmates during sharing time.

A teacher can also focus conference conversations on aspects of writing that might create a "forced success" for that student. In other words, what small hurdle can be jumped in the conference if you are there to support the writer? Can you quickly show a writer how to stay on topic and work through the piece with her to eliminate anything that does not stay on topic? At the end of the conference, you have something to praise the student about.

Some struggling writers will benefit from coaching conferences that allow them to talk through a writing idea before putting it on paper. If you can be the sounding board for these discussions, you can guide students in the prewriting/prethinking they do. If it is a help just to talk it through, allow the struggling writer to talk through the idea with other students, as well.

For some students, the ideas come without much trouble. But, if a student has to think through the idea while writing it down, there is often a gap. As teachers of students with many ability levels, we look for any way to support struggling writers. Could a student benefit from telling his story into a tape recorder? Could this student listen to the story through headphones, pausing the tape and writing what has been said, then pressing play to listen to the next part of the story? Working much the same as a dictation machine, the student could dictate his own story.

Many students are motivated by the opportunity to use a computer. Drafting on a computer is always an option. If you think the opportunity to draft on the keyboard would motivate or encourage any writer, it should be considered a tool. Again, it is one more resource you can utilize when trying to reach each student.

During conferences with struggling writers, teachers may play a more supportive role. For example, if a conference leads to a discussion of what a student needs to add to make a story better, you may make a bulleted list of details discussed during the conference. Then, you give this list to the student to help him remember what details were generated. The list will not have whole sentences or paragraphs but will provide the gist of the ideas, preventing the student from returning to his seat only to "forget" what he was going to add on.

He had thought that he had taken the glasses off ~~last night.~~ *the night before* So he kept them on and went to work on the ~~experiment,~~ *project* (the backpack jet pack). He was working very happily and was feeling wonderful. Unsyncable then felt an urge to do something radical. He was almost done with the experiment. The glasses told him where the last piece went. He was done. So he went to the test room in the school getting in with his spare key. He went to the test room and kept the glasses on. So he did not mess up when he tested the experiment. He slipped on the backpack and started it up. It worked great so he took it off and went to bed. Unsyncable awoke the next day and remembered that break was over. He went to school to start to teach. After class, he went to the front room to leave, but before that he had a chat with the secretary. When he left he saw that he had money in his hand. He did not remember taking any money out of his pocket. He then heard people saying, "Hey where is the money?" He started to think, could he have taken the money?

- <u>He</u>—maybe too many
  Could you use other pronouns or proper nouns?

- Paragraphs—Where should they start and end?

Writing in Big Blocks

Struggling writers are more likely to be interrupted during a conference with the teacher (Glasswell, Parr, McNaughton, and Carpenter, 2003). In addition, the content of these conferences tends to focus on the mechanics of the piece more often than on content. Your expectations for the struggling writers in your class influence the quality of the time you spend with them. Raising an awareness of quality during writing conference conversations may very well raise the achievement of the writer. The study by Glasswell, et al., did not find that less time was spent in conferences with struggling writers. In fact, in many cases, more time was spent. However, the interruptions were much more frequent, and the level of the conversation was much lower.

Whether or not they are struggling writers, all students in Big-Blocks classrooms need to write every single day in a variety of contexts. Of course, writing will occur in the Writing Block, but it will also occur in the Self-Selected Reading and Guided Reading Blocks, as well as in the various subject areas. So, even though the Writing Block may not take place each day, it is still expected that students will write each day. Quantity can certainly play into quality, and quantity helps writing fluency. Therefore, even our struggling writers need to achieve writing quantity. Quantity is typically what struggling writers lack, which helps to explain why they also lack fluency. In some cases, you may have to set short-term, achievable goals for the most struggling or resistant writers. As we've said before, the task of writing is not an option during the Writing Block. It is no more optional than doing your math during math time or your social studies during social studies time. In extreme cases, set a goal of how much writing a particular struggling writer must achieve during one Writing Block.

However, the real purpose in setting these goals is to make them achievable. Remember on page 84 when we mentioned "forced success"? Set an attainable goal for the amount a struggling student should write. Once she makes that goal, celebrate with her. Praise her for her hard work. For the next Writing Block, set a slightly longer goal. The goals are small, but won't you be happier with two lines (or two paragraphs) of text rather than no text and no engagement at all?

Some struggling writers are students who have fewer background experiences and limited vocabularies. In the Writing Block, teachers often encourage students to write about the things they have done and the things they know. For a child who has had few experiences, it is more difficult to find writing ideas. There are also students whose experiences weren't pleasant the first time around, and the students don't really care to relive the experiences through writing about them.

For those writers, retelling other things they know can be one safe way to build writing fluency. Could a struggling writer retell a movie or TV show? The characters are already developed, so there isn't a higher level of thinking, but there is thinking nonetheless. Students who retell movies or TV shows still have to choose their own words to tell what happened. Some may even try to take stories they know from movies or shows and make them their own. This can even be encouraged. If it is the type of writing chosen by a struggling writer, teach that student how to do that form of writing better.

Challenges to Writing

- **Some teachers perceive the Writing Block as an addition to "language arts" time.**

  The Writing Block is language arts instruction. In other words, what you teach in language arts lessons is usually what is needed for writing. This is not another layer to add, rather it replaces the traditional instruction that typically happens with a language arts book with instruction that shows students the context for learning about language arts.

- **Content area instruction becomes time intensive in upper grades, and writing may begin to take a backseat.**

  Writing takes time—most assuredly—as does anything worthwhile. Your students need instruction, and sometimes they will struggle to get better, just as there will be days you will struggle with the best approaches to make them better. However, writing is worth the investment because it is a "life thing" not just a "school thing." Take students beyond writing for the teacher and the grade. Show them how writing can and will be an integral part of their lives. When students "love" writing, it is often because of a wonderful writing teacher who shares his enthusiasm.

- **The state tests are another typical barrier to a Writer's Workshop format like the Writing Block of the Big-Blocks™ model.**

  Most states are now giving writing intensive assessments. Unfortunately, because these tests require students to write to a prompt, teachers often think that great chunks of instructional time need to be spent getting students ready for the test by writing to prompts. This is far from the truth. Will students ever need to write to a prompt to prepare for their state test? Certainly, but the most appropriate time to have students write to prompts is in the content areas. Real reasons to write are always better than writing just to practice for the test. Writing is thinking, and asking students to respond to short answer and extended answer questions in their content area studies lets them show teachers what they have learned and how they can apply or explain that knowledge.

- **Teachers don't see an improvement in student responses to prompts.**

  There will be times during the Writing Block when teachers will have students write to prompts in preparation for state tests. Not only will students need to do that work in a situation that mirrors that of the test, they also will need quality instruction on how to get better each time they practice in order to finally perform well on the test. The necessity of this is not being argued. The number of times this practice occurs is a concern.

  This need teachers have to require students to write to a prompt is perhaps the largest challenge to writing in the format we have described. Teachers should be assured that quality writing instruction, proper modeling of the process of writing, and an allotted time to teach specific forms of writing will improve students' ability to write coherently, express thoughts, and improve in the basic mechanics of writing (Hillocks, 1995). This improvement in writing will reflect in the state writing tests, too.

Writing in Big Blocks

Middle School

The interesting thing about the Writing Block of the Big-Blocks™ model for the upper grades is that the transition to middle school will be minimal. The block of writing time will be divided between the same elements: mini-lesson, independent student writing, teacher conferences during student writing time, and sharing. The amount of focused writing also remains the same. In fact, the instruction on writing genres may be reviews or more in-depth studies of genres previously taught.

The only element that might change is the frequency. If a middle school allows one 45-minute block of instruction for all language arts (including reading, spelling, and word work) in a grade level, then writing won't occur every day. These 45 minutes would need to be divided between writing and reading, with some time for word work, as well.

Some teachers might find it helpful to spend a week or two on writing, then a week or two on reading. Perhaps some teachers would even want trade-offs every grading period. Whatever the schedule, reading and writing must share in the instructional time frame.

Other middle schools have an 80-90 minute block of time for language arts. In this case, some teachers may decide to split the time between reading and writing each day. Other teachers still find it helpful to flip-flop and spend longer chunks of time on one or the other. Time is the basic element that changes in middle school. Other components of the Writing Block remain the same.

Professional Development Ideas

1. Whether in vertical teams (cross grade level) or grade-level teams, looking at student writing samples can be a powerful way to spend time. In as little as 10 minutes, you can gather ideas and have a quick discussion on one particular piece of writing. To do this, have one teacher bring along a writing sample with enough copies for each member of the team. Eliminate the student name to allow teachers to think more openly.

   Spend 2-3 minutes asking each teacher to make a list of things the writer does well and things the writer needs to work on. This 2-3 minutes should not include discussion. Each teacher makes her own list. Then, ask the team to talk about what the writer can do without mentioning mechanics. Teachers tend to focus on mechanics, and it can keep them from ever getting to the content. So, talk about positives in the content first, then move on to mechanics.

   After you have talked about what the writer does well, discuss what he needs help with. Identify appropriate conference topics and mini-lesson topics.

   Once you've made a list of things the student needs help with, talk about how you would decide on the one thing that could become the conference teaching point.

   Remember, you can't teach students about everything at once. Which of the things the team listed would help you make that student a better writer?

2. In grade-level or vertical teams, work together to develop writing mini-lessons to match your curriculum and state standards. Meet in the library so that you have access to the books in your building. Pull pieces of literature from the shelves and read through them to decide what would be a good lesson to teach. Sometimes, it works to do this in the opposite order, as well. Read the concepts you must teach and think about a book you've read that will help illustrate the point. If a

book won't be the most helpful teaching tool, but a piece of writing will, spend the time by starting to write the example you will use.

3. Visiting other teachers in your building and in other districts is a valuable professional development activity. Anytime you watch someone else's routines, organization, and conferences, you come away with new ideas. Force yourself to make the time to do this.

Recommended Professional Resources for Writing

Atwell, N. (1998). *In the Middle: New Understandings about Writing, Reading, and Learning, 2nd Edition.* Portsmouth, NH: Heinemann.

Calkins, Lucy M. (1994). *The Art of Teaching Writing, 2nd Edition.* Portsmouth, ME: Heinemann

Ray, K. W. (1999). *Wondrous Words.* Urbana, IL: NCTE.

Ray, K. W. (2001). *The Writing Workshop: Working Through the Hard Parts (And They're All Hard Parts).* Urbana, IL: NCTE.

Mini-Lesson Resources

Atwell, N. (2002). *Lessons That Change Writers.* Portsmouth, NH: Heinemann.

Fletcher, R. (1998). *Craft Lessons.* York, ME: Stenhouse.

Hall, D. P., Cunningham, P. M., and Arens, A. B. (2003). *Writing Mini-Lessons for the Upper Grades.* Greensboro, NC: Carson-Dellosa Publishing Company.

Portalupi, J. and Fletcher, R. (2001). *Nonfiction Craft Lessons.* Urbana, IL: Stenhouse.

Robb, L. (1999). *Brighten Up Boring Beginnings.* New York, NY: Scholastic, Inc.

Sample Mini-Lesson: Conclusions (Craft in Expository Text)

Purpose: Whether your students are writing reports/informational pieces that tie into your current social studies unit or you are teaching them how to properly respond to a prompt, conclusions are a necessary part of the instruction. Too often, students end their writing without wrapping things up or attempting to pull their ideas together.

"I thought we might go back and talk once again about how we have to end a piece of writing. Now today, I am really thinking about expository writing, you know—reports, information, articles—things like that. This would also work if you are writing a short answer to a question in social studies or science, or even if you are writing to a prompt. (Only use the word prompt if your students are familiar with the term.)

"I brought in a sample of writing to share with you. This sample was written by a seventh grader, and I know that is older than some of you, but I brought it in because the author did a very nice job of pulling her ideas together, or wrapping it up. You might even see that she was able to make a connection with her subjects. Let me share this with you.

"I won't read the whole thing, but I want to tell you about it. This student was asked to write about four women who lived during the time of the Civil War. The women were unusual for that time because they all acted as spies during the war. Two of the women lived in the South and spied for the Confederate Army, and the other two spied for the Union. The writer told about how the women went about spying in different ways. One of the women used her good looks to get information. One woman was a fine actress and was able to lie without people noticing. Another woman disguised herself as a man.

"Anyway, let me share with you the last two paragraphs of this piece of writing. I think the author did a nice job of pulling it all together.

'For the women in the Confederacy, the South was dead. The way of life they had always known was gone. Their sadness was replaced by a bitter anger. To the women of the Union, a great sadness swept through cities. The men and friends they had known and loved were gone. After President Lincoln was shot and killed, it seemed as if they had fought for nothing. It seemed as if they had won nothing.

'These women never knew each other, yet they were all connected. Connected through the daring work of espionage.'

"Do you hear how she pulled her ideas together? That is what a conclusion is for. It wraps up your information and finds a way to tell the reader what you, as the author, think your purpose of writing was. Let's look at one more piece of writing. Remember last fall when we wrote to a prompt? I saved those papers, and I borrowed one from another fourth-grade class to share. I think this piece has another good conclusion. (For this part of the mini-lesson, you can use any sample you might have that shows a well-written conclusion. Have students identify where the conclusion starts.)

"Does this conclusion wrap up the piece of writing? Do you know for sure what purpose the author had in writing?

"Let's stop for today so that you will have time to write. Please pull out your Big-Blocks Notebooks and turn to the Writing Handbook section. Let's make some notes about why your writing needs a conclusion. "We will copy the shorter example of a well-written conclusion, and I may even give you a copy of the one I showed you from the piece about the Civil War. But for now, let's write."

> A conclusion wraps up the piece of writing. It pulls together my ideas.
>
> It also helps my readers know my purpose.
>
> Example: These are the ways I could make the playground even more fun. I hope you will use my ideas.

Other ideas for mini-lessons on conclusions:

1. Show students a piece of writing that addresses the necessary points but lacks a conclusion. Work together to write an effective conclusion that is appropriate for the grade level you teach. If one sentence will conclude most of the writing they do, model one sentence. If your students are older and need to have more information in their conclusions, model your expectation.

2. When teaching students to write conclusions for a prompt, show them how it mirrors writing the lead. The language in the prompt establishes the purpose for writing. Therefore, borrow from the prompt when writing the lead and the conclusion. In prompt writing, it is relatively easy to write a conclusion without writing the rest of the piece. Try it with your students if you think they can work on it in isolation, without being confused by the task.

Sample Mini-Lesson: Beginning, Middle, and End as an Organizer

A simple graphic organizer with the headings Beginning, Middle, and End can provide a loose structure to get students started writing narratives or stories. By mapping out a story they know, students are able to connect to the premise that most stories can be divided up into these three categories. Then, by using the same graphic organizer to map out an original story, you can help students ensure sequential, telling tales. (See page 99 for a reproducible Beginning, Middle, and End graphic organizer.)

"Today, I am going to show you a very simple graphic organizer that you might choose to use when you are ready to write a new story. This graphic organizer asks us to divide a story into three parts: beginning, middle, and end. As we usually do, we are going to think about a story we all know and map it out using the graphic organizer. For today, why don't we think about the story of *Goldilocks and the Three Bears*? I know you are familiar with that story, even if it has been a while since you have thought about it. Quickly, let's map out the beginning, middle, and end of the story.

"What happens in the beginning of the story? Yes, that's right, the bears go for a walk because their breakfast is too hot. And while they are gone, Goldilocks comes into their house.

"What about the middle? Let's see, Goldilocks gets into everything during the middle, doesn't she? She tries the porridge, the chairs, and the beds, and then she falls asleep.

"Finally, at the end, what happens? Right, the bears come home, and Goldilocks runs away.

Writing Supplement

Beginning	Middle	End
Bears go for a walk Goldilocks comes into the house	Goldilocks eats porridge breaks the chairs tries the beds goes to sleep	Bears come home Goldilocks runs away

"Now as you can see, our organizer doesn't tell every detail of the story, but it gives us an idea of what happened. Most stories can be divided into this framework. Tomorrow, we are going to use the same framework to map out a new story. I have an idea for one I've wanted to write. But for today, you might just read back through the piece you are working on. If you are writing a story, does it have all three parts? What is missing?"

Day 2 of the same lesson:

"Today, I am going to use the same graphic organizer I used yesterday and show you my idea for a new story. Let's see . . . I think I want to write about the first time I went skiing. It was just this past Christmas, and we took our family skiing. I want to write a story about my first trip up in the lift.

"At the beginning of my story, I went to ski school for a day, but there were lots of people on the slopes and a couple of people in our group were having trouble, so we never got to ride the big lifts that take you in the air. We rode something called a Poma lift. It was like grabbing onto a long handle that pulled you up a small hill on your skis. So in my first box, labeled Beginning, I will write : ski school, Poma lift, first time ever on skis.

"The middle of my story moves to the second day of skiing. We weren't in ski school, so I went back to the small slopes with the Poma lifts to practice some more and get comfortable with stopping and turning before I went further up the mountain. It wasn't going so well, so I told my husband I would practice for a while and he could come back later to check on me. I was getting better at turning, but I still didn't feel very comfortable stopping. Then, I saw my five-year-old son and six-year-old niece heading to the ski lift for their first trip up. My husband came back by and convinced me to head up on the lift, too, so I could watch the little ones. So, in my second box, labeled Middle, I will write: practiced turning and stopping, still nervous, went to the lift to ride up at the same time as Lafe and Elinor.

"I am also going to add to the Middle that after we got to the top of the lift, I jumped off and skied over to the slope. I was terrified!!! The mountain was so much steeper than the small hills at the bottom. I really didn't know how I would get down. So, I will add this to my organizer: Too scared to ski down!

"Now for the end, I need to tell you how I got down the mountain. Once you go up on a ski lift there is only one way down. I also need to include my feelings about the trip. I want to tell you if Lafe and Elinor made it down the mountain. Wow, those are all good details to include in my ending. I think I also want to tell you how I ended my day, and whether or not I think I'll try skiing again. So, in the box labeled End, I will write: skiing down, falling down, walking down, being terrified, yelling at Jeff about being scared, seeing Lafe and Elinor with no fear, determined to try again, more ski school.

Beginning	Middle	End
Ski school Poma lift First time ever on skis	Practiced turning and stopping Still nervous Wanted to ride up when Lafe and Elinor went Too scared to ski down	Skiing down Falling down Walking down Being terrified Yelling at Jeff about being scared Seeing Lafe and Elinor with no fear Determined to try again More ski school

"Now, this graphic organizer doesn't have everything in it I will end up putting in my story, but it does have the basic details I want to include, and I know it will be sequential—or in the right order—because I used an organizer that helped me with that.

"Tomorrow, I will begin my story, and I will use my organizer to help me keep track of what should be included!"

Other Mini-Lesson Ideas for Beginning, Middle, End

1. If you have students who think "The End" is a good ending, or who want to use other contrived endings, or who just wear out and don't effectively wrap up everything in their endings, you can use the Beginning, Middle, End graphic organizer in the following manner. Once you have the beginning and middle filled in, ask students what they still want to know about in order to fill in the end. In the skiing example above, the teacher could have said, "What do you still want to know about my skiing adventure? What questions do you have?" Typically, students will have multiple questions, which models the idea that endings are not just one sentence. Instead, endings wrap up all of the loose ends.

2. As students get older, you also want to introduce more sophisticated techniques. Use the Beginning, Middle, End graphic organizer to organize the information for the text, but then model how a writer could start with the end. The story then goes back to the beginning to tell how you ended up where you are. You might also decide to start right in the middle of the action. The organizer is helpful as you decide how and when to include all of the story ideas.

3. When using the Beginning, Middle, End graphic organizer, many students start with the exciting part of the story. In other words, as they retell the story about skiing, they would write about being so terrified at the top of the mountain and wondering how they would get down. If this part of the story ends up in the box labeled beginning, realize that the setting and characters don't get established. Therefore, when using this graphic organizer to model, there are times when the "middle" box gets filled in first.

Writing Supplement

In other words, the mini-lesson might sound more like this:

"Well, today I really have a story I want to write about. I want to tell you about my first adventure skiing. I ended up at the top of one of the slopes, and I was absolutely terrified. So now, I am going to put that idea in my organizer. I think I will write it in the "middle" box because I think I should probably tell you how I got to the top of the slope and where we were, etc. So, now I need to go back and tell you what happened in the beginning."

By using the graphic organizer this way, you can show students that the exciting ideas they have probably belong in the middle. Then, they can use the beginning to set the stage, so to speak, for the rest of their stories.

Sample Mini-Lesson: Focused Writing—Persuasive

Persuasive writing is often a genre on the state tests at grade levels three and above. While that is the driving force behind most of the persuasive writing instruction you see, using persuasion is a powerful way to write. It is one type of expository text, and there are many forms of persuasion. For example, you can persuade your parents in a letter, you can convince someone to buy a product in an advertisement, and you can persuade someone to agree with you in a persuasive essay. Persuasive writing does not always have to be in essay form. If the main reason you are doing persuasive writing is the state test, and that state test will require an essay, it would make sense to teach students the essay format.

However, if you have some leeway, allow students to decide which form would be most appropriate for their argument and their audience.

Lesson 1
Mini-Lesson Focus: Looking at Examples of Persuasive Writing
Be sure to gather quality examples of persuasive writing in preparation for this mini-lesson. These examples can come from former students and professional publications. Each weekly issue of *TIME* Magazine has an essay. Read through several persuasive essays and find those whose topics would be suitable for examples with upper-grade students. Spend the mini-lesson reading and discussing the features of the persuasion. (This may take two days.)

Lesson 2
Mini-Lesson Focus: Choosing a Topic
Talk to students about topics you might write about. Spend time modeling the importance of choosing a topic in which you are knowledgeable and have strong feelings about. Persuasion is a lot easier to do if you really believe in the cause you are arguing for. Brainstorm some possible topics for and with your students, but don't limit their choices to those brainstorm topics. If you are connecting this focused piece to your content-area studies, talk about the possibilities of topics within those themes.

Lesson 3
Mini-Lesson Focus: Pros/Cons of the Topic
During your mini-lessons, you will use the topic you have chosen to model the process with the students. On this day, chart the pros and cons of your topic. Even if your feelings are definitely pro, you must be able to objectively look at the evidence against. Model the process of thinking through both sides. Persuasion is more effective when the writer knows how to defend against opposing arguments.

Lessons 4 and 5
Introduction/Arguments/Conclusion

For Lesson 4, talk about the format of the persuasive writing. These are three very basic components of the pieces students will write, but they are three very necessary pieces. The text will begin with an introduction to the topic along with a statement of the position the writer is taking. For this lesson, it might be helpful to look back at the examples from Lesson 1 and identify the parts of the text. How long is the introduction? How does the writer support his arguments? How effective and how long is the conclusion? Spend one day just looking at how these three components combine to provide the necessary information.

For Lesson 5, begin drafting your own ideas for the introduction, arguments, and conclusion. You might even try a three-part graphic organizer to take notes on. Show students you are not writing the entire piece now but are jotting down the things you know will have to be included.

Lesson 6
Appropriate Leads

If this focused writing genre is later in the year—which would be a good idea since it is a difficult genre to write—you will have already spent time talking about leads. Therefore, your conversation on leads for this mini-lesson will focus directly on the type of leads that would be most effective in a persuasive piece.

Freeman (1997) suggests the following as types of leads that work well in persuasive, or any type of expository writing: a question, an idiom, an anecdote, a definition, an exaggeration, a setting, a quotation, a pun or play on words, or a riddle. Choose any or all of these to model your own lead for your students to show how the leads work effectively.

Lesson 7
Arguments and Audience

Who will the writer be trying to persuade? If your topic is to argue the benefits of school uniforms, you will have different arguments if your audience is your students rather than the students' parents. Again, if the piece is tied to a content theme, you may determine the audience or topic. Otherwise, the student writers may determine the audience. Either way, spending time during the mini-lesson discussing audience and modeling who the audience is will make a difference in your piece of writing. This is another lesson where the students might benefit from going back to the examples you provided in Lesson 1. Who do students think the author was writing to in that piece? How would the argument have been different if the audience had been different? If you begin the lesson that way, it is likely this will be another two-day lesson.

Lesson 8
Supporting Details

Even though a persuasive piece is full of the author's opinion, the supporting details will include many facts. Students need to find statistics, provide concrete examples, use graphics like charts and tables, and even tell little stories or vignettes to support their own opinions. These details are how persuasive authors win someone over to their way of thinking.

Writing Supplement

Lesson 9
Other Techniques of Persuasion

What else do you know that works well to persuade someone? Use both your experience and the examples you read in Lesson 1 to decide on some techniques that seem consistent between the pieces. Appealing to someone's emotions is certainly a technique we've all tried when trying to be persuasive, whether in writing or in conversation. Think of other techniques your students might incorporate into their pieces.

Lesson 10
The Clincher Conclusion

In a persuasive piece, the conclusion does not need to be long, it simply needs to restate the author's views on the topic. As with any conclusion, it needs to wrap up the piece of writing. The arguments are where you will spend your time possibly restating or repeating in many ways. However, the conclusion will be brief and will more than likely refer back to the opening or the lead.

These mini-lesson descriptions lead you through some logical steps to teaching persuasive writing. Though they are not as detailed as the focused lessons provided in *Writing Mini-Lessons in the Upper Grades* (Hall, Cunningham, and Arens, 2003), they are here to show you that focused writing is a time consuming act with many deliberate lessons designed to teach the genre. Use these lessons as a guide. What do your students need? Do they need more of one thing and less of another? Do you have a state standard that requires another version of persuasive writing? Use those criteria also to guide your instruction.

Web Sites for Publishing Student Work

http://www.ucalgary.ca/~dkbrown/writings.html

http://www.discoverwriting.com

http://www.kidpub.org/kidpub/

http://www.scils.rutgers.edu/~kvander/childpublising.html

http://www.magickeys.com/books/link-pub.html

http://www.teenwriting.about.com/mbody.htm

http://www.poetry4kids.com/

http://www.arensconsulting.com

http://www.falcon.jmu.edu/~ramseyil/writing.htm

http://www.yahooligans.com/schoolbell/language arts/writing/Publishing on the web

http://www.ecis.org/links.writinglinks.htm

Quick Check

Name	Date													
1.														
2.														
3.														
4.														
5.														
6.														
7.														
8.														
9.														
10.														
11.														
12.														
13.														
14.														
15.														
16.														
17.														
18.														
19.														
20.														
21.														
22.														
23.														
24.														
25.														
26.														

R = revision   PC = peer conference   P = publishing   D = draft   B = brainstorming
E = self-edit   C = conference with teacher

Writing Record

Piece #	Date	Title	Genre

Conference Sheet

Name _____

Date	Title/Genre	Uses proper format	Conventions: grammar, spelling, capitalization, punctuation	Other observations Goals:

Name _Alexander_

Date	Title/Genre	Uses proper format	Conventions: grammar, spelling, capitalization, punctuation	Other observations Goals:	
October 17	How to Build with Legos (How to)		Used the checklist well	Discussed the format—doesn't have materials listed, etc. Goal: Will work on labeling or choosing a way to transition between steps in the process. Check it next conference	
October 26	How to Build with Legos (How to)	Format looks much better!		Walked through the revisions Alex made—good choices— much better piece Will take for final edit	
November 1	Poetry	Showed him some examples so he will draft in proper format		Is trying some free verse poetry about his first time skiing—reminded him what poetry looks like	

Chapter 4   Guided Reading in Big Blocks

The primary focus of the Guided Reading Block is comprehension. Reading is thinking—thinking abo the text, thinking about the reader's understanding of the text, thinking about the words, thinking abo the reader's own thinking, etc. Too often, Guided Reading instruction is focused on oral reading and presentation rather than complex thinking. Sometimes reading instruction is focused on answering literal questions rather than being thoughtful about the reader's understanding and the author's intent. Durkin (1978-79) and, more recently, Pressley (2000) identified that much of what was called comprehension instruction was actually comprehension assessment. Worksheets and fill-in-the-blank forms don't teach students how to think, they only assess whether students read the text well enough gather the information required in the blanks. Comprehension instruction requires thoughtful, focused attention on the complex processes that good readers use to understand text. This chapter will discus key comprehension strategies, formats, and activities to teach students to think about their reading. A comprehensive resource for Guided Reading is *Guided Reading the Four-Blocks® Way* by Cunningha Hall, and Cunningham (2000). Each section has specific recommendations for upper-grade teachers

Guided Reading is a "bossy" Block where the teacher is "large and in charge." The teacher determi what is to be read, the purpose for the reading, the skills and strategies to be learned and/or applie how students will engage in the reading, and how they will respond to the reading. The teacher selects texts at appropriate reading levels from a variety of types of reading materials—basal reader magazines, trade books, science and social studies texts, poetry, plays, etc. The teacher sets the purpose for the reading by identifying for, and with, students why they are reading the text and the outcome(s) intended for the reading. This should include the comprehension strategies students will learn or apply in the text. The teacher guides students to read in a variety of formats. Some days, the whole class will read together. On other days, students will read in small, flexible groups. Sometimes these groups are homogenous with students of similar reading abilities; sometimes these groups are heterogeneous with students of varying reading abilities. And finally, the teacher engages students in responding to the text through conversations and/or written responses.

In Big-Blocks™ classrooms, the Guided Reading Block—approximately 180 minutes per week— includes the following:

- **Before-Reading Phase**
  Before beginning a selection, students must access or build prior knowledge, make connections, learn key vocabulary, make predictions, and identify the purpose for reading. Readers must begi thinking about the text before they begin reading the text. Allington (2000) suggests that a brief amount of time spent building background knowledge is probably enough, leaving the majority o the Block free for actual reading.

- **During-Reading Phase**
  While reading, students must question and monitor what they are reading and thinking about, make inferences, visualize, and continue to make connections and set predictions. Students need uninterrupted periods of time to read and think, so this should be the longest phase of any Guide Reading lesson. Pearson and Fielding (1991) suggest that for every minute spent talking about reading (including before and after), students should spend at least one minute actually reading.

- **After-Reading Phase**
  After reading, students must follow-up on their predictions, connections, and purpose. They may need to summarize, identify important information, evaluate, or apply the information from the text to a specific problem or situation. They should be prepared to engage in conversations or written responses that reflect their thinking. The After-Reading activity should be substantive and challenging and move far beyond the "right answer" to the teacher's question. However, the After-Reading activity should not be so involved that it takes longer to respond than it did to read.

The goals of the Guided Reading Block in Big-Blocks classrooms are:

- to teach comprehension strategies
- to teach students how to read and respond to all types of literature including content texts
- to develop background knowledge and vocabulary
- to provide as much instructional-level material as possible
- to maintain the self-confidence and motivation of struggling readers

Guided Reading Is Multilevel

Guided Reading is the most challenging Block to make multilevel. The selection of a text (or even a dozen different texts) means the selected material will be on some students' reading levels but not all. To be most successful in the Guided Reading Block, you must know the reading level of students in your class and the average reading level for the class. The following are some common strategies you can use to make Guided Reading more multilevel:

- Alternate between texts that are at the average reading level of the class and texts that are below the average reading level of the class. All students benefit from reading easy text as it frees them to think about the text and develop fluency. The material you ask students to read should not be so challenging that most of the students in the class can't read it. If that is the case, it is not a good choice for Guided Reading. Consider reading aloud challenging material to students during content instruction if it is information they need to know but is in a format too difficult for them to read and understand.

- Select short texts and picture books. This allows you to design lessons that have students reread texts. Alter the purpose for each reading and select a different format. Rereading develops fluency of reading as well as fluency of thinking. Short texts also provide opportunities for many different types of texts to be read. If students only read chapter books in Guided Reading, there won't be time for a variety of texts.

- Vary the formats used during reading. Have students read as a whole class and in small, flexible groups including partners. When students are in small groups, match struggling readers with other students who can and will assist them in their reading.

- Occasionally schedule a small group to meet with you while other groups are reading. Small coaching groups allow you to focus on specific skills and strategies. These groups don't meet daily, nor do they only include struggling readers. These groups are truly flexible, meeting only when necessary and with different rosters of students. For more information on Coaching Groups, see *Guided Reading the Four-Blocks® Way* (Cunningham, Hall, and Cunningham, 2000).

Guided Reading in Big Blocks

All of the skills and strategies students learn in the Working with Words Block and all of the reading they do in the Self-Selected Reading Block assist them in reading and thinking about complex text. However, you must decide how to support your most struggling readers. (See page 145 for additional ideas.)

Teaching Students to Comprehend

There are some comprehension strategies all good readers use. Teaching students to understand and use these strategies will allow them to think critically about text. Strategies are systematic plans consciously adapted and monitored to improve students' performance in learning. Skills are the acquired abilities to perform well (Harris and Hodges, eds., 1995). Comprehension skills typically taught to students are main idea, important details, and sequencing. Once these skills are taught, it is assumed that students will know how and when to use them. A comprehension strategy that good readers use is summarizing. A good summary may include a main idea and important details in sequence. If you are summarizing what you read today for your spouse, it may sound different than if you are summarizing what you read today for your supervisor. Summarizing the key information from meeting may not require sequencing; however, summarizing key information for a review of a piece fiction would.

Pearson, Roehler, Dole, and Duffy (1992) identify three differences between skills and strategies:

- Students who use strategies are learners with conscious plans for comprehending; students who us skills do so without conscious planning.

- Students become more aware of their reasoning process as they use strategies to make sense out print; skills seldom involve self-awareness.

- Strategies change with the purpose for reading and the genre being read; skills are not adaptable

Cunningham, Hall, and Cunningham (2000) describe six strategies that seem to play a large part in how reading comprehension occurs:

- **Connecting**
  Readers connect what they know—their prior knowledge—to a text. This process begins in the selection of a text and/or in the initial thinking about a text. Readers make connections between text, their personal experiences, what they have read in other texts, and things they know about th world (Harvey and Goudvis, 2000).

- **Predicting/Anticipating**
  Readers use their prior knowledge to predict and anticipate what the text is about. While reading, they predict what the text may tell next and constantly revise their previous predictions based on new information. Connecting and predicting/anticipating are strategies that allow readers to mak sense of, enjoy, and learn from reading.

- **Summarizing/Concluding**
  While reading, readers draw conclusions, accumulate and keep important information, and subsume larger facts into generalizations. This synthesis of information is used to summarize—crec a brief retelling of—an entire text (Duffy, 2003). The summary is the reader's short version of the text.

- **Questioning/Monitoring**

Readers constantly ask themselves if what they are reading makes sense. They attend to irrelevant or erroneous information, words, thoughts, and ideas in text. When something disrupts the meaning, the brain sends up a red flag indicating a concern. Readers then engage in fix-up strategies to repair the meaning. More complex topics require readers to question/monitor more thoughtfully and carefully. However, too many questions may cause readers to lose interest and/or meaning.

- **Imaging/Inferring**

Reading requires the use of all of the senses—including the mind's eye and ears—to bring life to the text. For most readers, imaging is like seeing a movie while they read. Since descriptive language assists in imaging and descriptive language most often occurs in narrative text, imagery tends to be taught in conjunction with stories rather than expository text (Duffy, 2003).

Inferring is the ability to deduct important information the author did not explicitly state in the text. Inferring requires the reader to use background knowledge and an understanding of the text read so far to image, and from the image to infer situations.

- **Evaluating/Applying**

Readers do more than simply think about the author's message. They form opinions, make judgments, and sometimes take action based on their reading.

Although strategies can be isolated and defined, most often multiple strategies are used simultaneously. You need to teach students how to identify and use these multiple strategies in their own reading.

The most effective way to teach students about these strategies is to model how you use them in your reading. Thinking aloud while reading makes the internalized process of reading explicit for students. You should explain and model a particular comprehension strategy with text. After modeling, you should invite students to think along, sharing their thoughts and strategy use. You should then encourage students to use the strategy independently. You may have students write about their thinking and strategy use and/or make this a topic of conversation in Self-Selected Reading conferences. The transition from modeling a strategy to using it independently may take several weeks. Throughout the process, students must get the message that reading is thinking.

Formats for Grouping Students during Reading

You should plan for students to participate in various grouping formats. In an observational study, exemplary first- and fourth-grade teachers were found to teach lessons to the whole class, to small groups, and to individual students in one-on-one instruction (Pressley, Allington, Wharton-McDonald, Block, and Morrow, 2001). Guided Reading formats should vary based on the purpose of the lesson. Whole-group and small-group lessons may be used to focus on strategy introduction or practice, to introduce or use content knowledge, or highlight the attributes of a genre or author. One-on-one strategy instruction will most often occur in the Self-Selected Reading Block.

Whole Group, Multilevel Instruction

Any of the comprehension strategies may be introduced as part of a whole-group lesson. This allows you to provide a common vocabulary and set of experiences to students from which they can build strategy knowledge. Whole-group instruction may also be used to introduce a social studies or science

Guided Reading in Big Blocks

concept through text. Whole-group instruction may occur with class sets of books or materials which allow students access to the print and, when possible, a chance to highlight, mark, or place self-stick notes right on their own copies. A copy of a single text, such as a big book, an article copied and placed on an overhead projector, or text shown via a document camera, may also be used. Whole-group echo and choral reading may be used for fluency development. The whole-group lesson is made multilevel by the selection of a grade-level or easier text and multiple readings of the text.

Small, Flexible Heterogeneous Groups

Partner Reading

You may place each student with a partner to read a selection. Partnering allows students to read with others who can, and will, support them in their reading and thinking about texts. Most of the time, you will have all partners read the same text so that they can have before-reading and after-reading conversations with the whole class.

Partnering requires some thoughtful planning. Consider the following when using Partner Reading:

- **Carefully assign partners.** Partner struggling readers with good, solid, grade-level readers but not your best readers. Too great a disparity in ability does not make a good partnership. Once you have looked at current reading levels, then look at behaviors and dispositions. You may need to move students around a bit to accommodate likes and dislikes. Post the list of partners so that everyone can see with whom he is working.

- **Decide how often you need to change partners.** You may decide to keep partners together for multiple sessions and/or books. Partners should stay together long enough to develop good, working relationships. The goal of partner reading is not that every child can read with the other students in class. The goal of partner reading is so students can engage in quality reading experiences.

- **Decide where partners will meet.** Partners may work well at desks, or you may choose to have them use other seating in the room. Either way, students need to know where they are to sit, who is to move, etc. Post partner reading locations with the list of partners so that both can be easily seen from anywhere in the room.

- **Decide how to handle absent partners.** Will a student find a group on her own or will you assign her to a group? Can a student read alone or does he need to be with someone else?

- **Decide how partners will read each selection.** Partners can read selections in a variety of ways:

  ✔ **Take Turns**
  One partner reads a section or a page, and then the other partner reads the next section or page. Although this is the most common way for students to read in partners, it may not be the most effective since it is a bit like Round Robin Reading. (See page 124 for information on Round Robin Reading.)

  ✔ **Choral Read**
  Students can read the selection chorally. This may best be done as a rereading when students have read the selection silently first.

✔ **Ask Questions**

Both partners read each page silently or chorally. Then, each student asks her partner a question about what they read. Teach students to ask open-ended questions that require some thinking beyond the text.

✔ **Self-Stick Notes**

Give partners a limited number of self-stick notes to mark the places in the text where they applied the focus strategy or found something they thought was important. Partners must agree on where the notes are to be placed.

- **Make sure partners have a purpose for reading.** The format only tells students how they are to read, not what they are to think about. Partner reading is generally preceded by a whole-group lesson that focuses students on the purpose for reading. Be sure the partners are clear on why they are reading, what they are to think about, and what they should be ready to do after reading.

- **Set a time limit.** Be sure partners know how long they are to read and when they are expected to be done. Partner reading is generally followed by whole-group time that focuses on what was read and learned. Let students know when the after-reading conversation will begin.

- **Provide additional activities for partners who finish before the rest of the class:**

  ✔ **Do the Beach Ball**

  The Beach Ball has an open-ended question written on each of the panels. For fiction texts, the questions may be about story structure (Who was the main character? What was the setting? etc.), and for nonfiction texts, they may be about the information in the text (What is the main idea? Name three important details. etc.). Partners can toss the ball to each other and answer questions.

  ✔ **Graphic Organizers**

  Make a list of things to add to a graphic organizer.

  ✔ **Write Some "Why" and "How" Questions**

  These open-ended questions may be used in follow-up conversations.

  ✔ **Read Aloud**

  Practice reading a favorite page or favorite section aloud until it can be read perfectly with terrific expression.

  ✔ **Self-Stick Notes**

  Give each pair of partners a limited number of self-stick notes to mark important or interesting information.

  Each pair of partners does not have to have the same task. Make the tasks as open as possible, but when necessary, tailor the tasks to specific partners.

- **Model the expected behavior.** Before beginning, model, with a child as your partner, how to:

  ✔ move to the assigned seats

  ✔ review the purpose for reading

  ✔ read with a partner

  ✔ decide what to do if finished early

  ✔ find partners if one is absent

Guided Reading in Big Blocks

- **Be visible.** You should be circulating, listening in, asking probing questions, making notes to reference in the follow-up conversation, etc. Let students know you are interested and attentive to the partners. Highlight what partners are doing to support each other and their comprehension of text.

Reading Teams

Think of reading teams as two carefully selected partnerships making a foursome. The same benefits and concerns apply. Carefully select teams. They need to know how to read the text, what they should do after the reading, etc. Just as with partners, it would not be appropriate for one team member to do all of the reading and talking—in other words, the learning! Each team should have an assigned team leader who ensures that all members participate. This may not be your most proficient reader. In fact, this may be an opportunity for a struggling reader to be a strong participant on the team, depending on what the team leader needs to do that day. Teams may also need a recorder or a speaker. Think about what the teams will do with the information they read and decide what roles will be most beneficial.

After completing their reading, teams should do something with the information they learned. A team may develop a graphic organizer, discuss "How" and "Why" questions that you or partners developed on a previous day, or discuss Everyone Read To… statements. (See page 116 for a description of Everyone Read To . . . .) Most of the time, Reading Teams will all read the same text. You may engage the whole class in before- and after-reading conversations, or the before- and after-reading conversations may take place within the teams.

Small, Flexible Homogenous Groups

Three-Ring Circus

This format is a wonderful way to allow students to read a common selection in the most efficient way for them. In Three-Ring Circus, some students read by themselves (ring one), some students read with partners (ring two), and some students read with you (ring three). These groups are not static and should change with the reading selection. You will want to post assignments when assigning students to their reading ring since groups change frequently.

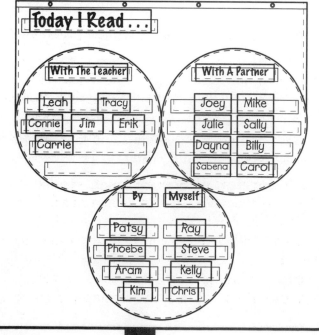

When planning for Three-Ring Circus, think about the difficulty of the text and the current reading levels of the students in your room. It would seem most appropriate to assign your proficient readers to read alone or with partners, assign your on-level readers to read with partners, and assign your struggling readers to read with you. Sometimes this is the best arrangement, but it won't be the only way you will assign students.

The group reading with you may be thought of as a coaching group. A coaching group will sometimes have struggling readers in it, especially if this is an easier (slightly below average reading level) selection. You can provide support and coach struggling readers since the material is closer to their reading level. Even then, include some good readers in the group. Think of the good readers as "salt," providing flavor through fluent reading and conversation. This also removes the stigma of being in the teacher's group if not all of them are the "low" readers. If the reading selection is on grade level (average reading level of the class), you may want to pair your struggling readers with competent readers and coach those students who are slightly below level, but who rarely get support. Again, include a couple of good readers to work with this group.

Partners and students reading alone may range from strugglers with competent partners to proficient readers. Assignments should change with each selection. Struggling readers may make great partners or even be able to read alone if they are "experts" on the topic. The purpose is to support each reader in a way that makes the most sense for that reader.

As with Partners and Reading Teams, have a plan for what students are to do if they get finished before other readers. The same suggestions (pages 106-107) apply for these groups, as well. You might also consider altering the reading assignment to match the groups. For example, while the students reading alone or in partners may be asked to identify seven important pieces of information, your coaching group may only identify three important pieces of information.

When students have worked in the Three-Ring Circus format for a while, you may let them choose which rings they will be in to read the selection. It will be important that students make good choices, however, so if you let them choose, you must also let them live with their choices. If they don't choose well, be sure they understand that they will be held accountable for the reading just like everyone else.

Book Club Groups
Books Club Groups offer an opportunity for students to read different texts at different reading levels that are all connected in some way. This format may take some time to locate sets of materials, but it is worth the effort! Teachers generally select several titles (three to five) that are connected by author, genre, topic, or theme. Book Club Groups are most successful when one of the selections is a bit easier and one is a little more challenging. Groups change with each book, and although this format provides materials at different reading levels, the groups may have varying abilities within them depending upon the text, student capacity, and interest.

To begin Book Club Groups, students preview each book before choosing the book they want to read. You will share how the selected books are connected and do a brief book talk on each book. Demonstrate how you sample a book before deciding to read it. (Look at the back cover, read the first few sentences, etc.) Let children indicate the books they want to read by ranking the choices. Then, form groups considering the choices made by the children and the difficulty of the books. If a struggling reader lists the hardest selection as his first choice, he may be placed in a group that will read another of his choices that is more appropriate. We call this "managed choice." If an advanced reader selects

Guided Reading in Big Blocks

the easiest book as his first choice, we may honor that request. He will provide a fluent model and support for the other readers in the group.

Once Book Club Groups are formed, the groups meet daily to read and discuss their book. Groups, or the teacher, will need to decide how they will read the text within the group. (See pages 106-107 for a list of suggestions.) However, Round Robin Reading within the group should not be a choice. (See page 124 for information on Round Robin Reading.) Teachers may choose to have before- and after-reading meetings with the whole class to discuss what groups are learning about the genre, topic, theme, or author; however groups will conduct some "before" and "after" conversations within the context of the groups.

One modification you may choose to use with older students is a Book Pass (adapted from Allen, 2000). Book Passes allow students to record their thoughts about each text as they preview it. The directions for Book Pass are:

1. Divide students by tables or into groups of three to five, depending upon the number of titles to be previewed.
2. Give each group one copy of each book.
3. Have each student take one book.
4. Choose a direction for passing.
5. Students should list the title and author of the book on the Pass.
6. Allow 1-2 minutes for students to look at their books.
7. At the end of 1-2 minutes, call "write." Students should make quick comments on the books they just looked at.
8. At the end of 30 seconds, call "pass." Students pass the books to the next students. The Book Pass continues until each student has previewed all of the titles.
9. After the Book Pass is finished, let students rank their choices.
10. Collect the Book Pass forms and assign a book to each student. Look at comments as well as number choice when assigning books.

Book Pass				
Name Kaitlin		Date May 2		
Author	Title	Comments		Choice
Berger	Chirping Crickets	interesting pictures, easy words, What is a nymph?		3
Hawes	Why Frogs Are Wet	good pictures, different kinds of frogs, easy words		2
Markle	Outside and Inside Sharks	lots of words, photographs, lots of teeth, shark being born alive		4
Simon	Snakes	photographs, snakes eating mice and other snakes, babies hatching from shell, just right words		1

Literature Circles

Literature Circles function like Book Club Groups in that students choose books and meet with small groups for discussion. However, in Literature Circles students generally:

- read on their own and only meet in groups to discuss what was read.

- determine as a group how much to read between meetings.

- have specific roles they play in the discussion groups. For example, there may be a Summarizer, a Discussion Director, a Vocabulary Enricher, an Illustrator, etc. These roles should rotate so that students learn all of the roles. At some point in time, the formal roles may fall away as students become proficient at playing each role.

- choose books connected by genre, author, theme, or topic.

Literature Circles are a wonderful way for students to read and engage in literate conversations. It does require students to be self-regulated and be able to read selected books without support. For additional information on Literature Circles see *Literature Circles: Voice and Choice in Book Clubs and Reading Groups, 2nd edition* (Daniels, 2002).

Comprehension and Fluency Strategies

The following activities are specific ways to encourage students to use the comprehension strategies identified on pages 104-105.

Connecting

T-Charts

Good readers make connections from the process of selecting or previewing text to completing the text. An activity that helps students make their connections explicit is a T-chart. On the left side of the T-chart, students write an entry from the text. On the right side, they respond to the text with their connections. (See page 149 for a reproducible T-chart.) Here is an example with text from *Because of Winn-Dixie* by Kate DiCamillo (Candlewick Press, 2001).

Text	Connection
That summer I found Winn-Dixie was also the summer me and the preacher moved to Naomi, Florida . . .	I moved to Iowa the summer of third grade.
"I don't even have friends because I had to leave them all behind when we moved here from Watley."	I didn't have any friends either. Not even my Dachshund. I had to leave him with my grandmother because we were renting a house that didn't allow pets.

Guided Reading in Big Blocks

Predicting/Anticipating

Guess Yes or No (Anticipation Guide)

Guess Yes or No (formerly called Anticipation Guides in *Guided Reading the Four-Blocks® Way*, Cunningham, Hall, and Cunningham, 2000) activities include statements about the text that guide students' thinking as they read. Prepare the Guess Yes or No lesson by writing some true and some false statements about the text with more true than false. Number the statements for later reference. Write only the number of statements students can read and respond to in any one session. Include important vocabulary students will need to know in order to understand the text. Although Guess Yes or No may be used with fiction, it is most commonly used with informational text. (See page 15 for a sample Guess Yes or No lesson.)

Guess Yes or No

Before   After

1. _____ Most Egyptians were farmers. _____

2. _____ All the houses were very close together, _____
   except for the wealthy.

3. _____ Egyptians dressed warmly because of _____
   their cool climate.

Introduce the statements by showing them to students on an overhead transparency, document camera, or individual copies. Read each statement aloud, discussing any important vocabulary. After each statement is read, have students indicate whether they believe it is true or false. This can be done with the whole class by signal or voice. Record the responses. In small groups, this can be done by the group members agreeing on a response for each statement and one member recording it. The responses may be recorded by writing a yes or no to the left of each statement. Some teachers develop forms for students to write on with a space to the left of each statement. A space to the right of each statement is used to record what is found out after reading. Once all of the statements have been labeled yes or no, students are ready to read the selection.

The selection may be read in any format (individually, partners, Reading Teams, Three-Ring Circus, etc.). During the reading, students identify the sections of the text that prove the Guess Yes or No statements are true or false. (Self-stick notes are helpful for this part!) When the reading is complete, revisit the statements. Discuss the statements again, identifying which are true and which are false. Have students read the marked sections from the text to support their responses. Reword all false statements so that they are true. The statements may then be used to write a summary of the reading or as notes for content study.

Prove It!

Prove It! can be used with fiction or nonfiction texts. Like Guess Yes or No, predictive statements are written about the text; however, Prove It! statements are developed by students. Before reading the text, have students preview the cover of the text, the title and/or headings, table of contents, visuals, etc., so that they can make predictions. If this is a whole-group lesson, write down students' predictions. If students are working in partners or groups, a recorder writes down the predictions for the group. All predictions are numbered for later reference. (See pages 138-139 for a sample Prove It! lesson.)

Students may read the text in any format you decide (individually, partners, Reading Teams, Three-Ring Circus, etc.). During the reading, students identify the sections of the text that prove or disprove the Prove It! Statements. (Once again, self-stick notes are helpful for this part!) When the reading is complete, revisit the statements. Discuss the statements again, identifying which are true and which are false. Have students read the marked sections from the text to support their responses. Reword all false statements so that they are true. Statements may then be used to write a summary of the text reading.

Summarizing/Concluding

GIST

Summarizing is the ability to retain only the most important information to create a brief synopsis of a text. Summary writing may be used as a means for increasing the understanding of complex topics and/or assessing student learning.

GIST is a group task designed to write a summary in 20 words or less. Students who participate in GIST lessons learn to develop a well-written summary. Explain to students that the gist of something is the main idea. Sometimes readers don't need to remember all of the details but just need to get the gist of the material. GIST usually works best with nonfiction text. The following steps will assist students to write the GIST:

- Provide students with copies of a short text (may be individual copies or on an overhead transparency). The text should be divided into two to three sections. Each section should contain no more than three paragraphs. There should be no more than one paragraph when you are doing GIST for the first time. The whole text shouldn't be more than six paragraphs.

- Draw 20 word-sized blanks on the board.

- Students read the first section, and then work with you to record the gist of what they have read.

- Students take turns telling you what to write. You lead the class in a discussion about how to put their ideas into sentences, allowing students to negotiate the construction of sentences.

- Do **not** write a 21st word.

- Now, read an additional section of the text and incorporate the information from both sections in just 20 words.

- It is possible to read one more section and condense the summary one more time.

Guided Reading in Big Blocks

GIST of "A Sweet Advance in Candy Packing" by Emily Sohn (*Science News for Kids*, online at *http://www.sciencenewsforkids.org/articles/20040218/Note3.asp*).

(after first paragraph)

More	M&M's	fit	into	a	bag	than
gumballs	of	the	same	size.	Squashed	spheres
pack	together	more	tightly	than	spheres.	

(after several paragraphs)

Squashed	spheres	pack	together	more	tightly	than
spheres.	Understanding	this	could	improve	heat	shields
for	furnaces	and	develop	clearer	glass.	

Choose the text carefully. If there is too much important information, it will be very difficult to condense it into a 20-word summary. Be prepared to walk students through the process of summarizing the first several times. They may have difficulty with the transition words and will have to give up some vocabulary words to make room for them. Once students are familiar with the process, they may construct GIST summaries in small groups.

Excitement Maps

An Excitement Map is a tool students use to discover the way stories come together with rising action, climax, and a resolution. Excitement Maps are used with narrative text. Rather than telling your student that stories do this or even sketching it out for them, this activity will bring them to that conclusion.

Bring out a piece of labeled chart paper and some lined and unlined self-stick notes. The chart paper labeled with the numbers 0-10 along the left side. Tell students that they will be retelling the story even with you. As students name the events, ask one student to quickly sketch a picture to represent the eve on an unlined self-stick note and ask another student to write a brief description of the event on a line self-stick note. Be sure to model this process by sketching and writing the first event. The written self-sti notes are lined up across the bottom of the chart paper. Below is an example of what this looks like.

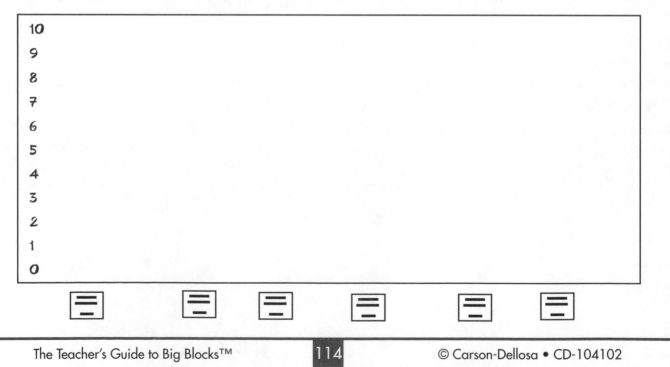

After students have retold the entire story, ask them to think about each event. How exciting was each event compared to the other things that happened in the story? As you take students through each event, they tell you approximately where the event falls in relation to excitement on a scale of 0-10. Place the picture self-stick note beside the correct number and directly above the corresponding description self-stick note.

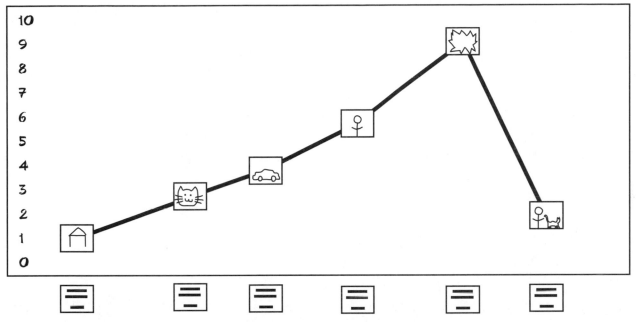

Once students have placed the pictures on the chart paper to represent how exciting each event is, connect the pictures with drawn lines. The result is a plot diagram that indicates rising action, climax, and resolution. Rather than just teaching those words and explaining that stories must do this, allow students to "discover" the concepts of climax and resolution. Each class will vote differently on the levels of excitement, but the story will always end up with a shape similar to that depicted in the excitement map above.

The same process may be used with a chapter book. Instead of listing the events of a story, students will briefly summarize each chapter and sketch a coordinating picture. For the best results, have students write the chapter summaries as soon as the chapter has been read. Don't wait until your students have read the entire book before having them write the individual chapter summaries.

You can either keep the chapter summaries or post them on the chart that will eventually be used for the excitement map. At the end of the book, go through the process of voting on each chapter's excitement level. Chapter books typically result in a little more variation across the chart. There may be a very exciting first chapter to draw you in or a smaller peak in the middle rather than a gradual climb to the climax.

Guided Reading in Big Blocks

Here is an example of an excitement map for a chapter book and an example of a typical self-stick note chapter summary. The chapter summary is from *The Sign of the Beaver* by Elizabeth George Speare (Yearling, 1994).

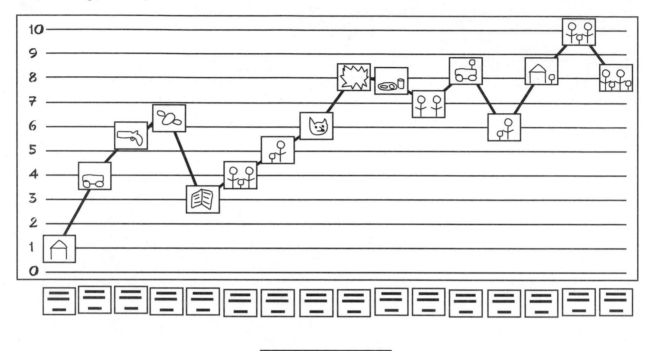

7. Attean teaches Matt to find his way and the sign of the beaver.

Inferring/Imaging

ERT (Everyone Read To...)

ERT is an activity that guides the whole class (or small groups) in reading a selection. Students do the initial reading on their own but stay together as a group for guidance and support in making inferences. For ERT, you lead students through the text a page or two at a time, having them read to find out important events or information. You provide written statements that tell students what to read for. Include statements that are literally stated ("Read to find out…"), as well as those that must be inferred ("Read to figure out…"). Some statements may have students read to find or figure out two things. Have students indicate when they read the part that helps them figure out an answer.

HINT

Each student may raise her hand (or hands if there are two things to read for), place her hand(s) flat on top of her desk, or move her pencil to let you know she has read and found the appropriate information. Find a nonverbal signal that lets you know students are ready but does not interfere with the reading and thinking of other students.

When most students are ready, ask a volunteer to give you the answer. Ask someone else to read the part(s) aloud that helped him find/figure out the answer. If the answer is not literally stated, ask students to read and explain how they figured it out.

(See pages 138-139 for a sample lesson using ERT.)

Graphic Organizers

Graphic organizers are powerful tools for collecting and organizing information from text. There are organizers that are helpful in gathering information from fiction and those that are helpful in gathering information from nonfiction. In the primary grades, teachers usually select the graphic organizer for students to complete. For the upper grades, we suggest that you post various examples of organizers and ask students to select the one that will gather the appropriate information for the task and the text. This may be best accomplished by having students preview or read the selection, and then select an organizer. This provides opportunities for students to reread materials for specific purposes.

Organizers for Fiction

A **Story Map** may be the most useful organizer to gather information from a fiction text. Story Maps have students attend to common fiction text features, such as main character(s), setting, problem, events, and resolution. They are helpful in assisting students in writing summaries of texts. A reproducible Story Map is on page 150.

A **Web** may be used to gather information about a particular scene, event, or character.

Here is a Web with character information from *Just a Dream* by Chris Van Allsburg (Houghton Mifflin Co., 1990).

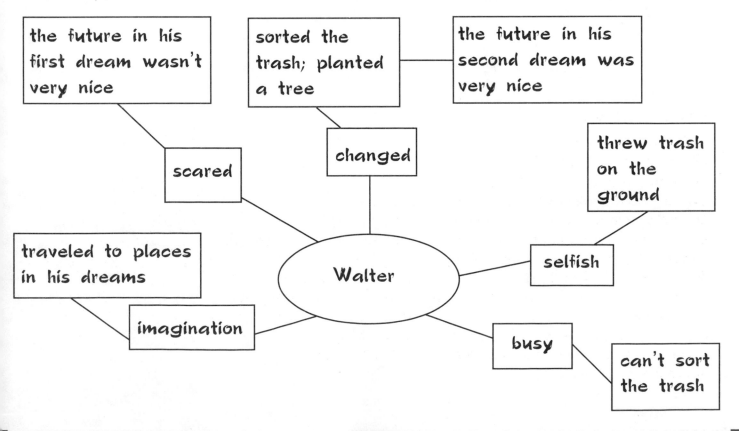

Guided Reading in Big Blocks

A **Venn Diagram** may used to compare and contrast two characters, books, authors, or themes. A reproducible Venn Diagram is on page 151.

Here is a Venn Diagram that compares characters from *Because of Winn-Dixie* by Kate DiCamillo (Candlewick Press, 2000) and *Lewis and Clark and Me: A Dog's Tale* by Laurie Myers (Henry Holt and Company, 2002).

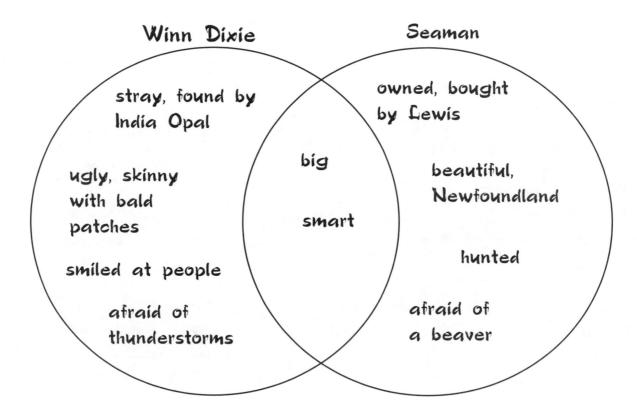

Winn Dixie   **Seaman**

stray, found by India Opal

owned, bought by Lewis

big

ugly, skinny with bald patches

beautiful, Newfoundland

smart

smiled at people

hunted

afraid of thunderstorms

afraid of a beaver

Organizers for Nonfiction
Informational text is generally organized in one of a few structures: main idea and details; compare and contrast; sequence; or cause and effect. The graphic organizer students choose should reflect the structure of the text.

Main Idea and Details
A **Web** may be used to gather information and organize it by details. The main idea would be listed in the center of the Web with details radiating as spokes.

Here is a Web with information from *We Are the Many: A Picture Book of American Indians* by Doreen Rappaport (HarperCollins, 2002).

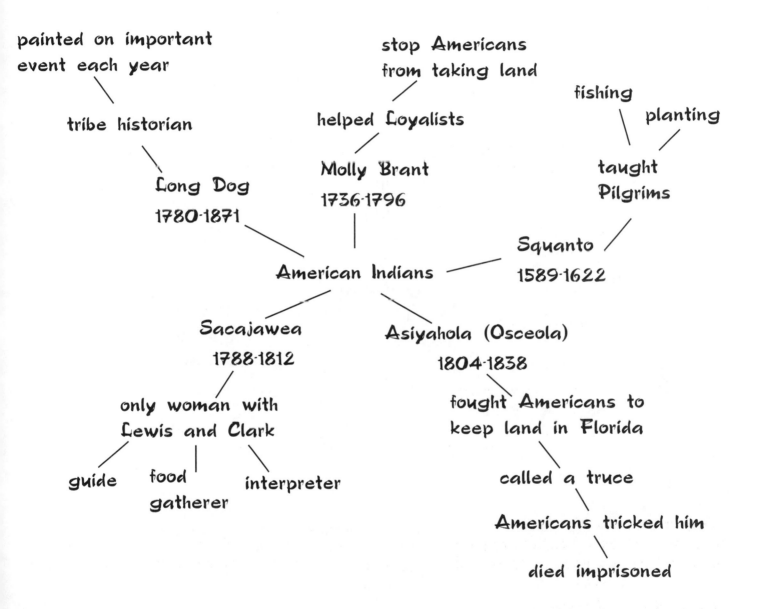

painted on important
event each year

tribe historian

Long Dog
1780-1871

stop Americans
from taking land

helped Loyalists

Molly Brant
1736-1796

fishing

planting

taught
Pilgrims

Squanto
1589-1622

American Indians

Sacajawea
1788-1812

only woman with
Lewis and Clark

guide

food
gatherer

interpreter

Asiyahola (Osceola)
1804-1838

fought Americans to
keep land in Florida

called a truce

Americans tricked him

died imprisoned

Guided Reading in Big Blocks

Compare and Contrast

A **Venn Diagram** is a visual used to compare and contrast two things. It can be used to compare concepts such as plants, animals, historical figures, or life today and in the past. A reproducible Venn Diagram is on page 151.

Here is a Venn Diagram comparing alligators (with information from *Outside and Inside Alligators* by Sandra Markle, Atheneum, 1998) and snakes (with information from *Snakes* by Seymour Simon, HarperTrophy, 1994).

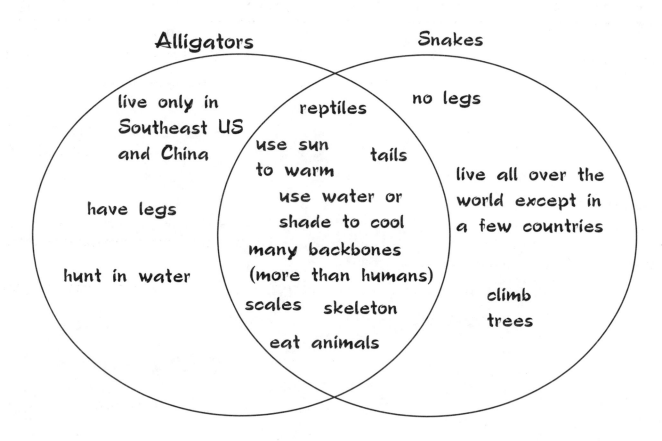

A **Feature Matrix** may be used to collect compare/contrast information on a topic. The features of the topic are listed on the left, and subtopics are listed across the top. Information from the matrix may be used to discuss specific features, write descriptive paragraphs, or write a summary of important information about the topic. You can also see more information for using a feature matrix in *Conversations in Four-Blocks® Classrooms* by Sharon Moore (2004) where they are referenced as Data Charts. You may also use Feature Matrices for writing. Examples of lessons using matrices in the focused lessons on biography and for informational writing are found in *Writing Mini-Lessons for the Upper Grades* by Hall, Cunningham, and Arens (2003). A reproducible Feature Matrix is on page 152. A sample lesson using a Feature Matrix can be found on pages 134-137.

Guided Reading in Big Blocks

Sequence

A **Time Line** may be important in collecting information from a biography, a historical event, or events leading to a scientific discovery.

Here is a Time Line with events from Paul Revere's life (with information found in *Paul Revere's Ride* by Lucia Raatma, Compass Point Books, 2003).

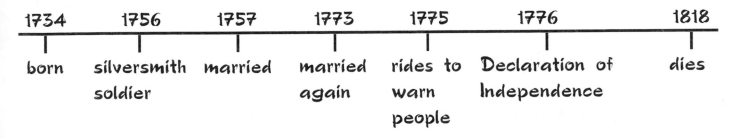

Cause/Effect

A Causal Chain may used to illustrate a series of events, such as the sequence of events (from bill to law), stages of something (a life cycle), or the steps in a linear process (how to conduct an experiment). A reproducible Causal Chain is on page 153.

Here is a Causal Chain with information from the book *A River Ran Wild* by Lynne Cherry (Voyager Books, 2002).

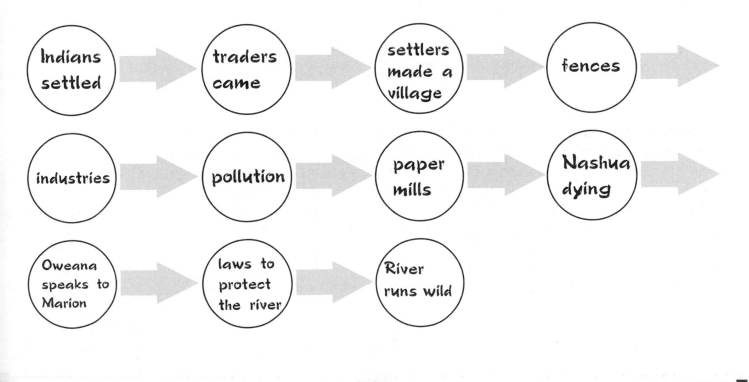

Guided Reading in Big Blocks

Other Organizers

A **KWL chart** may be used to help students activate their prior knowledge of a topic—what they **K**now—and determine what they **W**ant to learn as a result of their reading or study. When they have completed the reading or study, they list what they **L**earned.

Here is a KWL chart for *Outside and Inside Sharks* by Sandra Markle (Atheneum, 1996).

Know	Want to Learn	Learned
Sharks are mammals. Sharks are born alive. Sharks have two sets of teeth.	Where do they live? Do all sharks eat people?	Sharks are fish. Some sharks are born alive; others hatch from hard shells. Most sharks have 5 or more sets of teeth. Sharks live in oceans.

A **T–Chart** may be used to examine two facets of a topic—the pros and cons associated with it, its advantages and disadvantages, facts vs. opinions, etc.

A T–Chart may be used to record student responses to a reading by entering information from the text on the left and the students' responses or thinking on the right. A reproducible T–Chart is on page 149. A sample lesson using a T–Chart with multiple columns is on page 133 (also called multiple column notes).

Graphic organizers may be used to support students as they learn any comprehension strategy or read in any format. Information collected on the organizer assists in conversations and with written responses.

Fluency

Fluency is the ability to read text with appropriate pacing, phrasing, and intonation. It is the result of adequate word recognition and comprehension. Non-fluent readers rarely enjoy the process of reading. For them, it is a constant battle to get the words and/or retain the meaning. Although their lack of enjoyment is not limited to oral reading, it is most often associated with it since oral reading is used to assess fluency. Following are activities that promote and develop fluency.

Easy Text

One of the most valuable techniques for developing fluency is ensuring that students read a lot of easy text (Allington, 2001; Duffy, 2003). Easy text provides opportunities for students to hone their word recognition skills and strategies to automaticity. It also ensures that students are free to think about text rather than thinking about words.

Rereading

Another valuable technique is having students reread a text multiple times. This works best with short, easy text. Students may reread by themselves, with partners, or in teams. Students may be motivated to reread if a different purpose is set for each reading. A middle-school teacher in Missouri provides his students with short selections from the Internet and from magazines on topics relevant to their lives. He asks them to reread a selection four or five times, each time for a different purpose. On the final reading, he has them read the selection orally, sharing what they learned as well as demonstrating their fluent reading.

Pick a Page

Pick a Page is a fluency building activity used with a short text or a section (chapter) of a text. Divide students into the number of groups that equal the number of pages or sections of the text. Assign groups to read and reread their pages or sections until they can read them perfectly. Next, form new groups that contain one reader for each page or section. Like a puzzle, students will read the pages in order. Students listen or read as the story or article unfolds. (For more information on Pick a Page, see *Guided Reading the Four-Blocks® Way* by Cunningham, Hall, and Cunningham, 2000.)

Phrase Fluency

Another strategy for focusing on the fluency of individual readers, Phrase Fluency (Swaby, 1998), can be used with individuals during a Self-Selected Reading conference or with a whole group of students during Guided Reading. If you use Phrase Fluency with a whole group, use a piece of photocopied text as a class set. You might consider using poems, articles, or paragraphs from a text. These copies will be marked with high lighters.

If your students only need a basic idea of how fluent reading sounds, use two different colors of high lighters to mark the logical phrasing of a chosen piece of text. For example, you could use a pink and a blue high lighter to indicate each phrase as it should be read. The phrases may be whole sentences or portions of sentences depending on the text and how it should sound if read fluently.

HINT

Individual students can use the same process during a Self-Selected Reading conference. The difference is that the phrases may only be two or three words together if the reader tends to read word-by-word. This type of reader would need to work up to the natural phrasing of the text. Even reading two to three words together is better than word-by-word reading.

Guided Reading in Big Blocks

This highlighting gives students a "visual" cue for the phrasing they should use. For those students who have a difficult time hearing the phrases, explain that no pauses or breaths are allowed until they get to the end of the "pink," then they will read through the "blue" part of the text. Just as echo reading guides the process of phrasing and inflection, the colors will guide the phrasing of the readers and an echo isn't necessary.

Here is an example of text from *Mouse-Deer's Market* by Joanna Troughton (Peter Bedrick Books, 1984 marked for reading with Phrase Fluency.

One day Mouse-deer was out in the jungle, when suddenly she fell down a large hole! The sides were long and steep.

"How am I going to get out?" Mouse-deer asked herself. "I will be in here forever, until I am just a pile of bones. Help! Help!" she cried. But none of the animals took any notice.

No Round Robin Reading!

Most of the reading that students do should be silent reading with a focus on understanding and enjoying what they read (Cunningham and Allington, 2003). Armbruster and Wilkinson (1991) found that silent reading, compared to oral reading, enabled students to be more attentive during reading and have greater participation in follow-up conversations as students were better able to recall information from the text and locate specific examples to support their answers.

Oral reading may be used to develop fluency, for performances, and as part of reading assessment. If the oral reading is for a performance, such as a Readers' Theater, students need an opportunity to read the text silently several times before reading it aloud. If the purpose of the oral reading is assessment, it could be appropriate to ask a student to read a previously unread text, however, the only audience would be the teacher.

The practice of Round Robin Reading, one child reading at a time, is not an effective use of time or strategy practice. Opitz and Rasinski (1998) cite the following reasons why Round Robin Reading is not effective:

- It does not represent how people read aloud in everyday life.

- It can cause faulty reading habits, including poor fluency and subvocalization.

- It can cause inattentive behaviors since students are expected to follow along, yet rarely do. Students are either reading ahead or are engaged in other disruptive behaviors.

- It can lead to a correction of oral reading errors by others before the reader has an opportunity to self-correct. This is particularly true for struggling readers.

- It can be a source of anxiety and embarrassment. Students are so focused on "sounding" good they forget the purpose of the reading is to comprehend.

Guided Reading in Big Blocks

Round Robin Reading should be replaced with activities that focus students on comprehension or fluency. A very good resource is *Good-Bye Round Robin Reading: 25 Effective Oral Reading Strategies* (Opitz and Rasinski, 1998).

Strategies to Build Meaning Vocabulary

Vocabulary words are labels for concepts. Knowing labels has a direct effect on students' ability to comprehend text. Understanding the meaning of words and being able to quickly access that information are critical skills for all readers. These skills are particularly important for upper-grade readers as they encounter more complex words and more content-specific words. The least efficient way to help students learn vocabulary is to have them look up and write definitions from the dictionary. The most effective way to teach vocabulary is to "give students multiple opportunities to learn how words are conceptually related to one another in the material they are studying" (Vacca and Vacca, 2001).

Rivet

Rivet is one activity used to introduce key vocabulary to students and have them use those terms to develop predictions for the text. Rivet may be used with fiction or nonfiction text. To prepare for Rivet, select six to eight key vocabulary words from the text with an emphasis on difficult words and/or terms that will affect students' abilities to understand the text. On an overhead transparency or the board, draw blanks (similar to Hangman) for each letter in each of the words to be introduced.

— — — — — — — — —

— — — — — — — — — — — — — — —

— — — — — — — — — — — — —

— — — — — — —

— — — — — — — — — — — —

— — — — — — — — — — — —

— — — — — —

HINT

You may want to include a couple of words students are familiar with so that they have a basis for their predictions.

Guided Reading in Big Blocks

Unlike Hangman, this is a guided lesson, You fill in each letter of the word, one at a time, in order, as students watch. Stop after each letter and see if anyone can guess the word.

l e a _ _ _ _

Students are not guessing the letters but are trying to guess each word as soon as they think they know it.

l e a g u e s

When the correct word is guessed, have students help you finish spelling it and defining it. Discuss multiple meanings, if appropriate. Continue with each word.

l e a g u e s

e x t r a o r d i n a r y

s e g r e g a t i o n

r a c i a l

p r e j u d i c e

a p a t h e t i c

c r e e d

In the second step of the lesson, students make predictions based on the words. Encourage students to use all of the vocabulary words in their predictions, anticipating how these words might come together in the text. When students make six to eight predictions, have them read the selection in any format to see if their predictions are correct. After the reading, have students use the key words to write some things that happened in the story.

Guess the Covered Word

Guess the Covered Word is an activity that helps students cross-check using word meaning, word length, and the beginning letters up to the first vowel (Cunningham and Hall, 1998). In the primary grades, this activity is used to assist students in decoding. In the upper grades, it is used for decoding and learning key vocabulary. This activity uses paragraphs or short sections of textbooks, articles, or any other content material students need to understand.

1. Write or copy a paragraph related to something students are studying or a topic of general interest.

2. Select one word per sentence that begins with a consonant letter and cover that word a self-stick note torn into two pieces. The first piece covers all of the beginning consonant letters up to the vowel (onset) and the second piece covers the first vowel to the end of the word (rime).

3. Read the paragraph, one sentence at a time. Have students make three or four guesses about the covered word in the sentence before any letters are revealed. These guesses must make sense in the sentence and paragraph. Write down the guesses.

4. Remove the self-stick note that covers the beginning letter(s). Eliminate any guesses that don't fit. Have students make additional guesses for the word. This time, the guess must make sense and have all of the correct beginning letters. Discuss the words and word meanings.

5. When students can't think of any more words that meet both criteria, reveal the rest of the word and see if the covered word was guessed. Continue this process with each sentence in the paragraph.

6. Reread the paragraph when all of the words are uncovered, making sure students understand the words and the meaning of the text.

See pages 181-183 for examples of Guess the Covered Word lessons.

Many upper-grade teachers use Guess the Covered Word during or toward the end of a content study to determine how well their students are learning key vocabulary and concepts.

Maps and Sorts

Word Maps

A Word Map is a visual display of words that are related to one another. Here are the steps for creating a Word Map.

1. First, identify the main idea of the story. Then, select several vocabulary words that are directly related to the main idea and may be new to students. Draw a large oval and write a word (or phrase) that represents the main idea from the story.

2. Write one of the vocabulary words beside the oval. Think aloud about the vocabulary word and how it is related to the main idea. The out-loud conversation you have with yourself as you write the word and draw the connection is the most important part of the lesson.

3. Draw a box or oval around the vocabulary word, and then connect it with a line or arrow to the main idea. Continue writing and connecting vocabulary words to the main idea and/or to other vocabulary words.

Guided Reading in Big Blocks

Once students are familiar with the mapping process, they may work in groups to brainstorm as many words as they can think of that are related to the main idea of a book. Then, you can compile a class Word Map using the groups' results. Again, you think aloud and focus students' attention on the vocabulary words and their connections to the main idea. It will be necessary for you to add any vocabulary from the story you think is important that students don't come up with in their brainstorming

Here is a Word Map with vocabulary from *Let's Go Rock Collecting* by Roma Gans (HarperTrophy, 1997).

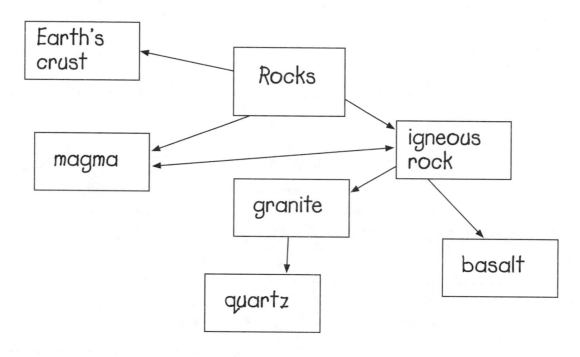

List-Group-Label

List-Group-Label (Taba, 1967) is an activity that engages students in sorting and labeling groups of words. This may be done with vocabulary lists generated by the teacher or vocabulary lists generated by students. It may be done with words familiar to students (at the end of a study or reading) or with words unfamiliar to students (to introduce words to students).

There are two kinds of sorting that can be done: open sorts and closed sorts. "Closed Sorts" are sorting activities with predetermined labels. In a closed sort, the teacher would provide the category labels, and students would place each word into a category. "Open Sorts" are sorting activities that require students to create and discuss their own categories.

Teacher-generated vocabulary:
Provide students with lists of words (or phrases) that have been discussed in class, that students will read, or that students have read in a selection. Have them work with partners or in Reading Teams of three to four to sort the words into groups or categories. Labels may be predetermined (closed) or determined by the group (open).

Student-generated vocabulary:
Students are given a topic and may generate their own words for a closed sort or an open sort. Student-generated words are a great way to end a topical study. This will assess how well students learned the vocabulary from the study.

HINT

Use teacher-generated words with an open sort to determine what students already know about a topic. Use student-generated words with an open sort to determine what students learned about a topic.

Here is an example of List-Group-Label with vocabulary from *The Hindenburg* by Patrick O'Brien (Henry Holt and Company, 2000).

| airship | voyage | luxurious | gigantic | dirigible | wondrous |
| zeppelins | stealthily | menace | transatlantic | hangar | wreckage |

Closed Sort categories (and words that fit each category):

Flying machines	Adjectives that describe flying machines	Fight	Flight
airship	luxurious	stealthily	voyage
dirigible	wondrous	menace	transatlantic
zeppelins	gigantic	wreckage	

Alphaboxes
The Alphabox is a before-reading activity for collecting related words. Alphaboxes are a modification of the activities suggested by Allen (1999) and Bone (2000). If, for example, you are about to read a text about tornadoes and hurricanes, you would ask students to tell you words they think will appear in the text. As they tell you the word, they must also tell you why that word is important to the study of these storms. After the explanation, write the word in the box on the Alphabox that corresponds with the first letter of the word. The Alphabox works well on an overhead transparency.

Guided Reading in Big Blocks

Students will show you their background knowledge on whatever topic you might be reading. As they give their explanations for how or why the word is important, they are also teaching other students who may not have the same background knowledge. This vocabulary activity allows you to get students thinking about their prior knowledge of a topic.

While students are reading, their purpose is to find more words they feel should be added to the collection. These words are jotted onto self-stick notes for the discussion after the reading. The following is an example of what the graphic might look like as students prepare to read a piece on hurricanes and tornadoes.

These are the words the students have generated.

A	B	C clouds	D
E	F	G	H hurricane
I	J	K	L lightning
M	N	O ocean	P
Q	R rain	S spring	T tornado thunderstorm
U	V	W wind	X·Y·Z

Once students have finished reading, they will come back and share any new words they feel should be added. Some of the new words added might include: twister, funnel, spinning, hail, Tornado Alley, meteorologists, pressure, eye, surge, dangerous, season, powerful, etc. As students collect these words and you write them on the Alphabox, the students are gaining background knowledge and vocabulary.

You might choose to make this Alphabox a content-area Word Wall. If you make photocopies of the transparency for students, they now possess a collection of words that will assist them while reading and writing during this new science unit.

Perhaps at the end of the unit, you might ask each student to write a paragraph or two about storms and what he has learned. Students could use the Alphabox to remember important words. They may even be required to use a certain number of words from the Alphabox in their paragraphs. The Alphabox, if used throughout the unit of study, becomes a great tool for review and reference. A reproducible Alphabox is on page 154.

Writing in Response to Reading

Writing in response to what has been read during Guided Reading is a highly appropriate after-reading activity. In fact, in Big Blocks, writing in response to reading should happen frequently. In Chapter 3, we discussed the necessity of teaching students to write to prompts. Most state tests have writing-intensive tests, and much of the work students complete for the test is writing to prompts for either short-answer, open responses, or longer open responses. For this reason, and because writing is thinking, it is only appropriate to have students write responses to what they have read.

We recommend this type of writing be done during Guided Reading rather than the Writing Block. This leaves the Writing Block for more in-depth writing. Here are some suggestions for writing responses after reading.

Quick Writes

Moore, Moore, Cunningham, and Cunningham (1997) refer to Quick Writes as the "least formal kind of writing, and in some ways, the easiest ones to fit into a crowded curriculum." Previously, Quick Writes were mentioned as an after-reading activity, but they can also be used before the reading.

Students are given a specific topic and a specified amount of time to complete the writing. The term Quick Writes lets you know the amount of writing time is short. You may tell students to write for 30 seconds or a minute. When content-area materials are being read for the Guided Reading lesson, it is a natural time to use a Quick Write as a preview. You might ask students to spend one minute writing everything they know or remember about the Civil War prior to reading the social studies chapter on that topic.

Some other examples of Quick Writes to be used before reading might include:

- "We are about to begin our unit on the regions of the United States. The first region we will read about is the Southwest. Take 45 seconds to tell me anything you know about the Southwest. What states would be in that region? Do you know anything about the weather or industry? Just write for 45 seconds."

- "Before we begin our study of the rain forest, take 30 seconds to list any animals you know that live in the rain forest. Thirty seconds . . . go."

Guided Reading in Big Blocks

- "Yesterday, we read that the northern states were called the Union. We also read that the southern states seceded from the Union. Take one minute to write what that means in your own words."

These opportunities for students to quickly put down their thoughts give you insight into their background knowledge. It is also nonthreatening for those students who might not know much. Thirty seconds won't let anyone write too much, and if the chosen questions and topics are appropriate, hopefully all students will have something to offer.

In addition to using Quick Writes before reading, they are a great way to review or respond after reading. The same technique is used. Students are given a specific requirement and a small amount of time to write. Here are some examples of Quick Writes that might be used after reading:

- "We have been reading about storms. Take 30 seconds to write as many storm-related words as possible."

- "After reading the first part of *Pink and Say* (Patricia Polacco, Philomel Books, 1994), write a prediction for what you think may happen between these two friends. You only have two minutes."

- "In 45 seconds, write some reasons you think the Civil War happened."

- "Take three minutes to tell me how you feel about the character in this story. How do her actions tell you what kind of person she is?"

If a Quick Write is used prior to any reading on a particular topic, save the students' writing. Then, at the end of the unit or study, give students the same amount of time and the same prompt and compare the two pieces of writing. Usually students and teacher alike are quite pleased with the results.

From specific information in nonfiction text to personal responses to narrative texts, the Quick Write is a great way to allow students to show you what they know and feel and to help develop fluent writing.

Summary

On page 113, you read about a strategy called GIST. In that strategy, the teacher guides the development of a very brief summary over a chosen piece of text. GIST is a great way to begin to move students toward the understanding that a summary is not a retelling and does not need to include every detail.

It is a good idea to use GIST as an introductory activity to teach students how to write a summary. Summary writing should be used with both narrative and expository texts. In narrative texts, students feel every event must be retold, and in expository texts, they are uncomfortable with deciding what is important and what can be left out.

In addition to doing GIST with students, write some whole-class summaries after reading a piece of text—a whole book or just a chapter. Discuss with students the things they think should be included in a good summary. If unnecessary information is offered, question the students and ask why they think that detail or piece of text should be included. See page 116 for an example of a one-sentence summary written for a chapter in a book as a part of an Excitement Map. With or without the map, one-sentence chapter summaries can be compiled as a summary of the entire text.

Journaling

One section of the Big-Blocks Notebook may be used to record a student's response to what he is reading in Guided Reading. Journal entries can range from a very informal, student-driven response to a very specific, teacher-directed response. If you are reading content-area materials for Guided Reading, you may decide to have students make a content-area subsection. This may be where they record summaries or quick writes. If students will be asked to do more formal pieces of focused writing on a topic of study, it would be very helpful to have the notes, responses, summaries, etc., all in one place when that writing begins. Informal responses may include a student's connections, questions, responses, etc.

One type of teacher-directed response is Two-Column Notes. Two-Column Notes is a useful tool and can actually be used in all three phases of Guided Reading. For example, to share important vocabulary words before students read, you might ask students to record those words in the left-hand column of the journal. During reading, ask students to mark the text with self-stick notes to show the places they encountered the words. Finally, after reading, have students write what the words mean in their own words, with or without partners. This last step can be done before or after a whole-class discussion of the words.

Other ideas for using Two-Column Notes with content-area reading could include main ideas on the left with details on the right or questions and dates on the left with answers and explanations on the right. If you are using Two-Column Notes while reading a story, you could have as many columns as you have topics (making Multiple-Column Notes). Below is an example of how multiple columns might be set up.

○				
	Character	Personality Traits	Actions to support	Page #

Two-Column (or Multiple-Column) Notes, summaries, and Quick Writes are just some of the ways a journal could be used in conjunction with reading. The journal serves as a place to organize thoughts and responses to reading. It is not the type of journal writing you may think of when a daily prompt is written on the board to get students writing "creatively." This type of journal is a response to reading.

Guided Reading in Big Blocks

Guided Reading in Social Studies and Science

Students spend more time in content-area studies as they get older, and often, this is the time when comprehension begins to break down. The purpose of Guided Reading is to support comprehension; therefore, it makes a great deal of sense to do that work in the texts that may have lots of new vocabulary and a heavy content focus. However, it would not be appropriate to use a textbook as a Guided Reading text if it is above the reading level of the class.

Approximately one-third of your Guided Reading time—across the span of a year—will be spent reading social studies materials and one-third will be spent reading science materials. These materials might include textbooks, current events articles from newspapers or other publications, or trade books and stories that connect to the topics of study.

At the beginning of this chapter, we describe several activities as being particularly useful in guiding students in reading nonfiction text. These are the strategies to consider when planning a Guided Reading lesson with content-area materials. You should also take into consideration your text. When will your students need the support? Are there some text items that would be better to read to your class? (If so, this would not occur during Guided Reading. You may choose to share that selection with students as a read aloud during content instruction.) Are there some sections that students will read with very few problems? (Those are the times when the reading may be done during Guided Reading, focusing students on comprehension.)

However, when you know the text is difficult because of vocabulary or the concept is relatively new, the support for comprehension is necessary and helpful. What can be done to ensure students will get the concepts that tie to your state standards or curriculum? The following examples illustrate the use of Guided Reading formats to support the reading. There are both social studies and science examples, as well as examples from textbooks, trade books, and literature.

Subject: Science

Topic: Weather

Text and Format: Book Club Groups

Questions and Answers About Weather by M. Jean Craig (Scholastic, Inc., 1996)

What Will the Weather Be? by Lynda DeWitt (HarperTrophy, 1993)

Do Tornadoes Really Twist?: Questions and Answers about Tornadoes and Hurricanes by Melvin and Gilda Berger (Scholastic, Inc., 2000)

The Magic School Bus: Inside a Hurricane by Joanna Cole, (Scholastic, Inc., 1995)

Comprehension Strategy: Compare/Contrast or Connecting text to text

Day 1:
Before Reading: The teacher introduces each text for the Book Club Groups. She selects a few illustrations to show and selects a few passages to read from each book. Each of these books offers information on weather, the science content the class is about to study. Not all of the books are on the same reading level.

The easiest text is *What Will the Weather Be?* It contains good information on fronts and other weather concepts. *Do Tornadoes Really Twist?* and *Questions and Answers About Weather* have comparable reading levels. *The Magic School Bus: Inside a Hurricane* is the most difficult title of the four. It is also the longest. Books in *The Magic School Bus* series are not easy texts to read. For a struggling reader, there is too much happening on any one page. There are always three things that occur: the continuous text that tells the story, the speech bubbles that carry the conversations of the characters, and the information in the margins that provides much of the factual information related to the topic. With all of this happening at once, it is easy for a reader to become confused.

HINT

When choosing books for Book Club Groups, it is important to choose texts that are related but are on a variety of reading levels. The different levels add to the multilevel instruction during Guided Reading.

During Reading: After the teacher gives a short book talk on each of the books, students are allowed to spend about five minutes with each of the four titles. Six to eight copies of each title are placed in four locations of the room. In randomly selected small groups, students spend five minutes with each title, selecting the books they think they would like. (You may want to consider using a Book Pass. This format includes having students record comments about each book before marking their top three choices. See page 110 for additional information and an example of a Book Pass.)

After Reading: It is time for students to write their top three title choices. By writing three choices, students are guaranteed not to have to read the one book they don't want to read, and the teacher is given wiggle room to place students with appropriate texts. (Day 1 of Book Club Groups may not take 40 minutes. Use the remaining time to build background knowledge or add time to Writing or Self-Selected Reading.) On the second day of Book Club Groups, the teacher will announce which students are in the groups.

Day 2:

Before Reading: Ahead of time, the teacher has marked a place in all of the books using paper clips. Students will not read beyond the paper clips today. The teacher gathers the whole class for the Before-Reading activity. She tells students, "After yesterday and your chance to glance through these books, you know we will be reading about weather and storms. Each of the books offers a few different ideas and different types of information about weather. You will be able to help each other learn about this topic.

"I thought you should record your information on a Feature Matrix. I have listed some headings that will help you record the information you need to remember. Let's take a look.

Guided Reading in Big Blocks

Weather Word	Define this condition or term	Important associated Weather Words	What makes it happen?	Are there certain places i happens?
cold front				
tornado				
hurricane				
thunder				
lightning				
meteorologist				

"Now that you have seen the matrix, you will get a copy to take to your group as you read today. You will not need to, or even be able to, fill in each box. Your book will only tell about some of these things and some of the things you won't read until tomorrow or the next day.

"As you read today, you will be reading with a partner. I've given each of you a partner within your Book Club Group. You and your partner will take turns reading paragraphs. At the bottom of each page, take the time to look at the matrix and decide if you came across any information you could use to help fill in the matrix. If that page does have information we will need, put a self-stick note on it so that you can easily come back to it.

"When you and your partner finish reading, work with the other members of your Book Club Group to fill in the information you read today on the matrix. Then, I will pull the whole group back together, and we will fill in our class matrix on the overhead."

During Reading: Students go off to read with partners, but each Book Club Group occupies a certain area. That way as partners finish their reading, they can easily join up with other members of their Book Club Group to fill in the matrix. The teacher monitors the work the partners are doing and makes the rounds to distribute the matrices and the self-stick notes.

After Reading: Once the groups have met and filled in any information they have gathered from the reading that day, the teacher pulls the whole group back together. She asks for information from students' reading to write on the matrix she has on an overhead transparency or on chart paper.

Here is an example of what the matrix might look like after one day of reading.

Weather Word	Define this condition or term	Important associated Weather Words	What makes it happen?	Are there certain places it happens?
cold front	cold air pushes against warm air	rising air vapor liquid	New air pushes against old air	
tornado	a severe windstorm	funnels thunderstorms waterspout	some thunderstorms make the twisting winds of a tornado	mostly the midsection of the US and Canada
hurricane				over the Atlantic Ocean or the Caribbean Sea
thunder	The sound of expanding air	lightning	Cold, dry air blows hard against very warm, wet air	
lightning	Clouds charged with electricity that jumps from one place to another	thunder	When the voltage in the clouds gets high enough	
meteorologist				

After the teacher fills in all of the great information students have shared, she collects their books and matrices and tells them that tomorrow they will continue reading and filling in the matrix together.

During the rest of the week, or for several days, students will read the same books, looking for more information to fill in the matrix. The boxes that are already filled in will be added to as other texts give additional information on the same topics. After the matrix is completed, students may use the gathered information to write answers to open-ended, compare/contrast questions. Or, students may write summaries of the things they have learned about weather. The column with related weather terms (Important associated Weather Words) could lead to additional study.

The weather Book Club Groups might be done as part of a unit on weather. This could be the prelude/background building for that unit of study.

Guided Reading in Big Blocks

Subject: Social Studies

Topic: Civil War

Text: *Voices from America's Past: Blue or Gray? A Family Divided* by Kate Connell (National Geographic Reading Expeditions, 2002)

Format: ERT (page 116) Most students will be reading independently.

Comprehension Strategy: Predictions with Prove It! Inferencing with ERT

Students will be reading the first 12 pages of the text today. This particular National Geographic book tells the story of families who were fighting against each other during the Civil War. It is told through letters written by two sisters; both have sons fighting for opposing sides.

Before Reading: The teacher will get students started on Prove It! with the first 12 pages of text. The teacher says, "In just a minute, we will spend some time previewing the book you will read today. It is a short chapter book, and you will be reading the first two chapters today, which is only 12 pages. We are going to do Prove It! before you read. You might remember that means you have two minutes to read the table of contents, headings, captions, and look through any pictures or graphics on the page stopping at page 12. You are not reading the text yet; you are just getting a little preview. Let me pass out the books, and I'll set the timer for two minutes."

The teacher passes out the books and lets students examine the cover. When he tells them to begin, students will use the two minutes to preview the first part of the text. Two minutes isn't long, and they will want to look at each page.

At the end of two minutes, the teacher asks students to close their books and share some predictions for what they will read about today. The teacher charts the predictions. After each prediction, the teacher asks the student how and/or why he thinks that is a possibility.

One student says, "I think the part about a house dividing is really going to be about the country dividing, because the picture on the page shows a map with the country divided into the North and the South." The teacher responds, "Okay, so I will write your prediction as:

1. A house dividing is another way to say the country is divided.

Is that okay? Is that what you meant?"

Another student offers a prediction:

2. The Shaws and the Abbotts will fight against each other.

"Why do you think that is a good prediction?"

"Well, on the page where I saw their pictures, one family was on gray and one was on blue, and those are the two colors of the different sides."

The teacher continues to call on a few more students and records the predictions they make. Students know that after they read, they will come back together as a class to check their predictions.

During Reading: Even though students will be reading to see if their predictions are correct, the teacher has decided to use an ERT (Everybody Read To . . .) format for the reading. This will allow the teacher to focus on key ideas and parts of the text where students may need to "read between the lines."

ERT is very structured, and students typically read small chunks of text before discussing what they found. In this lesson, the class will do that reading independently. ERT lessons are designed to help students read to "find out" and "figure out." A "figure out" statement requires students to infer or draw a conclusion. When writing the statements for ERT, use small, specific amounts of text. Here is an example for *Voices from America's Past: Blue or Gray? A Family Divided.*

1. Read page 4 to **find out** when Abraham Lincoln was elected and to **figure out** why South Carolina seceded from the Union.

2. Read the first paragraph on page 7 to **find out** which state was the seventh to join the Confederacy.

3. Read the next two paragraphs on page 7 to **find out** where the Shaws and the Abbotts lived.

4. Read the rest of page 7 to **find out** when the war started and what happened to let you know the war had begun.

5. Read the letter on page 8 to **find out** what Eli has chosen to do.

6. Read the letter on page 9 to **figure ou**t why Tennessee will now secede from the Union.

7. Read Sam's journal entries on page 10 to **find out** why Sam wants the war to last a little longer.

8. Read the letter on page 11 to **figure out** why Oberlin is an unusual school.

9. Read page 12 to **find out** at least three things women did to help with the war.

The teacher writes or uncovers the "find out" and "figure out" statements, one at a time, on the board or an overhead transparency. He reads these as specific instructions for each section of text to be read. The teacher does not give the statements to students all at once, and students don't complete this task like a worksheet. This is a teacher-directed activity. As students read to "find out" or "figure out," they raise their hands or use other nonverbal signals when they find an answer. Only one statement at a time is read and completed. This allows for discussion of the text and assures that all students are getting the ideas and information the teacher has deemed important.

After Reading: Today the after-reading activity is to go back to the predictions students made during Prove It! Students check to see if the reading they did proved or disproved the predictions made to begin with. The teacher guides them through the predictions, and they talk about the places in the text where they found proof for or against the predictions they made. The teacher rewrites any inaccurate statements. Today, because the students have only read a bit of the text, they write three-minute responses telling what they think will happen between Eli and Henry and between Edwina and Julie.

Guided Reading in Big Blocks

Guided Reading for Literary Purposes

Students in the upper grades need to continue to learn about literary elements. They need to learn the joy of reading for the sake of reading. They need to experience a variety of genres, not just those tied to their science and social studies themes. Although nonfiction text may be used to teach literary elements, it is not the only genre you will want to use. The following are examples of Guided Reading lessons using fiction and poetry from trade books and/or basals. Again, there are many other genres you will want to include in your Guided Reading that we have not included due to limitations of space.

Guided Reading Using Fiction and an Excitement Map

Text: *Two Bad Ants* by Chris Van Allsburg (Houghton Mifflin Company, 1988)

Format: Three-Ring Circus (pages 108-109)

Comprehension Strategy: Summarize/conclude

Before Reading: The teacher connects the after-reading activity to the work the class has already done with retellings and summaries. She reminds them, "You know we have been working on summaries and trying to keep those summaries brief and to the point. Today, when we finish reading, I am going to ask you to retell the events of the story, including a brief description of each event in the story. This retelling will not be as long as the story but longer than a summary.

"In addition, we are going to think about how exciting each event was. So, as you read, be thinking about the events that happen in the text. These ants go on quite an adventure. We will retell that adventure after we read today."

During Reading: Students have been put into the "three rings" for Three-Ring Circus (pages 108-109). Eight of the most independent readers have been assigned to read independently. Ten more students have been given assigned partners to read with. Six more students, four of whom need a great deal of support, have been placed in the "ring" with the teacher. This is a good coaching group since the book is slightly below the average reading level of the class. Students who read with the teacher will be doing a choral reading of the text. All readers are told that when they finish reading, if the teacher has not yet called them back together, they should talk about the events of the story.

After Reading: The teacher pulls the students back together to develop an Excitement Map. As they gather on the floor, the teacher brings out a sheet of labeled chart paper and a number of lined and unlined self-stick notes. She reminds students that they will be retelling the story events with her. As the students name the events, she asks one student to quickly sketch a picture to represent the event on an unlined self-stick note and another student to write a brief description of the event on a lined self-stick note. (The teacher actually does the first picture and description to model the process.)

For the first event, the teacher sketches and writes about the ants climbing into the window of the house. Then, students follow suit with subsequent events such as the two ants staying behind, ants falling in to the coffee, ants dropping into the toaster, ants spinning in the garbage disposal, and so on. They finish with the ants climbing into the electrical outlet and finally sleeping behind the canister and following their families home the next night.

After students have retold the entire story, the teacher asks them to think about each event. "How exciting was each event compared to the other things that happened in the story?" As she takes them through each event, students tell her about where the event falls in relation to excitement on a scale of

0-10. The teacher places each picture self-stick note beside the number that corresponds to the level of excitement for that event. The description self-stick note will be directly under the picture, along the bottom of the chart.

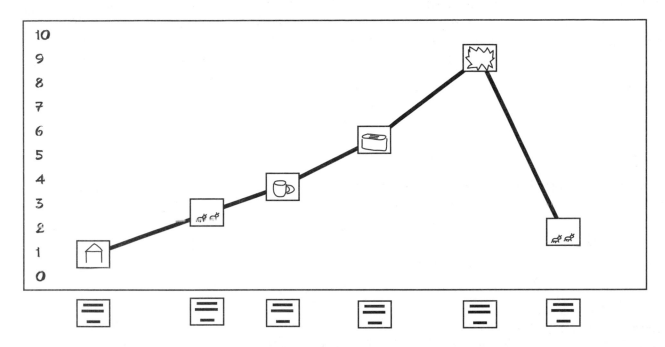

For this lesson, students agree that the most exciting event is when the ants crawl into the electrical outlet after being soaked in the sink. The story begins to wind down when the ants decide to sleep and then follow the other ants home the next evening, indicating the resolution.

Discussing the shape of the results leads the teacher to introduce or review terms such as rising action, climax, and resolution.

Guided Reading Using Poetry to Teach Visualization

Text: "Today" by Billy Collins (from the book *Picnic, Lightning*, University of Pittsburgh Press, 1998)

Format: Choral reading and echo reading, Reading Teams

Comprehension Strategy: Inferring/Imaging

Before Reading: The teacher gathers students together and shows them a single sheet of paper with the poem. She asks, "What kind of reading do you think we will be doing today?" Several students respond that the text on the paper is a poem. "How do you know it is poetry?" When the students begin to respond, the teacher labels a piece of chart paper with the word "Poetry" and begins to collect their ideas about what makes poetry different from other kinds of text.

Guided Reading in Big Blocks

> ### Poetry
>
> Looks different on the page
>
> Lots of punctuation, especially
> commas
>
> Different rules for capitalization
>
> Sometimes it rhymes, but it
> doesn't have to
>
> Usually they are short
>
> Chunks of writing with space
> (stanzas)

After this list is written with students, the teacher wants to bring up one more difference between poetry and other texts. "Did you all notice there are no pictures on this page? Sometimes the books of poetry we read have a few illustrations, but often there are no illustrations. If that is the case, where will the pictures come from? Where do we 'see' what is happening?"

One student shares that he "sees" the poems and books that he reads in his head. "Great! That is what good readers do. We imagine the stories or the poems in our minds. I like to call it mind pictures, or another word for it is visualizing. Today, I have a poem to read with you and as we read it, I want you to make mind pictures. Concentrate on what you are seeing. After we read, we will be talking about those mind pictures."

During Reading: "Today, we are going to start with an echo read. I know you all used to do a lot of echo reading when you were younger. But I want to do echo reading today because it really helps us read fluently, you know, smoothly and at just the right speed. So, I will read first, and then you will echo me as a whole class. Sometimes I might read a line, or two lines, or more. So, please make sure you listen so that you will know when I am finished reading."

The teacher leads the students in echo reading the poem twice. She asks between readings if students can "see" the poem in their minds. Then, the class does a choral reading of the same poem. After choral reading, students are sent to read the poem in Reading Teams. Students are told they may be asked to read the poem chorally with their team in front of the class, so they will want to practice choral reading as a team to make sure they read together using good speed and inflection.

The teacher circulates as the teams read. She listens in and encourages students to read together. She reminds them they are to read it over and over until she stops them. The more they read it, the more fluent they will get. Because this text is so short, students in this class will easily read the poem 10 times before the day is over.

After several minutes of circulating, the teacher stops the reading and asks for teams to volunteer to read the poem for the class. The teams must read it chorally. Most everyone wants a chance to be heard, and all of the teams sound very fluent since they have had so many opportunities to read the selection.

After Reading: After the teams have had opportunities to choral read for the whole group, the teacher asks students to return to their seats. She directs them to turn their poems over and to use the back of the blank paper to sketch their mind pictures. She tells them they will only have three minutes, and they are to use only pencils. "This is not about artistic ability; it is about showing the pictures you had in your head while reading."

The variety of pictures drawn is tremendous. The teacher asks a few students to share their drawings and to briefly explain what they were drawing and how it connected to the reading. After several students have shared, the teacher asks why everyone drew something different. "Is it okay to have different pictures?" The class agrees that it is fine to have different pictures in your head as you read, it is just important to have a picture.

Students are encouraged to take the poem home and read it to their parents. Or, this poem could be used for an additional Guided Reading lesson the next day.

Guided Reading with a Basal or Anthology

If your district is using a basal or an anthology, it is one more resource for Guided Reading. However, only the pieces of text are the necessary elements. Extra materials that come with the basal are often that—extra. Read through the selections and decide which before-, during-, and after-reading activity works best for any piece you choose to use with students. Look for a variety of genres to ensure students are learning to read all kinds of text. Many of the skills mentioned in a teacher's guide are unnecessary for all teachers to teach. The publishers of the guide don't know your students like you do. Your students' needs and your district's curriculum should guide your decision to use a piece of text and what to do with that piece of text to best support your readers. In addition, many of the stories in a basal are too difficult for all students to read, so we often supplement with easier text. A basal can be quite effective when used with trade books and other resources if you thoughtfully choose the best before- and after-reading activities for each piece of text you use.

Shared Reading with Big Books

The proliferation of big books has been a blessing to the classroom teacher. In fact, in recent years, not only are predictable, repetitive texts available for shared reading, but you can also find big books appropriate for upper-grade students. The enlarged format allows teachers to focus on the text structure of nonfiction text.

Several of *The Magic School Bus* books by Joanna Cole are now available in big book format. As we mentioned in the Book Club Groups lesson (pages 134-137), *The Magic School Bus* books are very difficult texts. The majority of the difficulty is due to the multiple forms of text on each page. Use a big book in the before-reading phase to point out the many things happening on each page. There are the speech bubble conversations between characters, the continuous text that tells the story, and the notebooks or informational text in the margins. All of these forms of text intermingle on the page, and for struggling readers, cause great apprehension as to what should be read first. A before-reading

Guided Reading in Big Blocks

phase with the big book would allow you to teach students to read the various forms of text one at a time. This particular lesson would be best if you have multiple copies of the book for students to read after looking at the big book. Otherwise, you must gather students close enough to read from your copy. If students can't see the text and you don't have multiple copies, make overhead transparencies of the text or use a document camera. A Guided Reading lesson must include students reading!

Environmental Print in the Upper Grades

When students are in the primary grades, teachers often connect to the environmental print those young children are familiar with. At a very early age, children can "read" the golden arches as McDonald's® the bull's-eye as Target®, and so on. However, as students move into the upper grades, they encounter new kinds of environmental print. This print includes: menus, pamphlets, schedules, programs, recipes, instructions, directions, etc.

The first time a student encounters this kind of text, it can be confusing. Guided Reading is a great time to bring in some of these real-life examples of text and provide lessons to guide the students through the process of comprehension. Find pamphlets connected to a social studies topic, labels in science, or a playbill from a production after reading a play.

Many hotels and local chambers of commerce have an abundance of pamphlets and brochures on interesting locations, historical information, and points of interest. Check with local restaurants to see if they would be willing to "share" their menus with you for a few days, or even allow you to borrow one to make copies. Some restaurants also have paper to-go menus that you could use. This environmental print is typically inexpensive and accessible.

These lessons should still include before-, during-, and after-activities. Your purpose for reading is determined by the type of environmental print you choose to share with your students. These real-life connections are motivating to students. They can see the life connection and the purpose of knowing how to read this type of text.

Struggling Readers

For many teachers, there is a concern when they use one piece of text for the entire class. Each time they do that, they know it will be difficult for some of their struggling readers. For that reason and others, the many different reading formats mentioned in this chapter help support the lower readers.

Partnering students, when done well, provides a continuous support throughout the reading of the text. Struggling readers can be partnered when the class reads independently. Choral reading and echo reading provide fluency practice for everyone and strong support for struggling readers. Strategies and formats such as Book Club Groups allow you to use texts at multiple levels. Three-Ring Circus provides time for you to meet with small flexible groups. And using content area texts for two-thirds of the instruction supports the struggling readers not only in their reading, but also in the learning of social studies and science concepts. All of these many structures are put into place with the struggling reader in mind.

Ways to Support Struggling Readers
- Vary the during-reading formats to support the struggling readers. Assign partners who can and will help.
- Use a variety of literature. Ensure that most text is at the instructional level of most of your class.
- Use Book Club Groups—the most multilevel format in this block—as often as you can.
- Use Three-Ring Circus to create time to meet with small flexible groups.

In the Guided Reading Block, students will also be exposed to all kinds of literature, which will help them know how to read the different genres when faced with them again in the future. Students will also be supported by the purpose for reading being introduced before reading.

Challenges to Guided Reading
- **Content-area instruction becomes time intensive in upper-grade classrooms, and reading instruction may begin to take a backseat.**

    Students have to have time to get engaged in texts in this Block, and more importantly, they have to have instruction on how to comprehend. Take time to set up the purpose for reading (before), give students ample time to read (during), and reserve enough time to pull everyone back together and check up on comprehension (after). "Buy" time by teaching content-area texts in the Guided Reading Block.

- **Many upper-grade classrooms have textbooks but limited numbers of other kinds of texts.**

    You don't need a class set of materials to have a successful Guided Reading Block lesson. Partner reading works fine with half-class sets. In Book Club Groups, only four to eight copies of each text are necessary. Online articles and other reproducible texts are wonderful sources of reading material. However, if you have only one copy of a text—and have no means of increasing that number—you are doing a read aloud, and a read aloud is not guided reading. Guided reading absolutely must include students engaged with text as readers.

- **Traditional methods of instruction may lead teachers to use Round Robin Reading.**

    When Round Robin is the format, students are not given enough reading time, have little engagement in text, and many feel a great apprehension in reading for the entire class.

    Use alternative formats and various activities so that students are constantly engaged in reading and thinking.

- **Another challenge to Guided Reading is a lack of emphasis in the other Blocks.**

    To improve reading comprehension, research indicates the following must be in place:
    - Decoding skills and strategies
    - Vocabulary
    - Opportunities to read to build world knowledge
    - Active comprehension strategies
    - Students are encouraged to monitor their comprehension (Pressley, 2000).

If any component, or Block, is missing, students will not be successful in comprehending text.

Guided Reading in Big Blocks

Middle School

In a true middle school where classes are departmentalized, the majority of Guided Reading takes place in the content areas. The social studies, science, and math teachers will need to find strategies and activities to support the reading comprehension of their students.

Less Guided Reading instruction will take place in the language arts (any course titles related to reading and writing) classroom since language arts teachers will be busy getting to Self-Selected Reading, Writing, and some Working with Words. Comprehension will be taught in language arts through mini-lessons before Self-Selected Reading. However, if content-area teachers are not teaching comprehension, the language arts teacher might occasionally include a Guided Reading lesson to ensure students are continuing to learn comprehension strategies.

Not every middle-school content lesson needs to be a Guided Reading lesson. Some content-area lessons will not require students to read a text. Instead, it might be appropriate to read the text to the class or provide the information through a video. This instruction would not be considered Guided Reading lessons. But, if the students will be asked to read from a text of any kind, and the teacher is concerned that comprehension may break down because of a lack of background knowledge or new vocabulary, it only makes sense to guide the reading.

Professional Development Ideas

1. Divide the hard work of developing Book Club Groups. The most difficult part is finding the resources with a connection. Divide content-area connections between grade-level teachers and ask that each person spend time looking for resources to support that strand for Book Club Groups. If each person develops one Book Club, the whole grade-level team will benefit.

2. Plan lessons together. Spend grade-level time looking closely at the books you have multiple copies of or any resources you will be using for Guided Reading. Everyone will bring different ideas to the table, and you'll find more variety in your lessons.

3. Do a group book study of *Guided Reading the Four-Blocks® Way* (Cunningham, Hall, and Cunningham, 2000).

Recommended Professional Resources

Beck, I. L., McKeown, M., Hamilton, R., and Kucan, L. (1997). *Questioning the Author: An Approach for Enhancing Student Engagement with Text*. Newark, DE: International Reading Association.

Cunningham, P. M., Hall, D. P., and Cunningham, J. W. (2000). *Guided Reading the Four-Blocks® Way*. Greensboro, NC: Carson-Dellosa Publishing Company.

Daniels, H. (2002). *Literature Circles: Voice and Choice in Book Clubs and Reading Groups, 2nd edition*. Portland, ME: Stenhouse Publishers.

Duffy, G. G. (2003). *Explaining Reading: A Resource for Teaching Concepts, Skills, and Strategies*. New York, NY: Guilford Press.

Harvey, S. and Goudvis, A. (2002). *Strategies That Work: Teaching Comprehension to Enhance Understanding*. Portland, ME: Stenhouse Publishers.

Lapp, D., Flood, J. and Farnan, N. J. (eds) (1995). *Content Area Reading and Learning: Instructional Strategies*. Boston, MA: Allyn and Bacon.

Moore, D. W., Moore, S. A., Cunningham, P. M., and Cunningham, J. W. (1997). *Developing Readers and Writers in the Content Areas K-12*. New York, NY: Addison-Wesley Publishing Company.

Moore, S. A. (2004). *Conversations in Four-Blocks® Classrooms*. Greensboro, NC: Carson-Dellosa Publishing Company.

Opitz, M. F. and Rasinski, T. V. (1998). *Goodbye Round Robin Reading: 25 Effective Oral Reading Strategies*. Portsmouth, DE: Heinemann.

Tovani, C. (2000). *I Read It, But I Don't Get It: Comprehension Strategies for Adolescent Readers*. Portland, ME: Stenhouse Publishers.

Vacca, R. T. and Vacca, J. L. (2001). *Content Area Reading: Literacy and Learning across the Curriculum, 7th edition*. Boston, MA: Allyn and Bacon.

Guided Reading in Big Blocks

Recommended Poetry Resources

Bolin, F. S. (1994). *Poetry for Young Children, Emily Dickinson.* New York, NY: Sterling Publishing.

Collins, B. (1998). *Picnic, Lightning.* Pittsburgh, PA: University of Pittsburgh Press.

Collins, B. (2002). *Nine Horses.* New York, NY: Random House.

Greenfield, E. (1978). *Honey, I Love.* New York, NY: Harper Collins.

Hughes, L. (1959). *Selected Poems of Langston Hughes.* New York, NY: Vintage Classics, a Division Random House.

Schmidt, G. D. (1994). *Poetry for Young Children, Robert Frost.* New York, NY: Sterling Publishing.

Schoonmaker, F. (2000). *Poetry for Young Children, Robert Louis Stevenson.* New York, NY: Sterling Publishing.

T-Chart

Text	Connection

Story Map

Title and Author

Setting

Characters (identify main character)

Problem

Events

Resolution

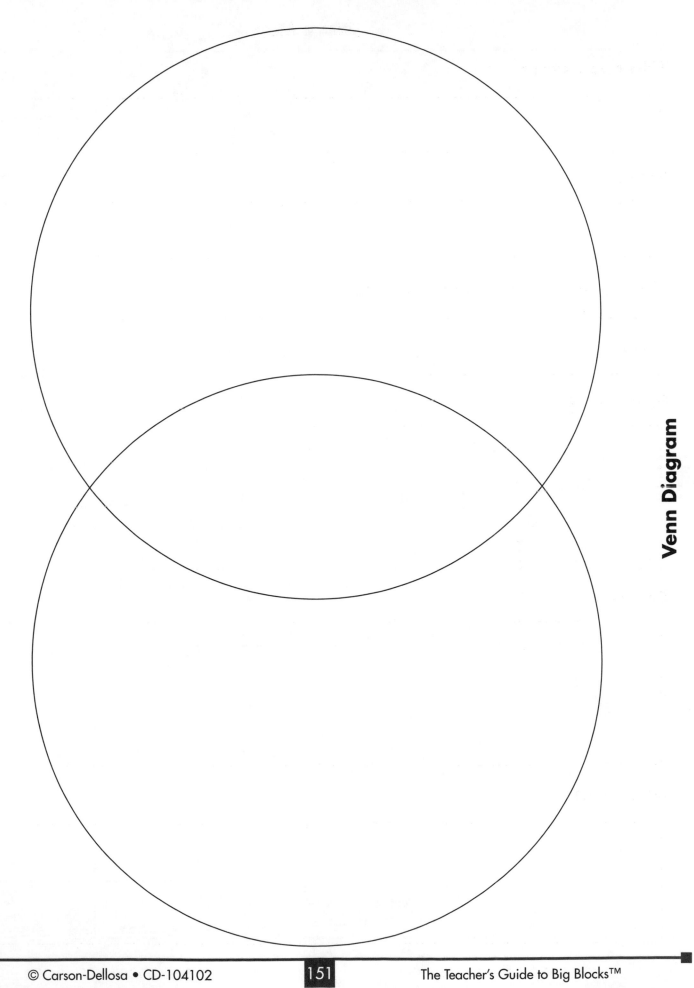

Venn Diagram

Feature Matrix

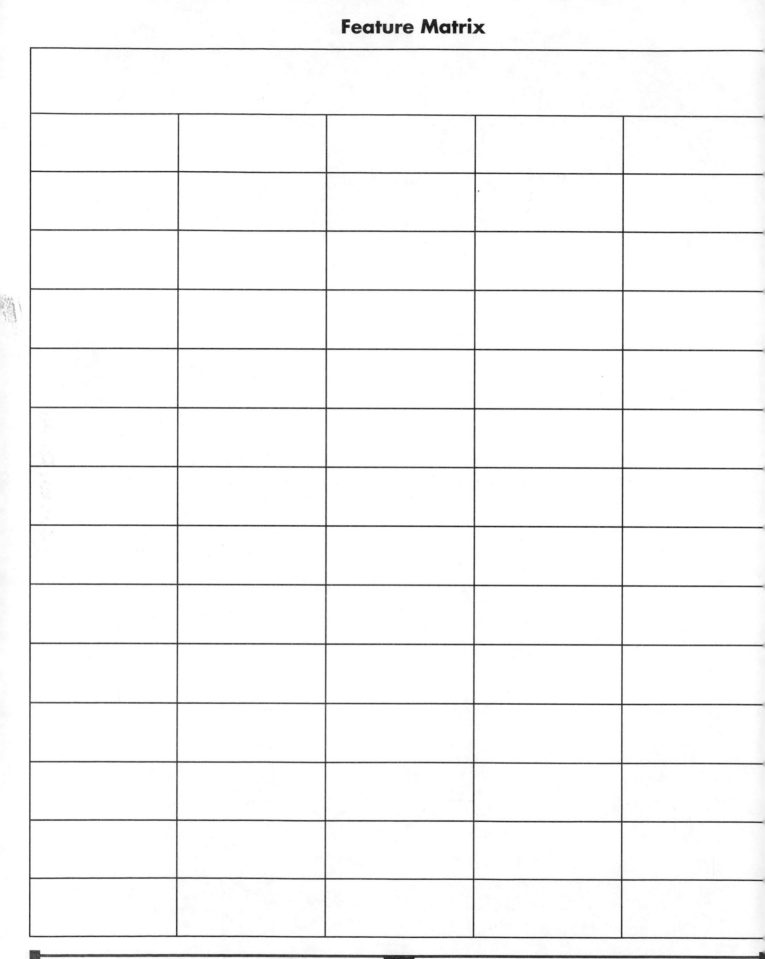

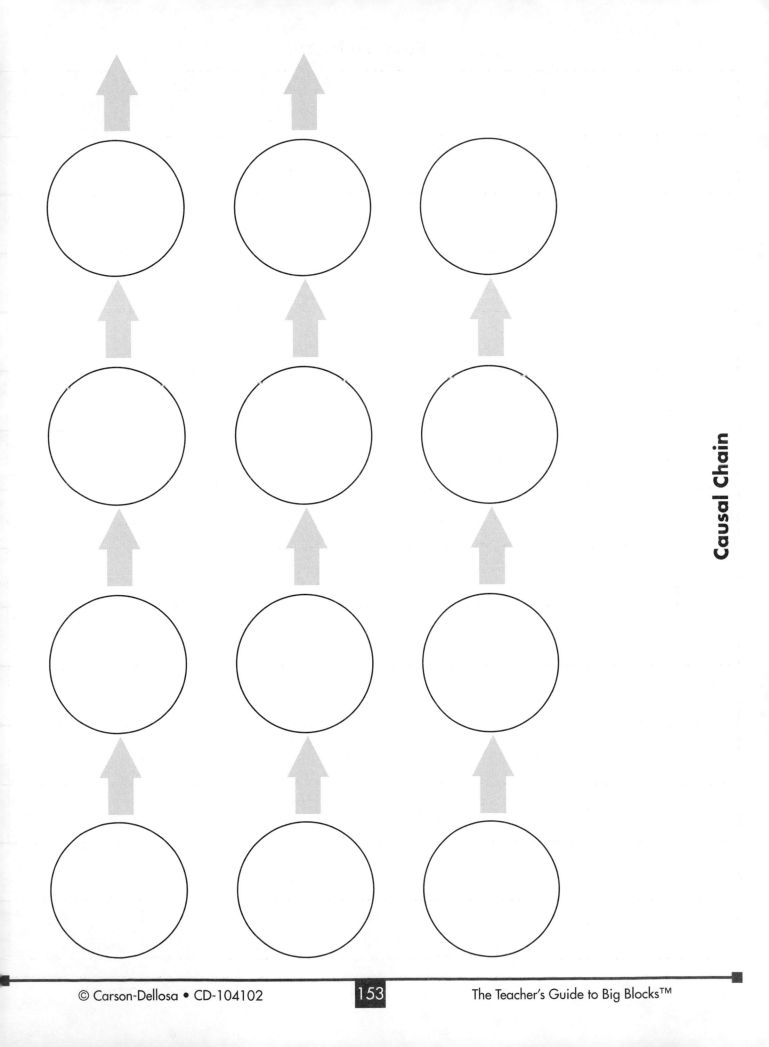

Causal Chain

Alphabox

A	B	C	D
E	F	G	H
I	J	K	L
M	N	O	P
Q	R	S	T
U	V	W	X-Y-Z

Upper-grade students still have much to learn about words and the English language. They need instruction and practice analyzing words for patterns, particularly within big words, and developing their vocabulary (Cunningham, 2004). Upper-grade texts contain words that students have trouble decoding because the words are longer and have prefixes and suffixes. They also contain words that students can't define, particularly in content-based materials. Students need instruction in strategies that focus on building word meanings and vocabulary, and using word parts, context, and morphological patterns to decode and spell big words.

In Big-Blocks™ classrooms, the Working with Words Block—approximately 60 minutes per week—includes the following each week:

- **Word Wall and Nifty Thrifty Fifty Word Introduction (20 minutes) and Practice (ongoing)**
  The week begins with the introduction of new words. Teachers may choose to introduce five Word Wall words one week and four Nifty Thrifty Fifty words the next week or a combination of the two each week. Word introduction includes an explanation and written practice. Students should be guided to review, chant, and write the posted words throughout the week, whenever there are a few minutes of available time.

- **Phonics/Spelling Activities (two 20-minute lessons)**
  The strategies readers use to decode unfamiliar words are the same strategies writers use to spell words. The activities suggested in this chapter teach students to use context and morphological patterns as they decode and spell, and word parts and meanings as they read.

There are several professional materials that will be referenced throughout this chapter:

- *Month-by-Month Phonics for Upper Grades* (Cunningham and Hall, 1998)

  This book is intended to help struggling readers—whether they are fourth graders or tenth graders—as well as those students who are learning English. Some of the activities are relevant for all upper-grade students and will be referenced throughout the chapter.

- *Making Big Words* (Cunningham and Hall, 1994) and *Making More Big Words* (Cunningham and Hall, 2000)

  Both books contain many step-by-step, sequential Making Words lessons in which students select letters to build short and long words.

- *Big Words for Big Kids* (Cunningham, 2003).

  This book contains 100 Making Words lessons, which teach 33 common roots and all of the common prefixes and suffixes.

These books will provide directions, as well as complete lessons, for many activities that promote phonics and spelling development for upper-grade readers.

Working with Words in Big Blocks

The goals of the Working with Words Block in Big-Blocks classrooms are:

- to teach students the correct spellings for high-frequency, often irregularly spelled words such as **they**, **friend**, **could**, **there**, **their**, **they're**, **right**, **write**, etc. Word Wall words and activities address this goal.

- to teach students key words containing the major prefixes, suffixes, and spelling changes and how to use these to decode, spell, and build meaning for many polysyllabic words. Nifty Thrifty Fifty lessons, Making Words, Word Sorts, Word Detectives, and Scavenger Hunts address this goal.

- to teach students that spelling rhyming words is not as easy as decoding them because some rhymes; such as **right/bite**, **claim/name**, and **toad/code** have two spelling patterns. Writers have to develop a visual checking system and learn to use a dictionary when they are unsure about which pattern is right. What Looks Right? lessons address this goal.

- to teach students to use cross-checking while reading and a visual checking system while writing to apply what they are learning in the Working with Words Block as they engage in meaningful reading and writing. Guess the Covered Word lessons address this goal.

Working with Words Is Multilevel

All of the activities in the Working with Words Block are multilevel by design, assisting struggling readers and writers and challenging proficient readers and writers.

- Word Wall words are selected because they are frequently misspelled (including high-frequency words and homophones) and/or they represent spelling patterns and morphological patterns that students can use to read and spell many other words.

- Some students will use prefixes, suffixes, and spelling changes to decode unfamiliar words. Others will use these word features as they spell new words and build meaning for unfamiliar words. The following multilevel activities support students learning prefixes, suffixes, and spelling changes:

  - Nifty Thrifty Fifty Words are multilevel because some students learn to read them and other students use the word parts to make many words.

  - Making Words lessons begin with short, easy words and progress to more challenging words. Lessons conclude with students sorting for patterns including prefixes, suffixes, and spelling changes.

  - Word Sorts begin with words that students easily recognize. More challenging words are introduced as the lesson progresses.

  - Word Detectives is a multilevel activity because students generate words that meet the Word Detectives criteria. The teacher guides students to look at meaning relationships among the generated words.

  - Scavenger Hunts are independent activities that have students find words with prefixes, suffixes, and common spelling changes in the context of books read in class. Scavenger Hunts may be made more multilevel by having some students work with you, some on the targeted prefix, suffix, or common spelling change, and others on all prefixes, suffixes, or common spelling changes learned to date.

- What Looks Right? lessons begin with easier words and graduate to more challenging words.
- Guess the Covered Word lessons require students use cross-checking strategies to read and understand key vocabulary from texts they will read or texts they have read.

Word Wall Words

It is estimated that a little over 100 words make up 50% of what people read and write. Many of these high-frequency words have irregular spellings. These words are often introduced and assessed as spelling words in the primary grades and then assumed that students know them before they advance to the upper grades. Many upper-grade teachers express concern that students spell **they** as **t-h-a-y** or **was** as **w-u-z** in their daily writing. Students also continue to confuse **there**, **their**, and **they're**, as well as other common homophones. If given a list of words to memorize and spell for a Friday spelling test, students generally do well on the test but continue to misspell the words in their everyday writing. These are not students who are lazy or are ignoring what they have learned. In fact, the brain has the remarkable ability to make things "automatic" after having processed them several times. Once something is put in the automatic part of the brain, it is carried out without any conscious thought.

This automatic function of the brain is a wonderful asset when it stores things automatically correct. Once a person has had lots of practice driving, he can shift, use turn signals, steer, etc., while talking to passengers, listening to the radio, planning dinner, or talking on the phone. The brain can do many automatic things at a time but only one nonautomatic thing at a time. When children are just beginning to write, they spell words the logical or phonetic way—**t-h-a-y (they)**, **s-e-d (said)**, **f-r-e-n-d (friend)**. Because these are high-frequency words, students write them many times. Each time they write them, they spell these words logically but incorrectly. After a certain number of times (it varies from brain to brain), the brain assumes that these are the correct spellings and puts these spellings in its automatic compartment! Later, the child learns the correct spellings for **they, said,** and **friend** as part of a spelling list, but they are only practiced one week for the test. The child doesn't get enough practice for the brain to replace the incorrect spellings in the automatic compartment. When a person is writing, the brain's nonautomatic function is focused on meaning, and except for an occasional new word, the brain's automatic compartment takes care of spelling. When the words in that automatic compartment are correct, this is a marvelous function of the brain. But, when the words in the automatic compartment are incorrect, it changes the adage from "Practice makes perfect" to "Perfect practice makes perfect."

Look at your students' first-draft writing to determine whether they need to correctly relearn the high-frequency words. In addition to high-frequency words, there are many other words students need to learn. Here are the word lists provided in this book, in order of priority:

- **First Priority:** High-Frequency, Commonly Misspelled Words (page 192)
- **Second Priority:** Common Contractions and Compounds—including words that are not compounds but which students write as compounds (page 192)
- **Third Priority:** Common Homophones (page 192)
- **Fourth Priority:** Spelling Change Examples—doubling letters, drop **-e**, change **y** to **i** (page 193)
- **Fifth Priority:** Other Homophones or Prefix/Suffix Examples (page 193)
- **Sixth Priority:** Less Common Homophones; Other Commonly Misspelled Words (paged 193-194)

Working with Words in Big Blocks

The focus of Word Wall activities is to get the correct spelling of words in the automatic compartment of the brain. This won't be a quick fix. Students may need to practice the words for several years before their brains accept the required changes. It is not necessary that your students practice all of the words on the lists. We recommend that you identify, practice, and post only 100 words. With the addition of the Nifty Thrifty Fifty words, there will be 150 words on your Word Wall by the end of the year. Select the words carefully. If there are words on the lists that students know and spell correctly, don't practice them or add them to the Word Wall.

Once a word has been added to the Word Wall, hold students accountable for spelling the word correctly. Once a word with a spelling change, prefix, root, or suffix is added to the Word Wall, students should be coached and encouraged to use those changes and patterns in their daily writing.

Because old habits are hard to break, only 8-10 "new" Word Wall words should be introduced and placed on the wall each month. For example, you may choose the following words for a group of fourth-grade students:

another	because	friends	laugh	people
they	want	getting	can't	said

Display the words, arranged by first letter, somewhere in the classroom. The words need to be big and bold so that students can easily see them from any point in the room. Write the words on index cards, construction paper, etc. Using different colors makes them more visible and attractive, and is particularly helpful for easily confused words (**their/they're/there**).

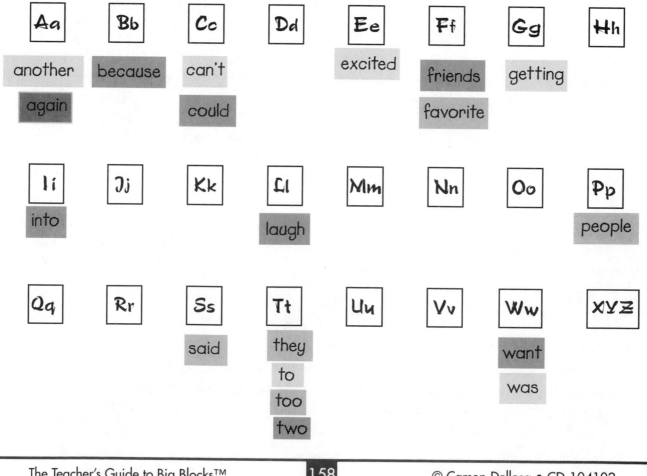

Working with Words in Big Blocks

In addition to the classroom display, you may choose to give each student a "portable" Word Wall to keep at his desk or to take home. Since the rule is Word Wall words must be spelled correctly in all writing in every subject—including homework—a portable Word Wall is very helpful. You can make portable Word Walls for students or have them make their own.

It isn't enough simply to post the most commonly misspelled words. Students must actively engage in writing and spelling the words correctly. As you introduce the words to be learned each month, explain to students that in English many of the most common words are not spelled logically. Have students look at each word and tell you what is illogical about it. Use questions to help them see that these words don't follow the usual patterns. Share with students what you know about the brain and automatic learning. Convince students that the problem is not with them but with the illogical nature of some English spellings. Let them know that with your help and lots of practice they can "wire their brains" to spell these words correctly. This "brain wiring" will happen in a couple of ways. First, you will highlight a set of words to be practiced each week. When there are a few minutes of available time, you and students will practice the words in a variety of ways. Second, whenever you see a Word Wall word misspelled on any student writing, you will write "1 WW" (or "2 WW" if two words were misspelled, etc.) on the paper and return it so that the student can find the word (or words), make corrections, and turn the piece back in to you.

For more differentiation, provide different levels of scaffolding with misspelled Word Wall words. Some students may need assistance in finding the misspelled words for a few weeks. These students might benefit if you write "WW" in the margin on the same line where the misspelling occurs. Once students are successful with this assistance, move to writing the WW at the top of the paper.

After discussing what makes the spelling of a new word illogical, ask students to say the letters in the word aloud in a rhythmic, chanting fashion. Students (and you) may be uncomfortable with this at first, but it is a vital part of relearning. The brain responds to sound and rhythm. Think of the number of jingles and raps you know. You remember these easily because they are set to short, rhythmic tunes or beats. Words may be chanted cheerleader style, clapped, snapped, tapped, etc. Once all of the new words have been chanted, have students write the words with careful attention to each letter and the sequence of letters. Don't assign students to write each word five times. They do this "mechanically" without attending to the individual letters. They may even copy them wrong five times, which compounds the issue! The words should be printed in manuscript, not written in cursive. Words that are to be committed to memory for later use should always be printed for easier recall.

If your curriculum requires cursive writing instruction, you may have students write the words in cursive beside the printed words. This would be for handwriting practice, not spelling practice.

This is a 20-minute lesson. If time allows, it is preferable that the writing occur in the context of the initial introduction. This means all modes of instruction are employed to teach the new word: visual (looking at the posted word), auditory (chanting), and kinesthetic (writing). Post the new words on the Word Wall

Working with Words in Big Blocks

once they have been introduced. That means you will begin the year with a blank wall. After the first week there will be five words, after the second week there will be 10 words, etc.

Some of the words you introduce will have spelling changes. It will be helpful to underline/highlight the spelling changes on the posted words so that students can transfer that information to other words they read and spell.

 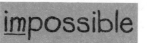 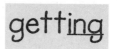

Review Activities with Word Wall Words

Riddles
Students often enjoy reviewing the Word Wall words through riddles. You can do this by giving them clues to the word(s) you want them to write. Have each student number a piece of paper to 10 (or the number of words you have time to review). If the suggested words this month are

another	because	friends	laugh	people
they	want	getting	can't	said

clues for the list of suggested words might include:

1. For number one, write the four-letter word that should be spelled like **say** and **pay**.
2. For number two, write the four-letter word whose pronunciation used to rhyme with **paid** and **braid**.
3. For number three, write the word that should rhyme with **ant**.
4. The number four word is a contraction.
5. For number five, write the only word with six letters.
6. For number six, write the seven-letter-word that has the word **cause** in it.
7. The word for number seven has three syllables.
8. For number eight, write the totally illogical five-letter word.
9. For number nine, write the **g** word.
10. To end this, write the word that ends with **ends**.

Have students check their own papers by chanting the letters aloud once more, underlining each letter as they say it. Throughout the month, use the chanting and writing activities (with various words and different clues!) when you have a few minutes of available time.

Be a Mind Reader
Be a Mind Reader is a favorite Word Wall review activity. In this activity you think of a word on the wall, and then give five clues about that word.

Working with Words in Big Blocks

Have students number their papers from 1-5. Tell them you are going to see who can read your mind and figure out which of the words on the Word Wall you are thinking of. By the fifth clue, everyone should guess the word.

The first clue is always the same.

1. It's one of the words on the Word Wall.

Students should write any word they think might be your word next to number one. Each succeeding clue will narrow the possibilities until the fifth and final clue, when there is only one possible word. Each clue builds on the previous clues so that students must be good listeners and spellers.

As you give the clues, students continue to write their guesses next to each number. If a succeeding clue confirms the word the student has written next to one number, then the student may write the same word next to the following number. Clues may include any features of the word you want students to notice (for example, "It has more than two letters." "It has two vowels." "It is a noun." "It begins with w." "It doesn't have a t."). The last clue usually has the word omitted from a sentence

Be a Mind Reader Example

1. It's one of the words on the Word Wall.

2. It begins with **t**.

3. It has four letters.

4. It has an **e**.

5. It belongs in the sentence, "I think _____ want pizza for lunch."

The Wheel

Like the game show Wheel of Fortune®, students will use the category and some letters to help them figure out which word is being reviewed (Cunningham, 2000). The rules for this version of The Wheel are:

1. Contestants guess all letters without considering if they are consonants or vowels.

2. They must have all letters filled in before they can say the word. (This encourages them to learn to spell the word.)

3. They will win paper clips instead of fabulous prizes.

4. Vanna will not be there to turn letters.

Begin by writing the category for the game on the board and draw blanks for each letter in the first word. Have a student begin by asking, "Is there a . . .?" If the student guesses a correct letter, fill that letter in. Give that student one paper clip for each time that letter occurs. Let the student continue to guess letters until he gets a "No." When a student asks for a letter that is not there, write the letter above the puzzle and go on to the next student.

Make sure that all letters are filled in before anyone is allowed to guess. (This really shows the importance of spelling and attending to common spelling patterns.) Give the person who correctly guesses the word five bonus paper clips. Just as in other games, if someone says the answer out of turn, immediately award the five bonus paper clips to the person whose turn it was. The student with the most paper clips at the end is the winner.

Working with Words in Big Blocks

Example of The Wheel:

"The category is contractions. The first word has 4 letters. I will give anyone who can correctly place the apostrophe a bonus paper clip. Kaitlin, ask for a letter."

Kaitlin asks for a **t**. Kaitlin gets a paper clip, then asks for an **n**. She gets another paper clip and tells the teacher the apostrophe comes between the **n** and the **t**. After getting her third paper clip, she asks for a **d**. There is no **d**, so it becomes Kyla's turn.

___ ___ n ' t

Kyla asks for a **c**. (She gets a paper clip.)

c ___ n ' t

Then, she asks for an **a**. (She gets another paper clip.)

c a n ' t

Kyla correctly pronounces **can't** and receives five bonus paper clips to make a total of seven paper clips.

Nifty Thrifty Fifty

Another group of words to be placed on the Word Wall are called the Nifty Thrifty Fifty. As students encounter more challenging text, they need to decode and spell polysyllabic (big!) words. Words with three or more syllables follow patterns that are more sophisticated than words whose patterns are onsets and rimes. The patterns in these "big" words are morphemic units commonly referred to as roots, prefixes, and suffixes. These word features require that students understand how words change in their spelling, pronunciation, and meaning as suffixes and prefixes are added. English is the most morphologically complex language. Linguists estimate that for every word you know, you can figure out how to decode, spell, and build meaning for six or seven other words by recognizing and using the morphemic patterns in words (Nagy and Anderson, 1984). The Nifty Thrifty Fifty consists of fifty words that provide examples of the most common prefixes and suffixes, as well as common spelling changes. More than two-thirds of fourth graders know 42 of the words. More than two-thirds of sixth to eighth graders know the remaining eight words (Dale and O'Rourke, 1981). The Nifty Thrifty Fifty words are on page 195. Activities with the Nifty Thrifty Fifty will help students learn to use these words and the patterns in them to decode, spell, and build meaning for thousands of other words.

Nifty Thrifty Fifty words will be introduced gradually over the course of the year. Students will do extensive work with these words until their spelling and decoding becomes automatic. Students will also see and practice lots of other words, which can be spelled using the patterns from the words on this list. A monthly list of words, along with examples and explanations, can be found in *Month-by-Month*

Phonics for Upper Grades (Cunningham and Hall, 1998). For example, the Nifty Thrifty Fifty Words introduced and practiced in August/September are:

composer	discovery	encouragement	hopeless
impossible	musician	richest	unfriendly

Teachers generally introduce four Nifty Thrifty Fifty words every other week (alternating weeks with Word Wall words). Another option is to introduce two Nifty Thrifty Fifty words every week, along with three Word Wall words. Students practice the new Nifty Thrifty Fifty words by saying the letters in each word aloud in a rhythmic, chanting fashion; analyzing the words; and then writing them with careful attention to each letter and the sequence of the letters. Upper-grade students (and teachers) may be reluctant to chant the words because it seems rather "elementary" however, the brain easily remembers words put to music and rhythm. Think of the number of jingles or raps you know. Did you work very hard to memorize them? The chanting may be nothing more than saying each letter in a rhythmic way. It may involve clapping, tapping a pencil or foot, or doing a different activity for the prefix, root, and suffix. Be as creative as you and your students are willing to be.

After chanting the word, talk about meaning; determine the root, prefix, and suffix; and note any spelling changes. These explanations are provided in *Month-by-Month Phonics for Upper Grades* (Cunningham and Hall, 1998). Finally, have students write each word one time, paying attention to the letters and the sequence of letters. Don't ask students to write each word five times. They do this "mechanically" without focusing on the individual letters. The words should also be printed in manuscript, not written in cursive. Words to be committed to memory and later use should always be printed for easier recall. This is a 20-minute lesson. If time allows, it is preferable that the writing occur in the context of the initial introduction. This means all modes of instruction are employed to teach the new word: visual (looking at the posted word), auditory (chanting), and kinesthetic (writing). Once words are introduced, they are posted on the Word Wall under the beginning letter of the word.

Review Activities for Nifty Thrifty Fifty
Throughout the month and year, use chanting and writing activities to practice the words when you have a few minutes of available time. As you are cheering and writing the spelling of each word, ask students to identify the root, prefix, and suffix, and talk about how the prefix and suffix affect the meaning of the root word. The same activities that are used to review Word Wall words may be used to review Nifty Thrifty Fifty words.

Riddles
See page 160 for directions. Clues provided in the *Month-by-Month Phonics for Upper Grades* for the August/September list of words are:

1. Number 1 is the opposite of **friendly**.
2. Number 2 is the opposite of **discouragement**.
3. Number 3 is the opposite of **hopeful**.
4. For number 4, write the word that tells what you are if you play the guitar.
5. For number 5, write what you are if you play the guitar but you also make up the songs you play.

Working with Words in Big Blocks

6. Number 6 is the opposite of **possible**.

7. For number 7, write the word that has **cover** for the root word.

8. Number 8 is what you are if you have the most money of any of your friends.

Be a Mind Reader

See page 160-161 for directions. Clues for Nifty Thrifty Fifty words may include prefix, suffix, and/or spelling changes you want students to notice.

Nifty Thrifty Fifty Be a Mind Reader Example

1. It's one of the words on the wall.

2. It has eight letters.

3. It has two syllables.

4. It only has a suffix.

5. It is the opposite of **hopeful**.

The Wheel

See page 161 for directions.

Nifty Thrifty Fifty The Wheel Example

"The category is a Nifty Thrifty Fifty adjective. The first word has 10 letters. Lafe, ask for a letter."

— — — — — — — — — —

Lafe asks for an **a**. There isn't an **a** in this word. Alex gets to go next. He asks for an **o**. After getting a paper clip he asks for an **n**. There isn't an **n**. Merrill is next. She asks for an **e**.

— — — o — — — — e

She gets a paper clip and tells the teacher she wants an **i**. She gets two paper clips for this letter! Then, she says **u**. There is no **u**, so it becomes Treydon's turn.

i — — o — — i — — e

Treydon asks for an **m** and then for a **p**, for a total of two paper clips.

i m p o — — i — — e

Then, Treydon asks for an **r**. There isn't an **r**, so it becomes Trent's turn. Trent asks for an **s**. He gets two paper clips for this one!

i m p o s s i — — e

Then, he asks for a **b** and finally an **l**.

i m p o s s i b l e

Trent correctly pronounces **impossible** and receives five bonus paper clips to make nine paper clips total.

Beyond Nifty Thrifty Fifty

Once students can automatically, quickly, and correctly spell all eight of the new Nifty Thrifty Fifty words and explain how they are composed, help them see how these words can assist them in decoding and spelling other words. Have students spell words that are contained in the eight new words. Next, tell students that they can combine some of the parts of the eight words to spell other words.

Help students use each word in a sentence and talk about the meaning relationships when appropriate. Don't assign students to write each of the words in a sentence. The only writing associated with Nifty Thrifty Fifty is writing each word when it is introduced, which helps students learn and recall it for later use.

Because there are so many words that can be made and spelled using the various roots, prefixes, and suffixes in the fifty words, we encourage both fourth- and fifth-grade teachers to teach the Nifty Thrifty Fifty lessons. Fifth-grade teachers will see students extend the use of the morphemic word parts as they become more familiar and confident with these complex patterns.

HINT

Students may enjoy combining the word parts using a manipulative activity. Jana Watkins, a fifth-grade teacher in Raytown, MO, has her students write the prefixes, roots, and suffixes of the Nifty Thrifty Fifty words introduced each month on different colored index cards: green for prefixes, yellow for roots, and pink for suffixes. Students can "mix and match" the word parts to make new words. The manipulative and visual support provided by writing the word parts on index cards helps students see many other words.

Working with Words in Big Blocks

Phonics/Spelling Activities

Making Words

Making Words is an active, hands-on manipulative activity in which students learn how adding letters and moving letters around create new words (Cunningham and Hall, 1994, 1997). Making Words lessons highlight patterns and demonstrate how changing one letter changes the whole word. For Big-Blocks classrooms, it will be important to select lessons that make words with common roots so that students can sort for prefixes, suffixes, and spelling changes. You will also want to select lessons with a secret word that is either a vocabulary word from a current content study, such as science or social studies, or a word that represents a particular part of speech.

To plan a Making Words lesson, begin with a "secret" word. The letters in the secret word are used to make the words in the lesson. For example, the secret word might be **classification** (lesson from *Big Words for Big Kids*, Cunningham, 2003). Using the letters in **classification**, choose 10-15 words that will provide some easy words, some harder words, some words with the same root, and some words with prefixes, suffixes, and/or spelling changes. Then, decide on the order in which words will be made, beginning with short words and building to longer words. Write the words on index cards to use in the sorting and transferring parts of the lesson. Write the letters on a strip, vowels first, then consonants, so as not to give away the secret word. Make a copy of the letter strip for each student.

HINT

It is easy to type the word cards in a 125-150 point font on the computer. Keep the words, overhead letter tiles, and a copy of the letter strip in a labeled manila envelope so that it is ready to use for next year.

To begin the lesson, give each student a copy of the letter strip and have him cut or tear the letters apart. Have students write the matching capital letter on the back of each letter. Place letter cards with the same letters in a pocket chart (or use clear letter tiles on the overhead projector). The letters are in alphabetical order with the vowels first, then the consonants. Assign one student to be the letter manipulator. As students make each word at their desks, the letter manipulator makes the word with the letters in the pocket chart (or on the overhead). You place the word card in the pocket chart (on the board, etc.) so that everyone can see it.

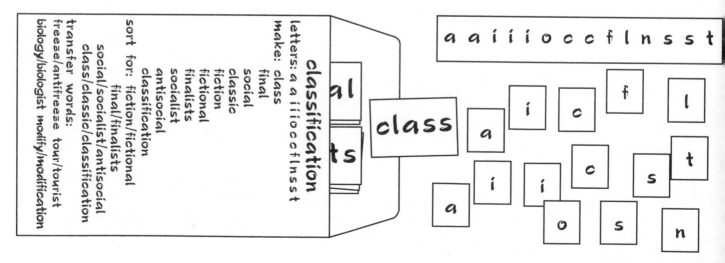

letters: a a i i i o c c f l n s s t

make: class
final
social
classic
fiction
fictional
finalists
socialist
antisocial
classification

sort for: fiction/fictional
final/finalists
social/socialist/antisocial
class/classic/classification

transfer words:
freeze/antifreeze tour/tourist
biology/biologist modify/modification

classification

class

Working with Words in Big Blocks

Make Words: As the lesson begins, the letters cards **a a i i i o c c f l n s s t** (**classification**) are visible at the front of the room, and students all have the same letters at their desks. Guide students to make the words by saying the following:

1. Take 5 letters and spell **class**. The **class** of 1994 was having a reunion.
2. Use 5 letters to spell **final**. We are playing in the **final** game of the season.
3. Use 6 letters to spell **social**. He was a very **social** person who had lots of friends.
4. Use 7 letters to spell **classic**. My uncle collects **classic** cars.
5. Use 7 letters to spell **fiction**. I like to read historical **fiction**.
6. Add 2 letters to spell **fictional**. The characters were all **fictional**, but they seemed very real.
7. Use 9 letters to spell **finalists**. There were four **finalists** in the last round of the math competition.
8. Use 9 letters to spell **socialist**. Many countries in Europe have **socialist** governments.
9. Use 10 letters to spell **antisocial**. Someone who doesn't like people is **antisocial**.
10. Now, use all of the letters to spell a special word.

When a student figures out **classification**, let that student spell it for the letter manipulator. If students can't figure out the secret word, give them a clue. Finally, tell students the secret word and have them all make it.

Sort: Once all of the words have been made, lead students to sort for patterns, including prefixes, roots, suffixes, and spelling changes. In the classification lesson, the first sort is for related words such as **fiction/fictional; final/finalists; social/socialist/antisocial; class/classic/classification**.

Transfer: For the last part of the lesson, have students use the sorted patterns to read and spell other words. This part of the lesson is critical, so don't overlook it! For the classification lesson, write the words **freeze/antifreeze; biology/biologist** on index cards. Show students the word **freeze**. Have someone in the class read it aloud. Tell students you are going to show them a word with a prefix that they just sorted for. They are not to say the word aloud but should read it silently to themselves. Show everyone the word **antifreeze**. Have a student place the word in the correct column under **antisocial**. Have students use the pattern to decode the new word. Now, have someone pronounce the word **biology**. Show students the word **biologist** and have a student place it under **finalists** and read it aloud. Finally, show the word **tour** and have someone read it aloud. This time, tell students you are going to say a related word they might use in their writing, and they are going to figure out how to spell it using one of the word patterns they sorted for. Say the word **tourist**. Again, students don't say the letters in the word aloud until you ask someone to spell it. As a student spells **tourist** aloud, show it on a card and have a student place it in the pocket chart. Do this again with **modify** and **modification**. End the lesson by reminding students that they can use prefixes and suffixes to help them read and spell words in their daily reading and writing.

The Working with Words Block should not last longer than 20 minutes. If the Making Words lesson you choose to do has several words to make and sort, don't make all of them. Select the words that will challenge your students and focus on prefixes, suffixes, and spelling changes. Be sure you do the sort and transfer portions of the lesson. Again, these are critical parts of the lesson, so don't overlook them when planning for time and strategy instruction.

Working with Words in Big Blocks

There are several resources available with grade-appropriate Making Words lessons: *Big Words for B Kids* (Cunningham, 2003); *Making Big Words* (Cunningham and Hall, 1994); and *Making More Big Words* (Cunningham and Hall, 2000). When selecting words for Making Words lessons, we suggest you look at content-specific words that are connected to a current topic of study (science, social studies or language study that highlights a particular part of speech) and words that allow students to build and sort for prefixes, roots, suffixes, and spelling changes. Although *Month-by-Month Phonics for Uppe Grades* is a valuable resource for other phonics/spelling activities, we don't suggest the Making Word lessons from that book for all students. Those lessons may be more appropriate for small groups of struggling readers since they are not challenging enough for proficient upper-grade students.

Word Sorts

Explicit instruction with prefixes, suffixes, and roots can benefit students in multiple ways. It will be important for students to connect these morphemes to words that occur in their independent reading and in their content-area studies.

With Nifty Thrifty Fifty, students learn a collection of words each month with a variety of morphemic connections. In Word Sorts, all of the words studied will have a common part.

This prefix lesson might be taught in (or after) February following the introduction of the Nifty Thrifty Fifty word **deodorize**.

1. Write the column headings for the ways this morpheme affects the root word. Begin by writing words in the columns that students will recognize.

meaning—opposite of or to take Prefix	spelling/pronunciation only part of the word	part of the word only
defrost	delete	decorate

2. Have students read the words you write in each column and discuss the meaning and the pronunciation of each word. For example, **defrost** is the opposite of **frost**, the **de** in **delete** helps with only the pronunciation and spelling of the word, and the word **decorate** begins with **de**, but the letters don't affect the meaning or help with spelling/pronunciation.

3. Have each student create a page in the Working with Words section of her Big-Blocks Notebook with the same labeled columns you have. Students will underline the common part in each of the words. In this example, the **de** is underlined.

4. Tell students you will be showing them some words. They will write each word in the column where they think it belongs. After each word, have students tell you where the word belongs and how it fits in that category. Here are some words to use:

dehydrate   deface   delegate   define

Working with Words in Big Blocks

The conversations you have in this lesson might sound like this,

Teacher: Look at the word **dehydrate**. Which column would it belong in? Yes. Now, why does it belong in the "opposite meaning" column?

Student: **Dehydrate** means to take away the hydration.

Teacher: What about the word **delegate**?

Student: It doesn't sound the same as **defrost**, so it won't help with the pronunciation or spelling. It should go in the last column.

Teacher: Now, look at the word **define**. Well, you are right. When we take the **de** off, we do see the word **fine**, which is a word we all know. But let's think about it, does **define** mean the opposite of **fine**?

Student: No, that doesn't make sense. **De** must just help us say the word this time.

This conversation continues with all of the words that are shown and the words that are said.

5. Next, tell students you will be reading them some words, and you want them to decide how they think they should spell the words and which columns they will belong in. Here are some words you might say:

degenerate   delight   delicate   defeat   degrade   deliver   dedicate

6. End this lesson by helping students see how knowing the ways **de** affects words will help them when they encounter new words beginning with those letters.

meaning—opposite of or to take Prefix	spelling/pronunciation only part of the word	part of the word only
defrost	delete	decorate
degrade	deliver	dedicate
dehydrate	delight	delicate
degenerate	define	delegate
deface		
defeat		

Working with Words in Big Blocks

Here is another prefix Word Sort and two suffix Word Sort lessons to help you get started.

This prefix lesson might be taught in (or after) October following the introduction of the Nifty Thrifty Fif
word **submarine**:

meaning–under Prefix	spelling/pronunciation only part of the word	part of the word only
subset	submit	subtle

Underline the common part (sub). Discuss the meaning and pronunciation of each word. Students should prepare their papers to match your example. Continue this lesson using the steps on pages 168 169. Here are the words students read:

subconscious   substitute   subtract   subtlety

Words students spell:

subtitle   sublime   subway   subcontract   subtotal

meaning–under Prefix	spelling/pronunciation only part of the word	part of the word only
subset	submit	subtle
subconscious	substitute	subtlety
subtitle	subtract	
subway	sublime	
subcontract		
subtotal		

Working with Words in Big Blocks

This suffix lesson might be taught in (or after) August/September following the introduction of the Nifty Thrifty Fifty word **composer**:

Suffix: **er** (lesson from *Phonics They Use: Words for Reading and Writing*, Cunningham, 2000)

Create the Word Sort columns using this example as a model.

Meaning – People who do suffix	Meaning – Things that do suffix	Meaning – More or greater suffix	Spelling/ pronunciation only Part of the word
reporter	computer	fatter	master
teacher	pointer	greater	cover

Underline the common part (**er**). Discuss the meaning and pronunciation of each word. Students should prepare their papers to match your example. Continue this lesson using the steps on pages 168-169. Here are the words students read:

never   heater   skinnier   photographer   dishwasher   after   typewriter

winner   manager   fighter   diaper

Here are the words students spell:

winter   murderer   runner   richer   under   heavier   copier

writer   air conditioner

Here is an example of the completed Word Sort table:

Meaning – People who do suffix	Meaning – Things that do suffix	Meaning – More or greater suffix	Spelling/ pronunciation only Part of the word
report**er**	comput**er**	fatt**er**	mast**er**
teach**er**	point**er**	great**er**	cov**er**
manag**er**	heat**er**	skinni**er**	nev**er**
fight**er**	typewrit**er**	rich**er**	diap**er**
winn**er**	dishwash**er**	heavi**er**	aft**er**
photograph**er**	copi**er**		und**er**
runn**er**	air condition**er**		wint**er**
murder**er**			
writ**er**			

Working with Words in Big Blocks

This suffix lesson might be taught in (or after) August/September following the introduction of the Nifty Thrifty Fifty word **encouragement**:

Suffix: **ment**

Create the Word Sort columns using this example as a model.

Meaning – Turns verb into a noun suffix	pronunciation/spelling only part of the word
amusement	ornament
amazement	instrument

Underline the common part (**ment**). Discuss the meaning and pronunciation of each word. Students should prepare their papers to match your example. Continue this lesson using the steps on pages 16 169. Here are the words students read:

excitement   predicament   comment   disappointment   encouragement

embezzlement   compliment   arrangement

Here are the words students spell:

government   fragment   development   involvement   improvement

experiment   appointment   punishment

Here is an example of the completed Word Sort table:

Meaning – Turns verb into a noun suffix	pronunciation/spelling only part of the word
amuse<u>ment</u>	orna<u>ment</u>
amaze<u>ment</u>	instr<u>um</u>ent
govern<u>ment</u>	comm<u>ent</u>
develop<u>ment</u>	exper<u>im</u>ent
excite<u>ment</u>	frag<u>ment</u>
predica<u>ment</u>	compl<u>im</u>ent
disappoint<u>ment</u>	
encourage<u>ment</u>	
involve<u>ment</u>	
embezzle<u>ment</u>	
appoint<u>ment</u>	
improve<u>ment</u>	
arrange<u>ment</u>	
punish<u>ment</u>	

Working with Words in Big Blocks

Word sorts that focus on root words allow students to see how knowing the root sometimes helps them with the meaning of the new word. Choose a root word that has many recognizable words associated with it. Students often enjoy seeing how many words they can read and write from just one root.

Root word lesson: **play** (lesson taken from *Phonics They Use: Words for Reading and Writing*)

Write the word **play** on the board. Talk about what the word means. Write several more words with the word **play** in them. Have the words pronounced and talk about how the meanings of the words change. Here are some examples:

plays	played	playing	player	players
playful	playfully	playable	replay	playfulness
misplay	ballplayer	overplay	playground	playhouse
playoff	playpen	playwright	screenplay	

This particular example is an easy connection for students to see between the word **play** and the meaning, pronunciation, and spelling for many other words containing **play**. After you provide multiple examples, ask students if they can think of more. Here are other roots that have many words (lessons taken from *Phonics They Use: Words for Reading and Writing*):

Root word lesson: **work**

workable	homework	network	rework	working
legwork	housework	outwork	workers	unworkable
nonworker	woodwork	teamwork	overworked	paperwork

Root word lesson: **agree**

agree	agreeable	agreeably	disagreement	agreed
agreement	non-agreement	agreeing	disagreeable	agreeableness
disagreeably				

Root word lesson: **create**

creatures	creates	created	recreation	creator
creative	creating	creatively	creativity	uncreative
creation	recreational			

Other sorts focused on root words may contain more complex roots. These roots will not always help with meaning but may only help with pronunciation and spelling (just as some of the prefix and suffix examples did). For these sorts, provide words that help students see the connection to meaning. After students read several words that contain the root word, show a few examples that don't carry the same meaning, and the common word part only helps with spelling and pronunciation.

Working with Words in Big Blocks

Root word lesson: **port**

port = to carry or take	port = spelling and pronunciation help
exp<u>ort</u>	su<u>pport</u>
im<u>port</u>	<u>Port</u>ugal
trans<u>port</u>	op<u>port</u>unity
<u>port</u>er	
sea<u>port</u>	
air<u>port</u>	
misre<u>port</u>	
de<u>port</u>	

Extending Word Sorts

You may end a Word Sort lesson by writing a sentence that contains an unfamiliar word with the word part that was studied. Ask students to use the context and the information learned to determine if the word part helped with meaning, spelling, and pronunciation only, or if the word part was only part of the word but not pronounced. For example, after doing the Word Sort for **sub** you might write this sentence on the whiteboard:

The subglacial ice began to crack.

Occasionally ask students to write about how they will use the information learned from Word Sorts in their daily reading and writing. Have them write this as an entry in the Working with Words section of their Big-Blocks Notebooks.

O	When I am reading, I can understand the word better when it is a prefix because then I know it means "under" something. If it is not a prefix, then I know how to spell it.

Word Detectives

Word Detectives (Cunningham, 2000) is an activity that encourages students to answer the questions:

"Do I know any other words that look and sound like this word?"

"Are any of these look-alike/sound-alike words related to each other?"

The answer to the first question should help students with pronouncing and spelling the word. The answer to the second question should help students discover what, if any, meaning relationships exist between this new word and other words in their meaning vocabularies. These lessons are particularly well-suited for content-based vocabulary instruction. For example, in a science lesson, students might encounter the new word **transformation**.

Give examples of transformation and help build meaning for the concept. Then, ask students to pronounce the word and see if they know any other words that look and sound like **transformation**.

Here are some words students may think of:

transformer	formation	form	information
transfer	nation	transportation	format
translation	translate	transition	cremation
motivation	realization	multiplication	simulation
transform	transport	motion	transcontinental

List the words, underlining the parts that look the same. Have students pronounce the words, emphasizing the parts that are pronounced the same. Point out that thinking of a word that looks and sounds the same as a new word will help them remember how to pronounce and spell the new word.

Explain that words, like people, sometimes look and sound alike but are not related. If this is the first time you use this analogy, you will want to spend some time talking about people with red hair, green eyes, etc. These people have some parts that look alike, but they are not related. Words work the same way. Words are related if there is something about their meanings that is the same. Encourage students to think of ways the words they generated might be in the same meaning family.

With your help, students might discover that **transformation**, **transformer**, **transform**, **formation**, **format**, and **form** are related because the root **form** is in all of them. **Form** is the nature, structure, or essence of a thing. A **transformation** is a complete change in **form**. The **transformation** may result in a change into something with an improved appearance or usefulness. However, in the study of science it may also be

HINT

If students suggest a word that sounds the same but doesn't look the same as the content vocabulary word, then write the word on the board so that students see that it doesn't look like the content word. For example, a student might suggest the word *cushion* because it sounds like *transformation*. By writing *cushion* on the board, you will show students that it doesn't look like *transformation*.

a modification of cells into cancer (biology), a change of one type of atom to another resulting in a nuclear reaction (physics), or a change in the flow of energy and matter in an ecosystem (ecology). A **transformer** is a device that transfers energy from one circuit to another with a change in form (voltage,

Working with Words in Big Blocks

current, phase, or impedance). **Transform**, in a scientific context, means to convert one form of energy to another. **Formation** is the process by which something develops or takes **form**. **Format** is the way in which something is presented, organized, or arranged.

Other words in the list are also related. **Transformer, transfer, transportation, translation, translate, transition, transform, transport**, and **transcontinental** all have the prefix **trans**. In the words **transformer, transfer, translation, translate, transition**, and **transform**, **trans** indicates a change or conversion. In **transportation, transport**, and **transcontinental**, **trans** means across or beyond.

The key to Word Detectives is in guiding students to look for spelling and meaning relationships among words. Because English is such a morphologically related language, most new words can be connected to other words by their spellings and pronunciations, and many new words contain meaning-related words already known to the student. It is helpful to guide students to see the important patterns in words and how these patterns can help them with pronouncing, spelling, and deriving meanings for words. Asking the two critical questions for key vocabulary introduced in content areas only adds a few minutes to vocabulary instruction and provides students with a valuable word strategy.

Extending Word Detectives
Occasionally ask students to write about how they will use the information learned from Word Detectives in their daily reading and writing. Have them write this in the Working With Words section of their Big-Blocks Notebooks.

Scavenger Hunts
Scavenger Hunts are activities that follow the introduction of important prefixes, suffixes, and spelling changes in Nifty Thrifty Fifty. Students need to see the use and value of the fifty words and their word parts beyond memorizing them. Sometime during the month, have students use their Guided Reading text for a Scavenger Hunt to find all of the words that have the prefixes, suffixes, or spelling changes represented by the Nifty Thrifty Fifty words introduced that month. Students will record their findings in their Big-Blocks Notebooks in the Working with Words section under "Scavenger Hunt."

> **HINT**
>
> Remember, you are teaching students to notice similarities in words. Sometimes these similar word parts help with meaning; they almost always help with spelling and pronunciation. Accept whatever words students give you and only provide one or two examples of your own. Your examples should include words that have chunks that just look and sound like the selected word but don't lend themselves to developing the meaning of the selected word, as well as words that have some chunks that help with meaning. You don't want to mislead students into thinking the chunks always give meaning.

For example, the words **excited, valuable**, and **nonliving** might be added to the Word Wall on Monday of this particular week. You highlight how the final **e** was dropped to add the suffixes. This week you are reading *Teammates* by Peter Golenbock (Voyager Books, 1992) in Guided Reading. On Wednesday, your phonics/spelling lesson is a Scavenger Hunt using *Teammates*. Give students 15 minutes to reread the text to find all of the words with a dropped final **e** and **-ed** added to the ending. Be sure to reference **excited**. Have students write the root word beside each word they find.

A student might find and record the following words in his notebook:

◯	Scavenger Hunt Teammates drop final e/add ed
	compared-compare dared-dare disgraced-disgrace
	moved-move spiked-spike received-receive
	circulated-circulate hated-hate striped-stripe
	believed-believe decided-decide smiled-smile
	outlined-outline refused-refuse

After students read and find words for 15 minutes, spend 5 minutes asking them which words were collected. Correct any misconceptions and ask students what was most challenging about the activity. For example, one student may offer **replied** as an example. It would be important to help that student see that **-ed** was added to the ending, but **reply** is the root. The spelling change is changing **y** to **i**, but there isn't a final **e** to drop. Another student may offer that the most challenging part was remembering—it wasn't just adding the **-ed** ending but dropping the final **e** first. End the lesson by reminding students that thinking about the root word when they write will help them know when to drop the final **e** to add an ending with a vowel.

HINT

Looking for words is an important phonics and spelling strategy, but it disrupts comprehension. Looking for words during Self-Selected Reading should only take a few minutes of reading time. Reading itself is the most important thing students can do.

Students might add words to their Scavenger Hunts during Self-Selected Reading. You may also want to ask students at the end of the week to share any new words they found.

Making Scavenger Hunts More Multilevel

You may choose to alter the lesson a bit to support and challenge students. Organize students into three groups, much like Three-Ring Circus (page 108). One group will look for the prefix, suffix, and spelling change with you. This will allow you to guide them as they scan for words and talk them through whether a selected word fits the pattern. One group will look for the prefix, suffix, and spelling change on their own. The third group will look for all prefix, suffix, and spelling changes introduced up to this point.

Working with Words in Big Blocks

A student from one of the first two groups may have a page in his notebook that looks like this when h[...]
scans *Teammates*:

○	Scavenger Hunt Teammates
	e/add ed e/add er
	compar¢ compared manag¢ manager
	dar¢ dared
	disgrac¢ disgraced
	mov¢ moved
	spik¢ spiked
	receiv¢ received
	circulat¢ circulated

A student from the third group may have this page in her notebook when she scans *Teammates*:

○	Scavenger Hunt Teammates
	e/add ed e/add er e/add ion
	compar¢ compared manag¢ manager dedicat¢ dedication
	dar¢ dared segregat¢ segregation
	disgrac¢ disgraced humiliat¢ humiliations
	mov¢ moved
	spik¢ spiked
	receiv¢ received
	circulat¢ circulated

Working with Words in Big Blocks

After 15 minutes, bring the class back together to discuss the words the groups all found that dropped the final **e** to add **-ed**. If time allows, have the third group share some of the words they found that fit previously studied prefixes, suffixes, and spelling changes.

Extending Scavenger Hunts
Occasionally ask students to write about how they will use the information learned from Scavenger Hunts in their daily reading and writing. Have them write this in the Working With Words section of their Big-Blocks Notebooks.

Charts
You may choose to make charts of words that have a particular prefix, root, or suffix. If the suffix involves spelling changes, you may want a few charts of the same suffix with its various spelling changes. Words students discover during their reading may be recorded on the charts. Students can add to the charts throughout the month and year.

---

drop the final e, add ed

draped (drape)	rattled (rattle)	surprised (surprise)
reserved (reserve)	smiled (smile)	announced (announce)
edged (edge)	curved (curve)	waved (wave)
promised (promise)	figured (figure)	whistled (whistle)
lived (live)	stared (stare)	soothed (soothe)
glanced (glance)	tired (tire)	pulsed (pulse)
separated (separate)	used (use)	anticipated (anticipate)
admired (admire)	moved (move)	wrinkled (wrinkle)

What Looks Right?
In English, words that have the same spelling pattern usually rhyme. The complication is that some rhymes have multiple spelling patterns, such as plight and trite. This is not a problem when students are trying to read unfamiliar words, but it is a big problem when students attempt to spell unfamiliar words. Good readers and writers generally write a word the way they think it should be spelled, and then decide if it "looks right." If it does, they continue to write. If it doesn't, they check their spelling in a dictionary. What Looks Right? lessons help students use these two important self-monitoring strategies.

Monthly What Looks Right? lessons may be found in *Month-by-Month Phonics for Upper Grades*. The first lesson for August/September uses the **ite/ight** pattern.

1. Write two words on the board with the same sound pattern but different spelling patterns. This example uses **bite** and **fight**.

Working with Words in Big Blocks

2. Have students notice the rhyme with different spelling patterns. Tell students that good spellers us a visual checking strategy to see if the word "looks right." If it doesn't look right, good spellers try another spelling pattern for the rhyme. If a writer needs to be sure, she looks it up in the dictionary.

3. Create two columns on a chart or overhead. Write **bite** and **fight** as the headings. Have student do the same on sheets of paper.

4. Tell students you are going to say and write words using both spelling patterns. Their job is to decide which one looks right and write only that one. Then, they will find the word in the dictionary to "prove" it is the correct spelling.

5. Once students have proven their spelling is correct or have written the correct spelling, erase or cross out the incorrect spelling on the chart or overhead.

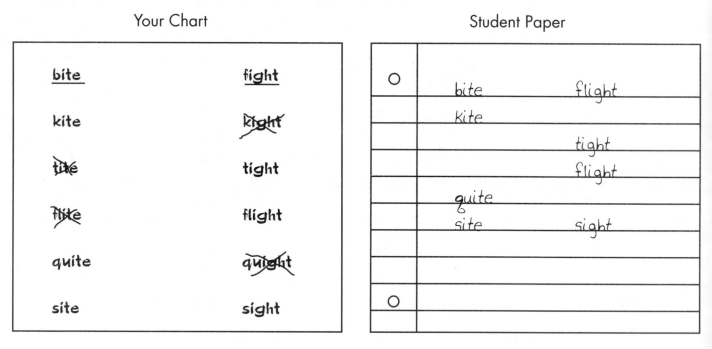

Your Chart · Student Paper

What Looks Right? lessons are written as two 20-minute sessions. Words introduced in the first session are more common, one-syllable words like those above. Words introduced in the second session are multisyllable words or words that students may not be familiar with, such as **trite**, **plight**, **dynamite**, an **excite**. Look at each lesson and decide how to select words to make one session. It is not necessary to do every word in both lessons.

Month-by-Month Phonics for Upper Grades has two What Looks Right? lessons each month. We recommend that fourth-grade teachers teach the first What Looks Right? lesson each month and that fifth-grade teachers teach the second lesson. (The exceptions are August/September and October, which has only one lesson and should be taught in both grades.) If you are teaching sixth grade, or if your students have developed the self-monitoring strategy for the more common words, you may choo to do just the multisyllabic or unfamiliar words. In addition to eliminating words that students already know, you may also choose to add multisyllabic (challenging) words. A list of additional multisyllabic words for each lesson may be found on pages 189-190.

Guess the Covered Word

Good readers use multiple cues to determine unknown words in text. They simultaneously cross-check for meaning, structure (or grammar), and visual information (letters and sounds). Guess the Covered Word is a guided activity that has students cross-check meaning (including structure), word length, and all of the beginning letters up to the vowel to figure out words in a game-like activity. Lessons may be developed using content texts or literature selections. To create a Guess the Covered Word lesson, copy a paragraph from a text students will read or have already read. The paragraph may be copied onto an overhead transparency, chart paper, or placed under a document camera. You may copy the selection by hand or use a copy machine. If you choose to use a copy machine and an overhead projector, you may want to enlarge the page so that it is easier to read. Select a key vocabulary word in each sentence of the paragraph that begins with a consonant. Cover that word with two self-stick notes. The first note covers all of the beginning consonant letters up to the vowel (onset) and the second note covers the remaining letters in the word (rime). Read each sentence and have students make three or four guesses about the missing word with all letters covered. Write down these guesses. If a student offers a guess that does not make sense in the context of the sentence or would not fit in the covered space, don't write it down. Rather, remind them they are answering the questions, "What Makes Sense? What Looks Right?" Guide students to make more appropriate guesses. Remove the self-stick note that covers the beginning letter(s) (onset). Erase or cross out any guesses that don't begin with the correct consonant(s). Have students make additional guesses for the word that both makes sense and have all the right beginning letters. When students can't think of any more words that meet both criteria, reveal the rest of the word and see if anyone guessed the covered word.

Guess the Covered Word lessons may come from content texts and focus on key vocabulary. For example, here is a Guess the Covered Word lesson adapted from *Everything You Need to Know About Science Homework* by Anne Zeman and Katie Kelly (Scholastic, Inc., 1994). The covered words are bold:

> The **moon** is the Earth's only natural satellite. A satellite is an object that orbits another body in **space**. The moon is a **giant** rock that follows an elliptical orbit. When the **point** of the moon's orbit is closest to Earth, it is perigee. The **farthest** point is apogee.

The key vocabulary words in these sentences might be **satellite**, **orbit**, **elliptical**, **perigee**, and **apogee**. If it is the beginning of a new unit of study, cover words that contribute to the meaning of key words but don't cover the key vocabulary words. Students may not know them, and they don't have enough information to guess all of them. Reasonable student guesses for the first sentence above might be **moon**, **sun**, or **Apollo**. When the guesses are written, uncover the first letter. Once the **m** is revealed,

Working with Words in Big Blocks

sun and **Apollo** would be eliminated. Then, ask students for other reasonable guesses that begin with **m**. They may not have any reasonable guesses other than **moon**. Once these guesses are written, reveal the rest of the word.

If it is the end of the study, cover vocabulary words students should have learned. Here is another example with the same paragraph adapted from *Everything You Need to Know About Science Homework*:

> The moon is the Earth's only natural **satellite**. A satellite is an object that orbits another **body** in space. The moon is a giant **rock** that follows an elliptical orbit. When the point of the moon's orbit is closest to Earth, it is **perigee**. The **farthest** point is apogee.

Although **elliptical** and **apogee** are key terms, it would not be appropriate to cover them for this activity because they begin with vowels.

Guess the Covered Word may also be used for the before-reading phase of a Guided Reading lesson. To develop a before-reading activity using Guess the Covered Word, you may choose to use a paragraph or paragraphs from a text students are going to read, or you may want to write a summary of what they are going to read. Creating a lesson using a paragraph copied from the text students will read introduces key vocabulary in context, previews enough of the text to help students develop reasonable predictions, and assists students in accessing prior knowledge. If the selection you choose is fiction, omit the ending. Include prediction as part of the Guess the Covered Word lesson by asking students to use the summary to predict how the selection will end.

A summary of a text students will read may look something like this:

Content Area: social studies

Text: *Journey to Freedom: A Story of the Underground Railroad* by Courtni C. Wright (Holiday House, 1997)

The Underground Railroad was actually a group of **people** who worked together to help slaves escape their masters. The people who helped the slaves on their way to **freedom** were called "station masters." The escaped **slaves** who went back to help others escape were called "conductors." In this story, Harriet Tubman, the most famous of conductors, helps a family try to make their way to **Canada**. Walking through snow in threadbare clothes makes the trip very **difficult**. After passing through many safe houses, the family will have to undergo a trip across Lake Erie on a **small** boat. The Underground Railroad was not an easy **journey**, and only the very brave and the very strong made it to their long-awaited freedom.

Lessons that utilize a summary of the text introduce key vocabulary in context, provide students an overview of the whole selection, and assist students in accessing prior knowledge.

Working with Words in Big Blocks

A before-reading Guided Reading activity with a summary of a piece of literature may look something like this:

Content Area: social studies

Text: summary of Chapters 2 and 3 from *Mummies in the Morning* by Mary Pope Osborne (Random House Books for Young Readers, 1993).

Jack and Annie see a parade with a sarcophagus and many **people**. But they think it is a **mirage** because the parade disappears. They follow a cat into a hole in the **pyramid**. Jack took out his book to find a way to the **burial** chamber. They hear a funny **sound**. Jack and Annie think they see something and wonder if it is a **mummy**.

Another way to use Guess the Covered Word is to focus on one part of speech in each sentence. It is not important to focus on the label for that part of speech, but rather to discuss the meaning these words add to each sentence. Here are two examples:

Content Area: social studies

Text: from *A Voice from the Border* by Pamela Smith Hill (HarperTrophy, 2000)

Adjectives:

"What a **joyless** day for all of us, Rebel or Yankee," she said gently, her voice suddenly thick. "So **many** friends gone. Your daddy and General Lyon shot **dead**. **Young** Percival Wilder, missing in action." (page 20)

Verbs:

Waves of darkness **pulsed** through my veins like poison. There **was** no meaning to this war. No good would ever **come** of it. Daddy was dead, and I **felt** certain Percival was gone, too. I would never see him again, never feel his hands reaching around my waist, his lips **brushing** against mine. (pages 121–122)

Struggling Readers and Spellers (and Those Who Have Not Had Four Blocks)

In each chapter, we have addressed the issue of struggling readers. The book *Month-by-Month Phonics for Upper Grades* is designed for struggling readers. Some of the activities in this chapter come from that resource (Word Wall, Nifty Thrifty Fifty, Making Words, and Guess the Covered Word). However, the examples provided in this chapter, with the exception of Nifty Thrifty Fifty, go beyond the lessons provided in *Month-by-Month Phonics for Upper Grades*. Here are some ways other teachers have supported struggling readers who need decoding and spelling support.

Most of Class Reading below Third-Grade Reading Level

If the majority of the class functions below a third-grade reading level, use the Four-Blocks® Literacy Model. That means 30 minutes of Working with Words instruction every day. The types of activities you will do with students differ from what has been shared in this chapter.

Working with Words in Big Blocks

Students Still Spell Letter by Letter

For students spelling letter by letter, there are several activities that will help them focus on patterns. *Reading/Writing Simple Rhymes* (Cunningham and Hall, 2003) gives students practice in using spelling patterns to decode and spell hundreds of words. *Systematic Sequential Phonics They Use* (Cunningham, 2001) helps readers of any age learn phonics through Word Wall and Making Words activities.

The *Systematic Sequential Phonics* lessons are available on a computer program called *Word Maker* (Don Johnston, Inc.). Brand Name Phonics, an activity included in *Month-by-Month Phonics for Upper Grades*, focuses students on common spelling patterns using familiar product names.

Students with Some Spelling/Decoding Skills but Struggling

In addition to the lessons offered in *Month-by-Month Phonics for Upper Grades*, there are other professional resources you will find helpful. *Prefixes and Suffixes: Systematic Sequential Phonics and Spelling* (Cunningham, 2002) is written with Word Wall and Making Words lessons that focus on the most common morphemes. These lessons are available on a computer program called *Word Maker II* (Don Johnston, Inc.). *Reading/Writing Complex Rhymes* (Cunningham and Hall, 2003) focuses on multiple ways to spell the same rhyme (for example, **ale** and **ail**) and connects to the What Looks Right? lessons students will be doing.

For struggling readers, as with all students, it is critical that each word activity end with a transfer. The two questions that lead to transfer are:

How will doing this make you a better reader?

How will doing this make you a better writer?

Many struggling students have been given additional "skills" instruction but lack the knowledge to see how the skill connects to the reading and writing they are trying to do. It is essential that whoever is providing this additional instruction assist students in making the transfer back to real reading and writing as often as they do word work.

HINT

Spelling is a visual skill. You may assist some struggling readers by having them look up toward the ceiling while they are chanting and clapping. This assists them in storing the information so that they can later retrieve it.

Instruction for struggling readers happens in addition to the instruction that is provided to the whole class. The best way to support struggling readers with their phonics work is to give them a double dose of instruction. Additional instruction may be offered by you, a resource teacher, a paraprofessional, or a volunteer.

If you are working with students who have never been in a Four-Blocks classroom, and therefore, have very little experience with Working with Words routines, you may find yourself needing to alter the amount and the type of phonics/Working with Words instruction you provide within the context of Big Blocks. The lessons and strategies in *Month-by-Month Phonics for Upper Grades* would also be appropriate for those students with little word work experience.

Challenges to Working with Words

- **Many upper-grade teachers begin to look for ways to save time and may consider phonics to be important only for younger students.**

  The type of phonics instruction is important to consider, and older students need instruction on morphemes. Spending only 60 minutes per week on phonics will have great payoff on students' ability to read and write well.

- **Using multiple resources to plan the lessons is a challenge.**

  There are many helpful professional resources, and that is good. However, it also means you will spend time consulting and searching out information as you develop lessons.

  Work with your grade-level team to divide responsibilities. Keep the lessons you develop this year and use them again next year.

- **Your own morpheme knowledge may be a challenge to instruction.**

  If this is an area where you feel uncomfortable, you may be tempted to avoid the instruction altogether.

  Rather than avoiding instruction in morphemes, use this chapter and the many other listed resources as a way to grow your own knowledge along with the students. See page 187 for professional development ideas to assist you in growing that knowledge.

- **Students aren't making the level of transfer you would like to see.**

  The two questions we typically ask are: Do you chant and write those words on a regular basis? Do you hold students accountable for the writing of those words in all of the writing they do? It is a challenge to force yourself to chant with students. You may feel foolish, or your students may resist. However, the lack of a rhythmic connection may contribute to the lack of transfer. And, telling the students they must spell the Word Wall words and Nifty Thrifty Fifty words correctly but not holding them accountable in any way will not convey the importance of these words to students.

  To make the most of the Working with Words Block, find the time, do all of the parts, and increase your own word knowledge.

Middle School

If you are dealing with middle-school students who have been in Four-Blocks and Big-Blocks classrooms, the need for a Word Wall should be minimal. You may still distribute a portable list of words you want students to consistently use correctly. But if this list comes from the words they've been receiving instruction on since first grade, you may not feel compelled to teach the words, but rather to provide the resource for those students who need a reference.

If, however, the students you work with have had little or no experience with Word Walls, you will need one. Choose the most appropriate list from those provided in this book (pages 191-194) or create your own list to reflect the words the majority of your students use frequently and still misspell.

As for some of the other activities described in this chapter—Word Sorts, Scavenger Hunts, Word Detectives, and Guess the Covered Word—these activities will be appropriate and will still need to be connected to the actual reading and writing your students are doing on a daily basis.

Working with Words in Big Blocks

If your middle-school students have never done the Nifty Thrifty Fifty, it would be quite appropriate and important to take them through those lessons, as well. Your middle-school decisions will be highly influenced by your students' previous experiences with words. As for how much time you should spend on Working With Words, you will again decide based on previous experiences. You may need three 20-minute lessons per week if students have little experience. However, you may find that two 20-minute lessons per week will suffice, or you may decide you need 50-60 minutes per week and that is divided into any number of 10-, 20-, and/or 30-minute lessons, depending on the activity.

Working with Words Connections to Other Blocks

Each of the Big Blocks connects and intersects with the other Blocks to assist students in transferring their learning from one Block to another. Here are a few ways the Working with Words Block connects to the other Blocks and ways you can help students transfer their learning about words to their reading and writing.

Working with Words Connection to Guided Reading

Students will read many materials with big words in them, particularly in Guided Reading materials with content connections.

- Help students identify when to use prefixes and suffixes to read a new word or create meaning for a new word.

- Show students how to use the Nifty Thrifty Fifty words to read and understand new words.

- Have students use Guided Reading materials to find words for Scavenger Hunts.

Working with Words Connection to Writing

As students' reading vocabularies increase so should their written vocabularies. At the same time, the common words students use need to be spelled correctly.

- Hold students accountable for always spelling posted words (Word Wall and Nifty Thrifty Fifty) correctly.

- Encourage and support students as they use the prefixes, suffixes, and spelling changes you introduce.

Working with Words Connection to Self-Selected Reading

Students need to transfer what they learn about words to their personal reading.

- Review decoding strategies during Self-Selected Reading mini-lessons on days when you don't have a phonics/spelling lesson.

- Have students keep track of words they find that are hard to decode and/or have unfamiliar meanings, which they have figured out. These words can be recorded in their Big-Blocks Notebooks or on self-stick notes.

- Students may keep track of words they read during Self-Selected Reading that have prefixes, suffixes, or spelling changes that match what has been studied. Be cautious! Focusing only on words may detract from students attending to meaning. If they identify a word incidentally, that is great; however, don't assign students to find words. Have them do that during a Scavenger Hunt phonics/spelling lesson.

- Have students share at least one "self-stick note/notebook" word in each Self-Selected Reading conference.

Professional Development Ideas

1. Prior to teaching the lessons in this chapter with students, teach one of each type to a group of adults.

   - **Word Sorts**
     Choose one of the prefixes or suffixes that isn't in this chapter. Use professional resources such as *The Reading Teacher's Book of Lists* (Fry, Kress, and Jossey-Bass, 2000), *Words Their Way* (Bear, Invernizzi, Templeton, and Johnston, 2003), dictionaries, and materials you think may be helpful. Determine how many columns will be appropriate and create headings for the columns. Work together in teams to find examples for each column. Be sure to include both words your students will recognize and words to extend their vocabularies.

   - **Scavenger Hunts**
     Look for one of the first examples of spelling changes or prefix/suffix words you will be teaching. Bring in a piece of text your students may be reading. Choose the type of word to look for (for example, words that drop the **-e** to add **-ed** or a word ending in **-tion**). Spend 5-7 minutes looking for examples. You will see how disruptive the task is to reading comprehension. This is the reason your students should do this activity as a reread of a text and not as a first read.

   - **Word Detectives**
     Choose a word that will connect to your content-area studies. As a group, brainstorm all of the words you can that both look like and sound like the chosen word.

     Having experiences in the same formats your students will experience gives you insight as a teacher. The time spent will also make you feel better about your own morphological knowledge.

2. Use the text *Phonics They Use: Words for Reading and Writing* (Cunningham, 2004) as a book study.

   In a meta-analysis of phonics instruction Stahl, Duffy-Hester, and Stahl (1998) summarized that good phonics instruction:

   - should not teach rules, need not use worksheets, should not dominate instruction, and does not have to be boring.

   - should provide sufficient practice in reading words—reading words in isolation, reading words in stories, and writing words.

   - should lead to automatic word recognition.

   - is only one part of reading instruction.

Working with Words for Big Blocks builds on these basic principles and expands to incorporate instruction in morphological patterns. This instruction will equip upper-grade students to read, understand, and spell complex words.

Working with Words in Big Blocks

Recommended Professional Resources

Cunningham, P. M. and Hall, D. P. (1998). *Month-by-Month Phonics for Upper Grades*. Greensboro, NC: Carson-Dellosa Publishing Company.

Cunningham, P. M. and Hall, D. P. (1994). *Making Big Words*. Parsippany, NJ: Good Apple.

Cunningham, P. M. and Hall, D. P. (2000). *Making More Big Words*. Parsippany, NJ: Good Apple.

Cunningham, P. M. (2003). *Big Words for Big Kids*. Greensboro, NC: Carson-Dellosa Publishing Company.

Cunningham, P. M. (2004). *Phonics They Use: Words for Reading and Writing, 4th edition*. New York, NY: Allyn and Bacon.

Cunningham, P. M. (2000). *Phonics They Use: Words for Reading and Writing, 3rd edition*. New York, NY: Addison-Wesley Educational Publishers Inc.

Young, S. (1997). *The Scholastic Rhyming Dictionary*. New York, NY: Scholastic, Inc.

Working with Words Supplement

August/September:
Additional words for What Looks Right?, page 25 in *Month-by-Month Phonics for Upper Grades*

appetite   twilight   impolite   meteorite   satellite   foresight   copyright

October:
Additional words for What Looks Right?, page 41 in *Month-by-Month Phonics for Upper Grades*

obtain   restrain   profane   inhumane   scatterbrain   sustain

November:
Additional words for What Looks Right?, page 56 in *Month-by-Month Phonics for Upper Grades*

Lesson 1: bittersweet   indiscreet   upbeat

Lesson 2: cartwheel   congeal   genteel   piecemeal

December:
Additional words for What Looks Right?, page 68 in *Month-by-Month Phonics for Upper Grades*

Lesson 1: petticoat   sugarcoat   rewrote   keynote   steamboat
anecdote

Lesson 2: renegade   escapade   nursemaid   masquerade   marmalade
centigrade   bridesmaid

January:
Additional words for What Looks Right?, page 80 in *Month-by-Month Phonics for Upper Grades*

Lesson 1: workplace   staircase   retrace   deface   erase

Lesson 2: buccaneer   musketeer   reappear   unclear

February:
Additional words for What Looks Right?, page 91 in *Month-by-Month Phonics for Upper Grades*

Lesson 1: none

Lesson 2: nosebleed   refereed   guaranteed

March:
Additional words for What Looks Right?, page 103 in *Month-by-Month Phonics for Upper Grades*

Lesson 1: camisole   console   enroll   loophole   porthole   unroll

Lesson 2: saxophone   telephone   monotone   overgrown   milestone   unknown

April:
Additional words for What Looks Right?, page 114 in *Month-by-Month Phonics for Upper Grades*

Lesson 1: airfare   welfare   debonair   impair   fanfare   midair

Lesson 2: curfew   corkscrew   kazoo   miscue   horseshoe   misconstrue

Working with Words Supplement

May:
Additional words for What Looks Right?, page 127 in *Month-by-Month Phonics for Upper Grades*

Lesson 1:
dimension	circulation	pension	constellation	immigration
digestion	legislation	nomination	migration	plantation
dissension	comprehension	adaptation	calculation	misapprehension
civilization	preservation	demonstration		

Lesson 2:
bottle	coddle	funnel	gavel	medal
kettle	Aristotle	travel	unravel	peddle
petal	pedal			

Word Wall Words for Grades 1-3 (Four Blocks)

about	discover	here	nice	some	wear
after	do	his	night	something	weather
again	doesn't	hole	no	sometimes	went
all	don't	hopeless	not	sports	were
almost	down	house	of	stop	we're
always	drink	how	off	talk	what
am	eat	hurt	old	teacher	when
and	eating	I	on	tell	where
another	enough	I'm	one	terrible	whether
animal	especially	impossible	or	than	who
anyone	every	in	other	thank	whole
are	everybody	independent	our	that	winner
at	everything	into	out	that's	with
be	except	is	outside	their	why
beautiful	exciting	it	over	them	will
because	favorite	it's	people	then	with
before	first	its	phone	there	won
best	float	joke	play	they	won't
big	for	journal	played	they're	wouldn't
black	found	jump	pretty	thing	write
boy	friend	junk	prettier	this	writing
brother	friendly	kick	prettiest	thought	you
brothers	friends	kicked	probably	those	your
bug	from	knew	question	threw	you're
but	fun	know	quit	through	zoo
buy	general	laughed	rain	to	
by	get	let's	really	too	
can	getting	like	recycle	trip	
can't	girl	line	ride	trouble	
car	give	little	right	truck	
caught	go	look	said	two	
children	good	lovable	sale	unhappiness	
city	governor	made	saw	until	
clock	green	mail	school	up	
come	gym	make	see	use	
community	had	many	she	usually	
confusion	has	me	shook	vacation	
could	have	more	sister	very	
countries	he	my	skate	want	
day	her	myself	slow	wanted	
did	hidden	name	small	was	
didn't	him	new	snap	we	

Working with Words Supplement

Words to Choose from for Upper-Grade Word Wall

First Priority: High-Frequency Commonly Misspelled Words

again	friends	terrible	when
are	favorite	thought	what
always	laugh	trouble	who
because	people	until	with
believe	perhaps	very	were
could	said	want	
during	they	was	
enough	then	went	

Second Priority: Common Contractions and Compounds

can't	that's	everybody	ourselves
don't	won't	something	sometimes
didn't	wouldn't	cannot	themselves
doesn't	another	however	throughout
let's	anyone	yourself	upon

Not Compounds but Students Write Them as Compounds

a lot

all right

no one

Third Priority: Common Homophones

accept	it's	right	they're
except	knew	write	we're
by	new	threw	wear
buy	know	through	where
hole	no	to	weather
whole	one	too (too much!)	whether
hour	won	two (#2)	your
our	quiet	their	you're
its	quite	there	

Fourth Priority: Spelling Change Examples: (doubling, drop e, y-i)

getting	swimming	tried	happiness
hidden	biggest	beautiful	
winner	exciting	funnier	
stopped	countries	prettiest	

Fifth Priority: Other Homophones

board	bear	flea	plain
bored	beat	flour	plane
close	beet	flower	road
clothes	berry	heal	rode
hear	bury	heel	sea
here	break	knot	see
heard	brake	not	son
herd	cell	knight	sun
piece	sell	night	stake
peace	cent	mail	steak
wait	sent	male	weak
weight	scent	sail	week
ate	dear	sale	wood
eight	deer	pail	would
bare	flee	pale	

Sixth Priority: Less Common Homophones; Other Commonly Misspelled Words

Less Common Homophones

desert	genes	principal	suite
dessert	jeans	principle	sweet
aloud	gorilla	rap	waist
allowed	guerilla	wrap	waste
capital	patience	scene	morning
capitol	patients	seen	mourning
compliment	pole	soar	pair
complement	poll	sore	pare
council	presence	stairs	pear
counsel	presents	stares	soared
			sword

Working with Words Supplement

Other Commonly Misspelled Words

although
America
beneath
between
bought
breathe
brought
caught
century
certain
committee
country
different

discussed
either
embarrassed
English
Europe
excellent
exercise
experience
field
foreign
happened
height
important

interesting
knowledge
language
machine
measure
millions
mountain
necessary
neighbor
once
particular
president
receive

recommend
remember
restaurant
serious
since
soldiers
special
temperature
thousands
together
until

The Nifty Thrifty Fifty

Word	Prefix	Suffix
antifreeze	anti	
beautiful		ful (y-i)
classify		ify
communities	com	es (y-i)
community	com	
composer	com	er
continuous	con	ous
conversation	con	tion
deodorize	de	ize
different		ent
discovery	dis	y
dishonest	dis	
electricity		ity
employee	em	ee
encouragement	en	ment
expensive	ex	ive
forecast	fore	
forgotten		en (double t)
governor		or
happiness		ness (y-i)
hopeless		less
illegal	il	
impossible	im	
impression	im	sion
independence	in	ence

Word	Prefix	Suffix
international	inter	al
invasion	in	sion
irresponsible	ir	ible
midnight	mid	
misunderstand	mis	
musician		ian
nonliving	non	ing (drop e)
overpower	over	
performance	per	ance
prehistoric	pre	ic
prettier		er (y-i)
rearrange	re	
replacement	re	ment
richest		est
semifinal	semi	
signature		ture
submarine	sub	
supermarkets	super	s
swimming		ing (double m)
transportation	trans	tion
underweight	under	
unfinished	un	ed
unfriendly	un	ly
unpleasant	un	ant (drop e)
valuable		able (drop e)

Chapter 6   Assessment and Evaluation

Teachers are being held more and more accountable for student learning. There is an increased expectation that all students will learn the content and curriculum for their grade level at high levels of mastery. Teachers are constantly asking, "Where in the Big-Blocks™ framework can we collect products for grades, and how can we report that information to parents and administrators?" We believe this is an important responsibility, and we will attempt to provide you with some suggestions for what you can collect and review for grades. However, we also believe that what you collect and review should do more than become a percentage or a letter in your grade book. We believe that what you collect and review should inform your instruction so that students make progress, and you are successful in helping them learn your content and curriculum. In this chapter, we will share information on assessment and evaluation.

There is a difference between assessment and evaluation. Assessment is the process used to determine what students know and what they need in order to change the instruction being provided. Evaluation is the process of reporting to parents, typically in the form of a percentage or letter grade, a student's performance. Grade cards are a record of evaluation.

Assessment

"Assessment drives instruction" is a very popular phrase. Unfortunately, many educators have yet to find a way to make it happen or have little understanding of how to make it happen. The following are opportunities where assessment is built into Big Blocks.

Assessment in Guided Reading

As students are reading, particularly in reading teams, with partners, and independently, you will be circulating to listen to the reading and the conversations taking place. Carry a notebook or clipboard along with you. Make notes of strategies students use or comments reflecting their comprehension.

HINT

The record-keeping forms found at the end of several chapters in this book are one way to gather assessment data.

When students are asked to respond to their reading through writing or drawing, you will have a chance to see what they understood and what needs more work. Add notes to your anecdotal records on individual students or jot down trends you happen to see in a class. These notes will help you assess what kind of work needs to happen in Guided Reading lessons in the future.

Assessment in Writing

When you assess students' writing, you are looking at what they can accomplish in order to make instructional decisions. On page 88, we suggested looking at student writing and creating a chart to show what the student can do well and what he needs help with. This strategy can help you see where to lead that student instructionally.

Weekly conferences help you decide what to talk about in future conferences and in future mini-lessons. There are forms in the Writing chapter that may help (pages 97-100). Any kind of anecdotal record keeping will work as long as you use it on a regular basis and refer back to it when planning for Writing.

Student self-assessment in writing can begin to happen with the development of scoring guides (rubrics). If you have developed a scoring guide for any piece of writing, students can use that guide to know how to improve their pieces of writing. It is a good way to get students involved in recognizing their own abilities. See the section on evaluation (pages 197-198) to see how to shift the scoring guide into evaluation.

Assessment in Self-Selected Reading
This Block also has conferencing built into the time allotted for the Block. You will have opportunities to talk with students and record the conversations. You should look for their use of strategies, particularly those strategies you have taught and modeled in Guided Reading. The work you do in Guided Reading will also help you decide what strategies to model for mini-lessons in Self-Selected Reading.

Students will be responding to their reading on a weekly basis. These written responses should be read with instruction in mind. What strategies do most of your students mention in their responses? Do they seem to use them well? If so, there is little need to spend much time on those strategies.

Between conferences and responses, you will have multiple opportunities to see what your students can do and the strategies they choose to use when reading. Occasionally, it would be appropriate to use the Self-Selected Reading Block to administer an informal reading inventory or other assessment measure. Students should not view this time as a "check up" but should look forward to this time to talk to the teacher.

Assessment in Working with Words
This Block is different. The place you look for transfer of the work you have done in Working with Words is in the other three Blocks.

You look at students' writing all week long. Are they spelling Word Wall words and Nifty Fifty Thrifty Words correctly? Are they using patterns and morphemes to spell other words? When you write notes during Writing conferences, these are things you will want to pay attention to. During Self-Selected Reading, students may share words they have figured out. They may be using patterns or morphemes to figure out how to say a word or what a word means. This is assessment information for the Working with Words Block. Guided Reading will also provide similar opportunities to see application of the strategies taught in the Working with Words Block.

You may also choose to collect their Big-Blocks Notebooks for assessment purposes. As students fill out Scavenger Hunts, Word Sorts, etc., you can see how well they understand the processes you have been teaching.

Evaluation
The most difficult questions teachers ask regarding Big Blocks are those dealing with evaluation. Each district has its own method of reporting, its own requirements for how to gather grades, and its own schedule for reporting to parents. How you share student progress with parents is a critical issue. Although grades and grade cards are the most prevalent reporting system in the upper grades, our own feelings and beliefs tell us that the most informative way of sharing growth and performance with parents would be through narrative scripts and/or conferences that share the tasks students have been involved in and how you, the teacher, know the student is doing.

Assessment and Evaluation

Many of the primary-grade teachers we work with are now using a checklist for assessment and evaluation. It is more effective than a letter grade in showing what students are working on and what they can and can't do. We also feel the checklist is more developmentally appropriate. However, very few upper-grade teachers we work with use checklists only. Some teachers complete checklists in addition to letter grades. Our experience is that most parents focus on the letter grades, if they are provided. Parents have more experience with letter grades than with checklists, so they stick to what they know.

Another issue that impacts what you evaluate and how you share it is the balance between effort and ability—both have a place when evaluating a student. When grading students, some consideration for effort must be made, otherwise hardworking students who are making great progress but are not on grade level will see no point in continuing to put forth effort. But, grading students solely on their effort means that hardworking students reading significantly below grade level receive A's and B's. This makes it difficult for parents to get a true picture of how well their child is reading. We can't offer the perfect formula for considering effort and ability when figuring grades. However, we do recommend that teachers and administrators have conversations around these issues and look carefully at determining the best way to share information on current ability and effort with parents and students.

HINT

A very general description of how to determine a student's reading level (his current ability) is given in *Classrooms That Work: They Can All Read and Write* (3rd edition) (Cunningham and Allington, 2002).

One final note . . . we evaluate that which we value. Be sure what you choose to grade and use as a reflection of student growth matches what you want parents and students to focus on. If you are working hard to get students to value reading for enjoyment and as a way to gain information, then you want to evaluate student work in a way that reflects those values. In this instance, you may not get your best information from book reports, computerized test results, number of pages read, number of points earned for reading a particular set of books, etc. These activities don't reflect how students value their reading. With that in mind, the remainder of this chapter will be lists of possible items to evaluate for grades.

Evaluation in Guided Reading

If you are required to give grades, you can ask students to do some after-reading activities independently and collect these for grades. Remember that the first few times you do any activity, it should be done with the whole class to provide support and to model the process. Then, when you do collect the independent work, it will be a reflection of the reader and not of whether or not she knows how to do the task.

You might have students complete Story Maps individually after several sessions of completing them as a whole class. This can also be done with written responses, other graphic organizers, a Guess Yes or No, etc. You might ask students to write down which Rivet predictions came true and to make true the remaining statements. These represent just a few evaluation opportunities for grades in Guided Reading.

Evaluation in Writing

If your grade card requires a letter grade in writing or language arts, carefully consider the places you will gather these grades. The first suggestion is that you realize you will not have as many grades in your grade book as you would if you were completing the many assignments in a language textbook. Instead, you will have grades for any published pieces of writing. You could take grades on the completion of the Writing Handbook section of the Big-Blocks Notebooks. If you have a weekly expectation for the number of pages students draft, collect writing notebooks and give grades on that expectation.

You may also give grades on the parts of a published piece. In other words, students are graded on rough drafts, on their own revision and editing processes, on final drafts, on meeting due dates, etc. Grades in writing should be reflective of student progress, effort, and ability. Those students who come in as good writers should still be expected to move forward.

When giving grades for Writing, it is easier to use a checklist or writing scale than it is to use a rubric or scoring guide. A scoring guide is a target for students. It allows them to self-assess and see how to improve. However, it doesn't always neatly transfer to a grade. Evaluate the items on the scoring guide and assign important items correlating point values. Weight the items according to the instruction you've provided. Use the checklist to determine letter grades or percentages.

Evaluation in Self-Selected Reading

Students will respond weekly to their reading in a section of the Big-Blocks Notebooks. This section could be graded for completion and for the quality of the responses. This may be another place for a checklist with point values. It would give the students targets to shoot for and make the evaluation more objective for you.

Record and reference conference conversations to indicate mastery of grade-level expectations or objectives. (See suggested conference forms on pages 52-55.) The Conference Summary Form and Reading Skills/Strategies Checklist may be used to record evidence of student mastery or evidence of a student struggling with a particular skill or strategy.

Evaluation in Working with Words

Students will be filling out many pages in the Working with Words section of their Big-Blocks Notebooks. These pages may be collected for assessment and evaluation. Look at Scavenger Hunts, What Looks Right?, Word Sorts, Word Detectives, and other lessons for information. Students should be asked occasionally to record how they will use what they are learning in Working with Words in their daily reading and writing. It will be appropriate to evaluate how well students articulate this transfer of learning. However, the majority of opportunities for evaluation occur in the remainder of the school day as students write.

HINT

Some teachers assign a certain point value to the paper. For example, if a student hasn't misspelled any words from the Word Wall, he will get five points. If the student misspells any Word Wall words, the score is 0. This seems tough, but the expectation is that once a word is on the Word Wall, students are responsible for spelling it correctly. If a student doesn't know how to spell the word, she has the Word Wall in the classroom, as well as a portable Word Wall, for reference.

Assessment and Evaluation

You may choose to collect a certain number of papers each week to give a Word Wall grade. Those papers may come from the Writing Block, social studies work, science, a response in Self-Selected Reading, etc. Check the paper for misspelled Word Wall words and Nifty Thrifty Fifty words.

Final Thoughts on Assessment and Evaluation

Assessment is permanently built into the Big Blocks. It is a critical part of teaching. If assessment doesn't occur, teachers continue to teach the things they think students need, rather than what they know students need. Conferences are not nearly as effective without written records, and those records are the assessment.

Evaluation is a much more difficult issue, and it is worth talking about at every school in every district. Work to make sure the information you report to parents is reflective of the work you do with students.

Children's Works Cited

Baby by Patricia MacLachlan (Delacorte Books for Young Readers, 1993)

Because of Winn-Dixie by Kate DiCamillo (Candlewick Press, 2001)

Betty Doll by Patricia Polacco (Philomel Books, 2001)

Blackberries in the Dark by Mavis Jukes (Yearling, 1994)

A Chocolate Moose for Dinner by Fred Gwynne (Aladdin, 1988)

Coretta Scott King by David and Patricia Armentrout (Rourke Publishing, 2003)

The Days of Summer by Eve Bunting (Harcourt Children's Books, 2001)

Do Tornadoes Really Twist?: Questions and Answers about Tornadoes and Hurricanes by Melvin and Gilda Berger (Scholastic, Inc., 2000)

Everything You Need to Know about Science Homework by Anne Zeman and Kate Kelly (Scholastic, Inc., 1994)

Free at Last! The Story of Martin Luther King, Jr. by Angela Bull (DK Publishing, Inc., 2000)

Grandfather's Journey by Allen Say (Houghton Mifflin Company, 1993)

The Hindenburg by Patrick O'Brien (Henry Holt and Company, 2000)

I Have a Dream: The Story of Martin Luther King by Margaret Davidson (Scholastic, Inc., 1994)

In the Time of Drums by Kim Sieglson (Jump Sun, 1999)

Journey to Freedom: A Story of the Underground Railroad by Courtni C. Wright (Holiday House, 1997)

Joyful Noise: Poems for Two Voices by Paul Fleischman (HarperTrophy, 1992)

Just a Dream by Chris Van Allsburg (Houghton Mifflin Company, 1990)

Just Plain Fancy by Patricia Polacco (Scholastic, Inc., 1990)

The Keeping Quilt by Patricia Polacco (Aladdin, 2001)

Letters from Rifka by Karen Hesse (Hyperion Books for Children, 1993)

Let's Go Rock Collecting by Roma Gans (HarperTrophy, 1997)

Lewis and Clark and Me: A Dog's Tale by Laurie Myers (Henry Holt and Company, 2002)

Lightning by Seymour Simon (HarperTrophy, 1999)

Loser by Jerry Spinelli (HarperTrophy, 2003)

The Lucky Stone by Lucille Clifton (Yearling Books, 1986)

The Magic School Bus: Inside a Hurricane by Joanna Cole (Scholastic, Inc., 1995)

Maniac Magee by Jerry Spinelli (Little, Brown and Co., 1999)

Children's Works Cited

Martin Luther King, Jr.: A Man of Peace by Garnet Jackson (Scholastic, Inc., 2001)

Maya Angelou: Journey of the Heart by Jayne Pettit (Puffin Books, 1998)

Mouse-Deer's Market by Joanna Troughton (Peter Bedrick Books, 1984)

Mr. Lincoln's Way by Patricia Polacco (Philomel Books, 2001)

Mummies in the Morning by Mary Pope Osborne (Random House Books for Young Readers, 1993)

My Dream of Martin Luther King by Faith Ringgold (Dragonfly Books, 1998)

My Rotten Red-Headed Older Brother by Patricia Polacco (Aladdin, 1998)

Outside and Inside Alligators by Sandra Markle (Atheneum, 1998)

Outside and Inside Sharks by Sandra Markle (Aladdin, 1999)

Paul Revere's Ride by Lucia Raatma (Compass Point Books, 2003)

Picnic, Lightning by Billy Collins (University of Pittsburgh Press, 1998)

A Picture Book of Martin Luther King, Jr. by David A. Adler (Holiday House, 1990)

Pink and Say by Patricia Polacco (Philomel Books, 1994)

Poetry for Young Children: Robert Frost edited by Gary D. Schmidt (Sterling Publishing, 1994)

Questions and Answers about Weather by M. Jean Craig (Scholastic Inc., 1996)

A River Ran Wild by Lynne Cherry (Voyager Books, 2002)

Rosa Parks: From the Back of the Bus to the Front of a Movement by Camila Wilson (Scholastic, Inc., 2001)

Sharks by Sandra Markle (Scholastic, Inc., 1996)

Sideways Stories from Wayside School by Louis Sachar (HarperTrophy, 1998)

Snakes by Seymour Simon (HarperTrophy, 1994)

Star Girl by Jerry Spinelli (Knopf Books for Young Readers, 2002)

Stateswoman to the World: A Story about Eleanor Roosevelt by Maryann N. Weidt (Carolrhoda Books, 1992)

The Stranger by Chris Van Allsburg (Houghton Mifflin Company, 1986)

"A Sweet Advance in Candy Packing" by Emily Sohn (*Science News for Kids*, February 18, 2004) *http://www.sciencenewsforkids.org/articles/20040218/Note3.asp*

Teammates by Peter Golenbock (Voyager Books, 1992)

Thank You, Mr. Falker by Patricia Polacco (Philomel Books, 2001)

Through My Eyes by Ruby Bridges (Scholastic, Inc., 1999)

Thundercake by Patricia Polacco (A PaperStar Book, 1997)

Two Bad Ants by Chris Van Allsburg (Houghton Mifflin Company, 1988)

Two-Minute Mysteries Collection by Donald J. Sobol (Scholastic, Inc., 2004)

The Van Gogh Café by Cynthia Rylant (Scholastic, Inc., 1999)

A Voice from the Border by Pamela Smith Hill (HarperTrophy, 2000)

Voices from America's Past: Blue or Gray? A Family Divided by Kate Connell (National Geographic Reading Expeditions, 2002)

Wayside School Gets a Little Stranger by Louis Sachar (HarperTrophy, 1996)

We Are the Many: A Picture Book of American Indians by Doreen Rappaport (HarperCollins, 2002)

What Will the Weather Be? by Lynda DeWitt (HarperTrophy, 1993)

When Lightning Comes in a Jar by Patricia Polacco (Philomel Books, 2002)

Wringer by Jerry Spinelli (HarperTrophy, 1998)

Other Literature Citations

The No. 1 Ladies' Detective Agency by Alexander McCall Smith (Anchor, 2003)

Professional References

A Thousand and One Formulas by Sydney Gernsback (Lindsay Publications, 1920)

Allen, J. (1999). *Words, Words, Words: Teaching Vocabulary in Grades 4-12*. York, ME: Stenhouse Publishers.

Allen, J. (2000). *Yellow Brick Roads: Shared and Guide Paths to Independent Reading 4-12*. Portland, ME: Stenhouse Publishers.

Allington, R. L. (1975). "Sustained Approaches to Reading and Writing." *Language Arts, 52,* 813-815.

Allington, R. L. (1994). "The Schools We Have: The School We Need." *The Reading Teacher, 48,* 14-29.

Allington, R. L. (2001). *What Matters Most to Struggling Readers: Designing Research-Based Program.* New York, NY: Addison-Wesley.

Anderson, C. (2000). *How's It Going?* Portsmouth, NH: Heinemann.

Anderson, R. C., Wilson, P. T., and Fielding, L. G. (1988). "Growth in Reading and How Children Spent Their Time Outside School." *Reading Research Quarterly, 23,* 285-303.

Armbruster, B. and Wilkinson, I. (1991). "Silent Reading, Oral Reading, and Learning from Text." *The Reading Teacher, 45,* 154-155.

Atwell, N. (1998). *In the Middle: New Understandings about Writing, Reading, and Learning, 2nd edition*. Portsmouth, NH: Heinemann.

Atwell, N. (1987). *In the Middle: New Understandings about Writing, Reading, and Learning.* Portsmouth, NH: Heinemann.

Atwell, N. (2002). *Lessons That Change Writers.* Portsmouth, NH: Heinemann.

Bear, D., Invernizzi, M., Templeton, S. and Johnston, F. (2003). *Words Their Way, 2nd edition*. Upper Saddle River, NJ: Prentice Hall.

Beck, I. L., McKeown, M., Hamilton, R., and Kucan, L. (1997). *Questioning the Author: An Approach for Enhancing Student Engagement with Text.* Newark, DE: International Reading Association.

Block, C. C. (2001). "Case for Exemplary Instruction Especially for Students Who Begin School without the Precursors for Literacy Success." *National Reading Conference Yearbook, 49,* 110-122.

Block, C. C. and Mangieri, J. N. (2002). "Recreational Reading: 20 Years Later." *The Reading Teacher, 55,* 572-580.

Bone, B. (2000). "Lessons from a Vocabulary Journal." *Voices from the Middle, (7)4 ,* 18-23.

Calkins, L. (1994). *The Art of Teaching Writing, 2nd edition*. Portsmouth, NH: Heinemann.

Cunningham, P. M. (2003). *Big Words for Big Kids.* Greensboro, NC: Carson-Dellosa Publishing Company.

Professional References

Cunningham, P. M. (2004). *Phonics They Use: Words for Reading and Writing, 4th edition.* New York, NY: Allyn and Bacon.

Cunningham, P. M. (2000). *Phonics They Use: Words for Reading and Writing, 3rd edition.* New York, NY: Addison-Wesley Educational Publishers Inc.

Cunningham, P. M. and Cunningham, J. W. (2004). "What We Know about How to Teach Phonics." *Four-Blocks Leadership Conference Notes.*

Cunningham, P. M. and Allington, R. L. (2003). *Classrooms That Work: They Can All Read and Write, 3rd edition.* Boston, MA: Allyn and Bacon.

Cunningham, P. M., Hall, D. P., and Cunningham, J. (2002). *Guided Reading the Four-Blocks® Way.* Greensboro, NC: Carson-Dellosa Publishing Company.

Cunningham, P. M., Hall, D. P., and Defee, M. (1998). "Nonability Grouped, Multilevel Instruction: Eight Years Later." *Reading Teacher 44.*

Cunningham, P. M., Hall, D. P., and Gambrell, L. B. (2002). *Self-Selected Reading the Four-Blocks® Way.* Greensboro, NC: Carson-Dellosa Publishing Company.

Cunningham, P. M. (2001). *Systematic Sequential Phonics They Use.* Greensboro, NC: Carson-Dellosa Publishing Company.

Cunningham, P. M. (2002). *Prefixes and Suffixes: Systematic Sequential Phonics and Spelling.* Greensboro, NC: Carson-Dellosa Publishing Company.

Cunningham, P. M. (2004). *WordMaker.* Volo, IL: Don Johnston, Inc.

Cunningham, P. M. (2005). *WordMaker II.* Volo, IL: Don Johnston, Inc.

Cunningham, P. M. and Hall, D. P. (1994). *Making Big Words.* Parsippany, NJ: Good Apple.

Cunningham, P. M. and Hall, D. P. (1998). *Month-by-Month Phonics for Upper Grades.* Greensboro, NC: Carson-Dellosa Publishing Company.

Cunningham, P. M. and Hall, D. P. (2000). *Making More Big Words.* Parsippany, NJ: Good Apple

Cunningham, P. M. and Hall, D. P. (2003). *Reading/Writing Simple Rhymes.* Greensboro, NC: Carson-Dellosa Publishing Company.

Cunningham, P. M. and Hall, D. P. (2003). *Reading/Writing Complex Rhymes.* Greensboro, NC: Carson-Dellosa Publishing Company.

Dale, E. and O'Rourke, J. (1981). *The Living Word Vocabulary.* Chicago, IL: Worldbook.

Daniels, H. (2002). *Literature Circles: Voice and Choice in Book Clubs and Reading Groups, 2nd edition.* Portland, ME: Stenhouse Publishers.

Duffy, G. G. (2003). *Explaining Reading: A Resource for Teaching Concepts, Skills, and Strategies.* New York, NY: Guilford Press.

Professional References

Durkin, D. (1978-79). "What Classroom Observations Reveal about Reading Comprehension Instruction." *Reading Research Quarterly, 14,* 481-533.

Educational Research Service (1999). *Reading at the Middle and High School Levels: Building Active Readers Across the Curriculum, 2nd Edition.* Arlington, VA: Educational Research Service.

Fielding, L. and Pearson, D. (1992). "Reading Comprehension: What Works." *Educational Leadership, 51,* 62-68.

Fletcher, R. (1998). *Craft Lessons.* York, ME: Stenhouse.

Fractor, J. S., Woodruff, M. C., Martinez, M. G., and Teale, W. H. (1993). "Let's Not Miss Opportunities to Promote Voluntary Reading: Classroom Libraries in the Elementary School." *Reading Teacher, 46,* 476-484.

Freeman, M. (1997). *Listen to This: Developing an Ear for Expository.* Gainesville, FL: Maupin House.

Fry, E. B., Kress, J. E., and Fountoukidis D. L. (2000). *The Reading Teacher's Book of Lists, 4th edition.* Paramus, NJ: Prentice Hall.

Gambrell, L. B. (1996). "Creating Classroom Cultures That Foster Reading Motivation." *The Reading Teacher, 50,* 14-25.

Glasswell, K., Parr, J. M., McNaughton, S., and Carpenter, M. (2003). "Four Ways to Work Against Yourself When Conferencing with Struggling Writers." *Language Arts, 80,* 291-298.

Graves, D. (1995). *A Fresh Look at Writing.* Portsmouth, NH: Heinemann.

Greaney, V. (1980). "Factors Related to the Amount and Type of Leisure-Time Reading." *Reading Research Quarterly, 3,* 337-357.

Hagerty, P. J. (1992). *Readers' Workshop.* New York, NY: Scholastic.

Hall, D. P., Cunningham, P. M., and Arens A. B. (2003). *Writing Mini-Lessons for the Upper Grades.* Greensboro, NC: Carson-Dellosa Publishing Company.

Harris, T. and Hodges, R. eds., (1995). *The Literacy Dictionary: The Vocabulary of Reading and Writing.* Newark, DE: International Reading Association.

Harvey, S. and Goudvis, A. (2000). *Strategies That Work: Teaching Comprehension to Enhance Understanding.* Portland, ME: Stenhouse Publishers.

Hillocks, G., Jr. (1986). *Research on Written Composition: New Directions for Teaching.* Urbana, IL: National Conference on Research in English/ERIC Clearinghouse on Reading and Communication Skills.

Hillocks, G., Jr. (1995). *Teaching Writing as Reflective Practice.* New York, NY: Teachers College Press.

Ivey, G. and Broaddus, K. (2000). "Tailoring the Fit: Reading Instruction and Middle School Readers." *The Reading Teacher, 54,* 68-78.

Ivey, G. and Broaddus, K. (2001). "'Just Plain Reading': A Survey of What Makes Students Want to Read in Middle School Classrooms." *Reading Research Quarterly, 36,* 350-377.

Kohn, A. (1992). *No Contest: The Case Against Competition*. New York, NY: Mariner Books.

Kohn, A. (1999). *Punished by Rewards: The Trouble with Gold Stars, Incentive Plans, A's, Praise, and Other Bribes*. New York, NY: Mariner Books.

Krashen, S. D. (2004). *The Power of Reading: Insights from the Research, 2nd edition*. Portsmouth, NH: Heinemann.

Lapp, D., Flood, J. and Farnan, N. J. (eds) (1995). *Content Area Reading and Learning: Instructional Strategies*. Boston, MA: Allyn and Bacon.

Letgers, N., McDill, E., and McPartland, J. (1993, October). "Section II: Rising to the Challenge: Emerging Strategies for Educating Students at Risk." In *Educational Reforms and Students at Risk: A Review of the Current State of the Art* (pp. 47-92). Washington, D.C.: U.S. Department of Education, Office of Educational Research and Improvement.

Moore, D. W., Moore, S. A., Cunningham, P. M., and Cunningham, J. W. (1997). *Developing Readers and Writers in the Content Areas K-12*. New York, NY: Addison-Wesley Publishing Company.

Moore, S. A. (2004). *Conversations in Four-Blocks® Classrooms*. Greensboro, NC: Carson-Dellosa Publishing Company.

Morrow, L.M. (1991). "Promoting Voluntary Reading." In J. Jensen, D. Lapp, J. Flood, and J. Squire (Eds.), *Handbook of Research on Teaching the English Language Arts*, (pp.681-690). New York, NY: Macmillan.

Nagy, W. and Anderson, R. C. (1984). "How Many Words Are There in Printed School English?" *Reading Research Quarterly, 19*, 304-330.

National Center for Education Statistics (2003). *The Nation's Report Card: Reading Highlights 2003*. Washington, D.C.: U.S. Department of Education.

Opitz, M. and Rasinski, T. (1998). *Goodbye Round Robin Reading: 25 Effective Oral Reading Strategies*. Portsmouth, DE: Heinemann.

Palmer, B. M., Codling, R. M., and Gambrell, L. B. (1994). "In Their Own Words: What Elementary Students Have to Say about Motivation to Read." *The Reading Teacher, 48*, 176-178.

Pearson, P. D. and Fielding, L. (1991). "Comprehension Instruction." In *Handbook of Reading Research, Vol. 2.*, Barr, R., Kamil, M., Mosenthal, P., and Pearson, P. D., (Eds.), (pp. 815-860). New York, NY: Longman.

Pearson, P. D., Roehler, L. R., Dole, J. A., and Duffy, G. G. (1992). "Developing Expertise in Reading Comprehension." In J. Samuals and A. Farstrup (Eds.), *What Research Has to Say about Reading Instruction, 2nd edition*. Newark, DE: International Reading Association.

Pilgreen, J. L. (2000). *The SSR Handbook: How to Organize and Manage a Sustained Silent Reading Program*. Portsmouth, NH: Heinemann.

Portalupi, J. and Fletcher, R. (2001). *Non-Fiction Craft Lessons*. Urbana, IL: Stenhouse.

Professional References

Pressley, M., Allington, R. L., Wharton-McDonald, R., Block, L. C., and Morrow, L. (2001). *Learning to Read: Lessons from Exemplary First-Grade Classrooms*. New York, NY: Guilford Press.

Pressley, M. (2000). "Comprehension Instruction: What Makes Sense Now, What Might Make Sense Soon." (2004). *www.readingonline.org/articles/handbook/pressley/index.html*.

Ray, K. W. (1999). *Wondrous Words*. Urbana, IL: NCTE.

Ray, K. W. (2001). *The Writing Workshop: Working Through the Hard Parts (And They're All Hard Parts)*. Urbana, IL: NCTE.

Reif, L. (1992). *Seeking Diversity: Language Arts with Adolescents*. Portsmouth, NH: Heinemann.

Robb, L. (1999). *Brighten Up Boring Beginnings*. New York, NY: Scholastic, Inc.

Routman, R. (1995). *Invitations, 2nd edition*. Portsmouth, NH: Heinemann.

Serafini, F. (2001). *The Reading Workshop: Creating Space for Readers*. Portsmouth, NH: Heinemann.

Stahl, S. A., Duffy-Hester, A. M., and Stahl, K. A. (1998). "Everything You Wanted to Know about Phonics (But Were Afraid to Ask)." *Reading Research Quarterly, 33*, 338-355.

Stanovich, K. (1986). "Matthew Effects in Reading: Some Consequences of Individual Differences in the Acquisition of Literacy." *Reading Research Quarterly, 21*, 360-406.

Swaby, B., January 22, 1998, *Comprehension Series Instructional Session #2*, Jefferson City, MO (teleconference), "Comprehension Failure Due to Lack of Fluency."

Taba, H. (1967). *Teacher's Handbook for Elementary Social Studies*. Palo Alto, CA: Addison Wesley.

Topping, K. J. (1987). "Paired Reading: A Powerful Technique for Parent Use." *The Reading Teacher, 40*, 608-614.

Topping, K. J. and Ehly, S. (Eds.). (1998). *Peer-Assisted Learning*. Mahwah, NJ: Erlbaum.

Tovani, C. (2000). *I Read It, But I Don't Get It: Comprehension Strategies for Adolescent Readers*. Portland, ME: Stenhouse Publishers.

Vacca, R. T., and Vacca, J. L. (2001). *Content Area Reading: Literacy and Learning across the Curriculum, 7th edition*. Boston, MA: Allyn and Bacon.

Veatch, J. (1959). *Individualizing Your Reading Program*. New York, NY: Putnam.

Worthy, J. (1996). "Removing Barriers to Voluntary Reading for Reluctant Readers: The Role of School and Classroom Libraries." *Language Arts, 73*, 483-492.

Worthy, J. (2002). "What Makes Intermediate-Grade Students Want to Read?" *The Reading Teacher, 55*, 568-569.

Worthy, J., Turner, M., and Moorman, M. (1998). "The Precarious Place of Self-Selected Reading." *Language Arts, 75*, 296-304.

Young, S. (1997). *The Scholastic Rhyming Dictionary*. New York, NY: Scholastic, Inc.